THE BUDDHA
Karmapa Con

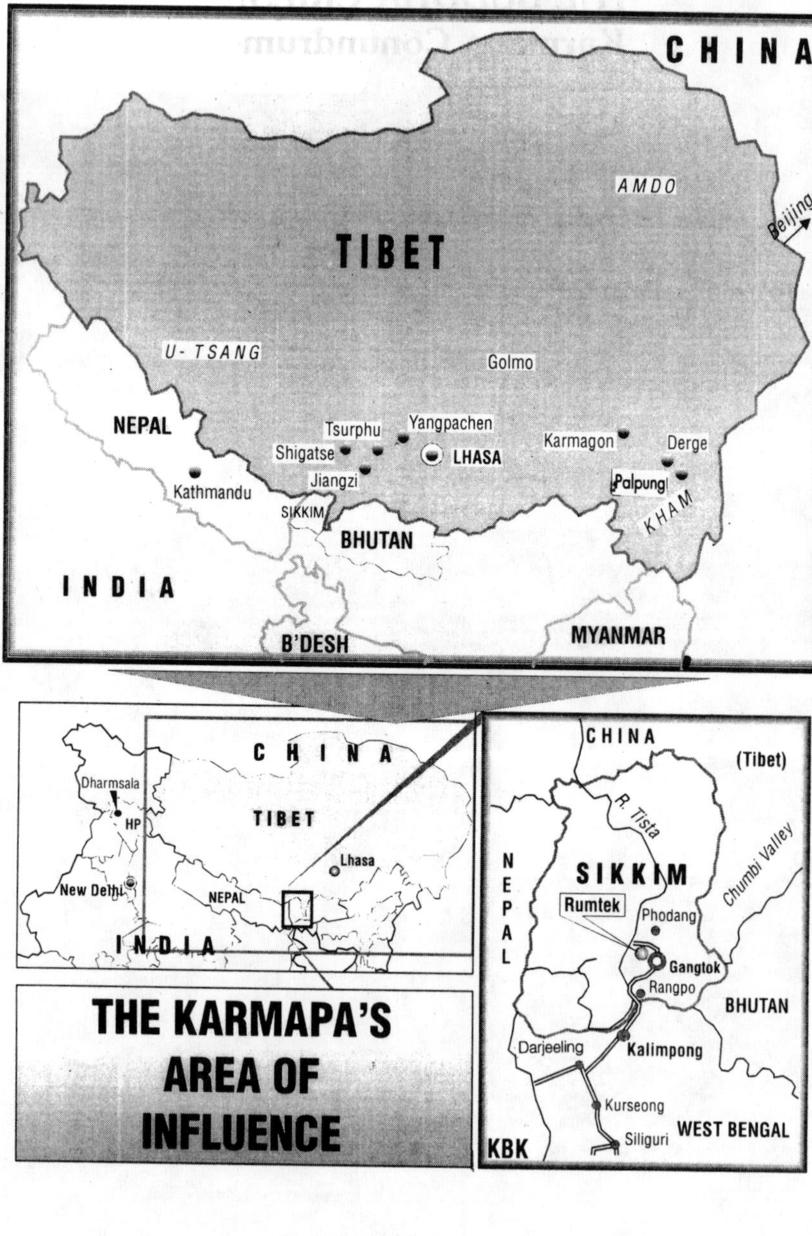
CHINA
AMDO
Beijing
TIBET
U-TSANG
Golmo
NEPAL
Tsurphu
Yangpachen
Shigatse
LHASA
Karmagon
Derge
Jiangzi
Palpung
Kathmandu
SIKKIM
KHAM
BHUTAN
INDIA
MYANMAR
B'DESH
CHINA
TIBET
Dharmsala
HP
Lhasa
New Delhi
NEPAL
INDIA
CHINA
(Tibet)
R. Tista
Chumbi Valley
NEPAL
SIKKIM
Rumtek
Phodang
Gangtok
Rangpo
BHUTAN
Darjeeling
Kalimpong
Kurseong
WEST BENGAL
Siliguri
KBK
THE KARMAPA'S AREA OF INFLUENCE

THE BUDDHA CRIES!
Karmapa Conundrum

Anil Maheshwari

UBSPD
UBS Publishers' Distributors Ltd.
New Delhi • Bangalore • Chennai
Calcutta • Patna • Kanpur • London

UBS PUBLISHERS' DISTRIBUTORS LTD.
5 Ansari Road, New Delhi-110 002
Phones : 3273601, 3266646 • *Cable* : ALLBOOKS • *Fax* : 3276593, 3274261
e-mail: ubspd@gobookshopping.com • Website: www.gobookshopping.com
10 First Main Road, Gandhi Nagar, Bangalore-560 009
Phones : 2263901, 2263902, 2253903 • *Cable* : ALLBOOKS • *Fax* : 2263904
e-mail: ubspdbng@bgl.vsnl.net.in
6, Sivaganga Road, Nungambakkam, Chennai-600 034
Phone : 8276355 • *Cable* : UBSIPUB • *Fax* : 8270189
e-mail: ubspdche@md4.vsnl.net.in
8/1-B, Chowringhee Lane, Calcutta-700 016
Phones : 2441821, 2442910, 2449473 • *Cable* : UBSIPUBS • *Fax* : 2450027
e-mail: ubspdcal@cal.vsnl.net.in
5 A, Rajendra Nagar, Patna-800 016
Phones : 686170, 672856 • *Cable* : UBSPUB • *Fax* : 686169
e-mail: ubspdpat@dte.vsnl.net.in
80, Noronha Road, Cantonment, Kanpur-208 004
Phones : 369124, 362665, 357488 • *Fax* : 315122
e-mail: ubskup@lw1.vsnl.net.in

Overseas Contact:
475 North Circular Road, Neasden, London NW2 7QG
Phone: 020-8450-8667 • *Fax*: 020-8452-6612 *Attn*: UBS

Distributors for Western India:
M/s Preface Books
Unit No. 223, 2nd Floor, Cama Industrial Estate,
Sun Mill Compound,Lower Parel (West), Mumbai 400 013
Phone: 022-4988054 • *Telefax*: 022-4988048 • e-mail: Preface@vsnl.com

First Published **2000**

Cover Design : UBS Art Studio

The photographs on the cover are Ugyen Trinley Dorji (left) and Trinley Thaye Dorje (right).

Printed at Rajkamal Electric Press, Delhi

Preface

As Tibetologists of the day would confirm, the period between the death of a high lama of monastic order and the reincarnation of his sccessor has always been marked by rivalries, struggles, intrigues and what have you — more so when the reincarnation happens to be that of the Karmapa. Considering the prevailing political scenario, and the strained relations between India and China, the Karmapa conundrum has become a 'chronicle of rogues in robes' that highlights the seamy image of the high-ranking Tibetan Buddhist lamas in their struggle to instal their choice — Trinley Thaye Dorje or Ugyen Trinley Dorji — as the 17th Karmapa. The struggle has assumed the shape of a game of chess, with India as the chessboard on which the murky moves and counter-moves are being played.

The Buddha Cries! is an update on the Karmapa episode that has all the 'spice' of clashes, machinations and mud slinging that have rocked the world spiritual to which the top echelons of Tibetan religious institutions profess to belong.

Contents

MAIN CHARACTERS

The Dalai Lama: Temporal leader of Tibetan Buddhists.

The Karmapa/The Gyalwa Karmapa: Head of the Kagyu order of Tibetan Buddhism.

Shamar/Shamar Rinpoche/Kunzig Shamar Rinpoche.

Shamarpa: Second in hierarchy of the Kagyu order. Senior regent.

Situ/Situ Rinpoche/*Tai Situ Rinpoche/Kenting Tai Situ Rinpoche*.

Situpa: Third in Hierarchy of the Kagyu Order.

Jamgon Kongtrul Rinpoche/Jamgon Kongtrul: Fourth in Hierarchy of the Kagyu order.

Gyaltsab/Gyaltsab Rinpoche/Goshir Gyaltsab Rinpoche.

Gyaltsabpa: Fifth in hierarchy of the Kagyu order.

Topga/Topgala/Topga Rinpoche/Topga Yulgyal/Topga Trangpa.

Jewon Takpoo Yulgyal: Former General Secretary of Rumtek Administration.

Kagyu/Karma Kagyu/Kagyupa/Kargudpa: The Second Oldest Order of Tibetan Buddhism.

MAIN PLACES

Potala: The great palace of the Dalai Lama, perched on a high mountain in Lhasa, largely built in the seventeenth century, overlooking the city. The majestic Potala was the traditional seat of the Dalai Lama's Tibetan government.

Tsurphu: The traditional seat of the Karmapa in Tibet

Rumtek: The headquarters of the Karmapa in Sikkim (India) after exile of the XVIth Karmapa from Tibet.

Dharamsala: The seat of the Dalai Lama in Himachal Pradesh (India); headquarters of the Tibetan Government-in-exile.

KIBI: The Karmapa International Buddhist Institute at New Delhi.

altsab Rinpoche

Situ Rinpoche

amar and Jamgon Kongtrul Rinpoches

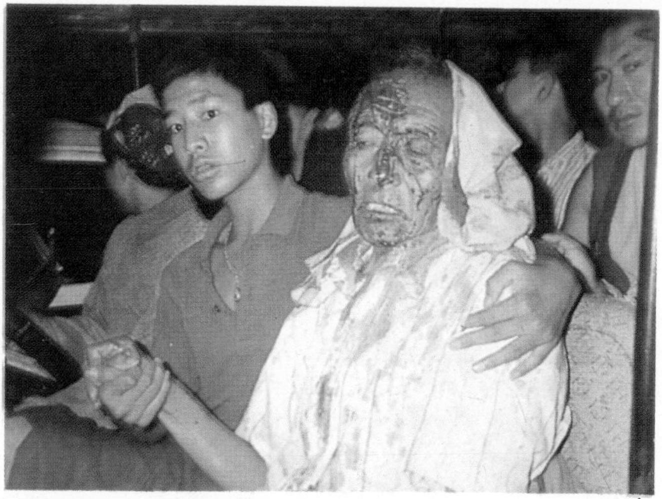

Apa Tsewang, an elderly man who was attacked by miscreants

In the company of Chinese officials, Akong Rinpoche enjoys his glass of local br

Situ and Gyaltsab Rinpoc
in a meeting with the Chin
officials at Lhasa

1

Karmapa — The Living Buddha

This is the chronicle of rogues in robes, and it has the ingredients of a racy potboiler depicting the seamy, uncompromising struggle in which the protagonists — high-ranking and respected Tibetan Buddhist lamas — are embroiled in clashes, machinations and mud-slinging that would better suit the temporal world of crooked politics than the spiritual world to which the top echelons of religious institutions profess to belong.

The study unfolds an uninterrupted chain of events and circumstances starting several centuries ago and leading to the present-day Tibetan camps and monasteries in the Himalayas of Nepal and India, Tibet, China as well as to modern Tibetan Buddhist centres in the West.

Nyingma, Kagyu, Sakya and Gelug are the four orders of Tibetan Buddhism. The Dalai Lama enjoys the status of the temporal leader of Tibet. His religious writs run only in his own Gelug order.

Strength-wise, among the four orders, Kagyu has the largest following in the West. The number of its non-Tibetan followers all over the world is over three hundred thousand as per a conservative estimate. Besides, the number of followers of this order in Tibet under Chinese occupation is estimated at one million.

The head of the Kagyu order is the Karmapa. On 5 November 1981, the XVIth Karmapa died of cancer in Chicago, USA, leaving behind property worth about US $.1.2 billion, a network of more than 430 centres worldwide, and a money-spinning machine where donations pour in incessantly.

Only a reincarnation of the Karmapa can inherit the title — and the wealth. The issue of reincarnation of the Karmapa has the main regents of the Kagyu order at loggerheads. They are divided into separate camps and, at the moment, at least two candidates have vied for the title.

One is Ugyen Trinley who 'escaped' from Chinese captivity in January 2000. Shamar Rinpoche, the senior regent of the Kagyu order, has described the escape of Ugyen Trinley Dorje as a Chinese ploy to claim the property of the Karmapa. Situ and Gyaltshab Rinpoches have investigated his antecedents. The Dalai Lama too has put the seal of approval on him. Trinley is supported by several lamas within the school and has been accepted by a section of the disciples of the late Karmapa. Curiously also, though avowed atheists, the Chinese too made a conciliatory gesture towards the faithfuls in Tibet by recognising Ugyen Trinley. It was the first such endorsement by China since the abortive Tibetan revolt of 1959 against the Chinese Communists. However, the announcement by China stressed that the Karmapas had regularly paid tribute to the (Chinese) emperors of the Yuan (1271-1368), Ming (1368-1644) and Qing (1644-1911) dynasties and had received imperial titles many times. Thus, on the one hand, while China shows a facade of tolerance towards religious tradition, on the other, it is obsessed with creating new evidence of its ancient sovereignty over Tibet and therefore pays special attention to Kagyu matters.

The Kagyu order predates the Gelug, the order of the Dalai Lama, by about 300 years. (See Appendix C for more details.) A tame Karmapa under Beijing's control would be a boon for China, as it would allow it to dominate his followers. With the young Karmapa's acquiescence, China would, at a stroke, legitimise its current claim of rule over Tibet dating back to the twelfth or thirteenth century. It was a near take-over by Communist China of the Kagyu order by proxy in which Chinese political expediency saw fit to create a unanimity of views with the Dalai Lama though the fact remains that the confirmation by the Dalai Lama of Ugyen Trinley as the reincarnation of the XVIth Karmapa came a full three weeks before the Chinese 'approval'.

The Dalai Lama's coterie was already itching to settle scores with the Kagyu order. It was also deluding itself with hopes of getting concessions from China regarding the reincarnation of the Panchen Lama, the second in hierarchy in the ruling Gelug order of the Dalai Lama. To the disappointment of the coterie, China did not oblige.

The only Buddhist lama who sidestepped the Chinese trap was Shamar Rinpoche, the senior regent in the Kagyu order. Brushing aside all overtures of the Chinese Embassy in New Delhi, he searched Trinley Thaye Dorje, a Tibet-born boy and, before declaring him as the reincarnation of the Karmapa, he smuggled the boy along with his parents into India. Trinley Thaye Dorje has been approved by several teachers within the Kagyu order and by a sizeable section of the students of the XVIth Karmapa in western countries.

India, a secular country, does not interfere in sacerdotal traditions. However, it could not remain aloof from this controversy. The headquarters of the Kagyu order is at Rumtek in Sikkim, a state bordering China, and China till date refuses to recognise Sikkim as an integral part of India. Were the 'Karmapa' recognised by China to be allowed access to Rumtek, the headquarters of the Karmapa in Sikkim (India), the decision would certainly have political repercussions for India. Understandably, India is covertly siding with Shamar Rinpoche while the Sikkim politicians, despite their differences, by and large, are kowtowing to Situ Rinpoche, the number three in the hierarchy of the Kagyu order.

Isolation has been a distinctive feature of Tibet for centuries. The country's geographical inaccessibility and the genuine desire of its inhabitants to have few contacts with outsiders created an ideal situation for seclusion. However, the asylum of Tibetans in India, Nepal, Europe and America was crucial for the survival of Tibetan culture. Considering that the Tibetans fleeing Tibet had little experience of the outside world, they managed the transition from obscurity to modernism well. But in exile they had to work hard to protect their culture from that of the host countries. This problem was exacerbated by the very success Tibetan Buddhism achieved outside Tibet. Tibetan Buddhism did not isolate itself in exile. Instead, by the late 1960s, it emerged as an active proselytizing movement in the West. For people with spiritual inclinations in the West who were not drawn towards the institutionally less embedded Hindu gurus and were more fascinated with 'miracles', Tibetan Buddhism appeared as an authentic and authoritative Asian religious alternative.

The present-day loyalties, rivalries, and hostilities among the Himalayan lamas have a direct connection with what happened inside Tibet and also China during the last several hundred years. The Tibetan history presents a tangled web of religion, politics, myths and miracles. It is critical to separate these threads to distinguish facts from fiction. (See Appendix D for Tibetan history.)

Little wonder, actions and thoughts of majority of Tibetans are governed, to a large extent, by episodes from the past. Tibetologists say that the intervening period between the death of a high lama heading a monastic order and confirmation of his reincarnation has almost always been marked by rivalries, struggles and intrigues — and also, machinations. The whole process of reincarnation of lamas and the metaphysical transmission of religious and temporal authority in a Tibetan monastic order possibly has political undertones.

The social fabric of old Tibet was very much determined by the institution of the *tulku*, the tradition of recognising a lama's consecutive rebirths. The idea of reincarnation is a unique Tibetan religio-political institution dating back to the twelfth century in the Kagyu order. It was borrowed by the Gelug order. The Nyingma order faced competing reincarnations in 1992. The Dalai Lama backed one nominee as the reincarnation of Dujom Rinpoche, the highest Nyingma lama. On the other hand, Nyingma Chadrel Rinpoche recognised another candidate, and all Nyingma disciples followed their own order's choice. The head of Sakya has always been a *tantric* practitioner, like the Nyingma lamas. He is allowed to marry and keep his plait of hair. As a true follower of *tantric* doctrine, he is believed to be a voluntary impotent for he does not discharge semen. However, if he feels it necessary to have a successor, he invites the soul of a dead holy person to enter into the womb of his wife. In former times, the Sakya lamas sent too many such invitations, which led to the division in the 'celestial family' into two parts. Later on, quarrelsome rifts generated by their ignorant staff created an unhappy relationship between the two divided families. The present reigning lama Ngawang Kunga Theckchen Rinpoche (Sakya Tridzen) is from the House of Dolma Phodrang. He stays at Dehra Dun in India. Two other lamas from the House of Phuntsok Phodrang work in Seattle, USA. Sakya Lama's priesthood is hereditary. The head of the Gelug order hands over his Ganden throne to a successor chosen by him before his death. The tradition continues till today. The 99th successor of the Ganden throne and the religious head of the Gelug order is Yeshi Dhondup. He lives in exile at the Kaden monastery in Karnataka (India).

The main secular function of *tulku* was to institutionalise the charisma of some individual lamas with extraordinary achievements. The idea is based on the Buddhist (or Hindu) concept of rebirth, which all persons are supposed to undergo after death. However, *bodhisattvas*, whose reincarnations most of the high lamas claim, are superior beings who are on the threshold of enlightenment but who have deliberately postponed it in order to be present in the world and help the suffering human beings to become enlightened.

What has set Tibet apart from the rest of the world is the fact that the country was able to continue the unbroken and living transmission of the teachings of the Buddha. These include the highest instructions about the ultimate nature of reality along with methods of its realisation. And while the average Tibetan goes about his or her business without giving much thought to the highest truth — leaving all such exalted matters to the attention of their lamas and institutions — a small number of individuals use the unique techniques available and achieve better results. Out of a few million people, a precious handful of lamas and *yogis* are able to fulfil, generation after generation, the highest potential of the human mind.

As such, Tibetans believe that such high lamas have a certain degree of freedom over death and rebirth, especially when it comes to when and where to be reborn. It is this mysterious jigsaw puzzle that lamas try to solve after the death of every high lama — through dreams and visions, oracles and divinations, mysterious signs and close observations.

The Karmapa has kept coming back in an unbroken sequence of embodiments that has spanned 900 years till now. Similarly, other highly realized lamas started to reincarnate consciously and were then recognised by their accomplished disciples. Life after life, a lama's enlightened qualities came into contact with his students. Hundreds of different *tulku* lines manifested throughout Tibet and the whole system served as a unique mechanism for preserving an unbroken transmission of the Buddha's teachings.

Over the centuries, however, monasteries and their *tulkus* have grown in wealth and wield considerable influence over the social and political life of the country. A number of *tulkus* have assumed the role of political figures augmenting their role as religious teachers. To locate and deliver the new reincarnation of a prominent *tulku* to his old monastery means gain of power. Since in many cases the criteria according to which reincarnates are recognised leave much room for manoeuvre, the process becomes an instrument for political infighting. The traditional method of scrutiny whereby the young hopefuls have to identity objects belonging to the predecessors is often bypassed. Outstanding masters are not always consulted. Political influence, money or the edge of the sword have become the decisive factors instead, and the rank of authentic *tulkus* has begun to dwindle.

It is not at all uncommon to have two or more candidates — each backed by a powerful faction — openly and violently challenging a well-known *tulku* seat. While the young aspirants may have little idea about the fray that goes on behind their backs, their mighty patrons are even ready to go to war to see their choice prevail.

Once the throne of a *tulku* for a contestant is won, his education begins, strictly in accordance with the role he has to play in his mature years. Surrounded by an all-male entourage of hereditary tutors and servants, the young reincarnate is generally subjected to severe discipline and left exclusively in the custody of his circle of zealous attendants. This is to enable the *tulku* to receive a transmission of the Buddha's teachings in its purest form, as much as it is to guard him as the monastery's most valuable possession. More often than not, consequently, the seclusion results in the *tulku's* somewhat vague knowledge about life outside his monastery's walls. At the same time, those around him play a far more dominant role than the benefit of his seat would require, pursuing sometimes their vested interests over the head of their master. Such a state of affairs is, of course, fertile ground for foreign interference.

With foreign as well as domestic meddling close at hand, the religious choice for a *tulku* has, over the centuries, become an exception rather than the rule. Authentic lamas have, of course, manifested. Tibetan history is rich in examples of highly accomplished *tulku* lines and, in theory, the whole system is geared towards bringing forward and taking care of such things. Yet, the same system, after centuries of abuse, has allowed a great number of reincarnates to become political puppets or absolute princes. They become instruments in the hands of their households whose members, while fervently guarding access to the former's ears, scheme their own intrigues. Reincarnates often behave like politicians and remain accountable to none. Advised by whosoever has gained their favour, they plunge often unprepared into the choppy waters of political passion. As a consequence, a throng of inept individuals often governs the affairs though their only qualification is the possession of a title or affiliation to a name.

The narrative that follows is to be perceived against this particular setting. The inflammable mixture of a touch of personal animosity, hostility and, eventually, hatred has added spice to an otherwise dry historical process.

The emerald-green mountains and the snow-white clouds above the Rumtek monastery turn dark gray as sunlight dissolves in the distant horizon. The deepening darkness renders the base murky. The bells toll a sombre note and the traditional ornate gongs resound at a slow and graceful pace. The multi-hued prayer pennants flutter in the gentle breeze that whiffs around the majestic monastery nestling on the mountain. An air of oriental mysticism pervades the place and spontaneously evokes feelings of deep devotion and awe. Tibetan ascetics and their disciples are there. So are the murals, tapestries and *thankas* (scroll paintings) embroidered with traditional and religious motifs. But, the pristine serene atmosphere of the *gompa* has soured to the extent that it seems to be beyond redemption. The canker has set in and, like gangrene, inch by inch, the flesh is putrefying though the spirit is ever so willing.

2

The Buddha Cries Again!

Shamar and Jamgon Kongtrul Rinpoches, second and fourth in the Kagyu hierarchy, respectively, had sponsored the construction of a Buddha statue for the Rumtek monastery's main assembly hall. On completion in early 1992, the gold-plated precious form stood a majestic fourteen feet high in the huge ornate prayer hall. During the consecration ceremony, drops of water suddenly began to drip from the statue. It was considered an ominous sign. Everyone apprehended major obstacles.

The last time a statue had 'cried' was in Lhasa before the Chinese invasion, as if anticipating the catastrophic event. Another statue of the Wisdom Buddha Manjushri from the Nalanda Institute above the Rumtek monastery had dropped its sword a few days earlier. Fearing more such ominous signs, the two regents expeditiously performed special prayers. To the modern and sceptical ear, any such extraordinary phenomenon may appear highly suspicious and one would rather not hear about them, and certainly not mention them as the great and ultimate proof of Buddhism's uniqueness. But for Tibetans, weaned to a diet of legends and mythology, such miraculous tales are their daily bread and butter.

A few weeks after this incident, Jamgon Kongtrul Rinpoche died in a tragic car accident. The Rumtek monastery was already on fire. The XVIth Karmapa had passed away in America. Forty-five days later, on 20 December 1981, the Karmapa's official cremation ceremony was held at Rumtek. During this period, the body of the Karmapa had shrunk considerably. Minutes after the body was consigned to flames, a 'blue-black ball' suddenly rolled out of an opening in the pyre. The mysterious object came to a stop on the northern side of the cremation place, facing Tibet, where one of the confidants of the Karmapa and two other lamas were standing. The incident sparked off hysterical excitement and speculation. Nobody knew exactly what to make of the mysterious object, and the puzzled lamas ran for advice to Kalu Rinpoche, the oldest and presumably the wisest in the gathering. After carefully examining the intricate 'ball', the rinpoche nodded in knowledgeable approval but 'wisely' remained mum just as the others in the illustrious assembly were. By now people realised the object resembled a human organ, and so the confidant of the Karmapa placed it high up on the side of the stupa.

At that moment, Situ Rinpoche emerged from an adjacent room with offerings to be burnt in the fire. He noticed the commotion but got no clue as to what was happening. He grabbed the object and disappeared into the main shrine room while others stood dazed and confused. Later that night, operating on a less ceremonial note, he quietly transferred the object to his private quarters.

Three days later, a big Kagyu conference was held in Rumtek. Situ Rinpoche rose from his chair and addressed the distinguished gathering of traditional Tibetan lamas in English. He first disclosed that what he had secured in his room was, actually, the Karmapa's heart. "The heart flew from the north door of the pyre and landed in my palm," he proudly claimed, exposing his right palm for everyone to admire. "It now belongs to me," he concluded. He then announced that he would build a two-to-three foot high stupa of solid gold in Sherab Ling, his monastery in Himachal Pradesh, to house the precious relic. It was all Greek to the lamas who looked on impassively as they were unable to understand even a word of his speech, rendered in English for reasons best known to Situ Rinpoche only. The few Western disciples gaped at the speaker in speechless astonishment. Smugly, the rinpoche scanned the silent assembly and resumed his seat with a satisfied air.

"Rinpoche, you should speak in Tibetan," a challenging voice resounded in the packed hall. It was Shamar Rinpoche. He had arrived half-way through his peer's sermon, just in time to hear how the heart had sailed from the pyre into Situ's palm. Visibly ill at ease, Situ Rinpoche again rose from his seat. "Shamar Rinpoche has rightly reminded me that I forgot to speak in Tibetan," he acknowledged and trotted out the story in his mother tongue.

Enter Dhamchoe Youngdu, the Rumtek's old general secretary. Less than impressed by the biased version of events from the cremation ceremony, and in no mood to let the unusual relic slip out of Rumtek, he boldly declared that the heart had not flown into anybody's palm. He then rallied his forces to challenge Situ's attempt to take away the relic to his monastery. Speaking on behalf of the Rumtek administration, he pledged to raise funds — if required — to erect a five-foot gold stupa. As caretaker of the Karmapa's seat, he firmly demanded that all items that had to do with the welfare and future prosperity of the lineage be left, in keeping with the Karmapa's wishes, in Rumtek. Without a moment's delay, he led a procession to Situ's room and quickly removed the relic from the shelf. His resolute action and decisive outbidding of Situ's offer carried the day. Barring him, nobody dared accuse a high lama of a lie. Perhaps it was not possible.

The story of Situ Rinpoche prophetically receiving and carrying away the relic would achieve the status of holy proof that he was indeed the senior peer of the lineage, selected by the Karmapa himself to bring forth his next reincarnation. And that could not be permitted.

Chagrined at losing hold of the Karmapa's heart, Situ Rinpoche then sought to take possession of the Karmapa's practice book instead. He argued that his monastery needed a special blessing from his teacher and a book that the Karmapa used was just the thing he had been looking for. This time, again, the general secretary strongly confronted Situ's new fancy. "He is going to produce a false prediction letter about the next

Karmapa out of it." Situ got nowhere with his lobbying and, eventually, had to leave Rumtek empty-handed. The Karmapa's belongings remained at his seat.

Situ Rinpoche's retinue lost no opportunity to poison the ears of their master. The seeds of contention had been sown. The Karmapa's two foremost disciples, Shamar and Situ Rinpoches, embarked, from that time on, on a competitive and hostile path.

The high *tulkus* did not forget how they — each one the absolute master of his monastery — used to hold undisputed sway over their respective regions. Their present condition was but a shadow of their former splendour. Following the urge to revive such small kingdoms, the embittered lamas started to plot to set up their own hierarchical organisations in exile. They displayed this blind tendency to duplicate their former structures in the new, foreign environment. At the same time, they showed an irresistible appetite for each other's portions. A case in point here is the ill-devised attempts of several Kagyu teachers to cut a piece out of the Karmapa's cake while ardently claiming to work in his name.

On 10 December 1982, Dhamchoe Youngdu passed away. The XVIth Karmapa, way back in 1968, had named Jewon Takpoo Yondu alias Topga Yulgyal, as another general secretary who was to look after the Kagyu affairs in Bhutan.

On 8 April 1983, the Department of Ecclesiastical Affairs of the Government of Sikkim acknowledged that, as per tradition, the four Eminences (the Shamar, Situ, Jamgon Kongtrul and Gyaltshab Rinpoches) had taken over as seat-holders of the Gyalwa Karmapa subsequent to his passing away. The department had issued a notification that:

> The four seat-holders formed a committee among themselves with the agreement that one of them would act as chairman for a period of three years in rotation. Dhamchoe Youngdu, the general secretary of the Karmapa administration, continued to be the general secretary to the four seat-holders. He passed away on 10 December 1982, leaving the post vacant. On 22 January 1983, with the consent of all the four seat-holders, Topga Yulgyal was appointed general

secretary and Tenzin Namgyal deputy general secretary to the Karmapa and all institutions of the Karmapa.

Till 1966, Topga Yulgyal was the *dorje lopon* (vajra master) of the Rumtek monastery. He was called rinpoche. In 1966 he married Ashi Chokyi Wangchuck, an aunt of the present king of Bhutan. Situ's supporters allege that for this act the Karmapa removed him from Rumtek itself. However, they admit that in 1968, the Karmapa, during one of his visits to Bhutan, conceded the title of general secretary to Topga Yulgyal, which earned him the right to wear the red scarf, the insignia of the upper class. Otherwise, he was entitled to wear only the white scarf, signifying a person of lower rank. In January 1983, on his own, Topga Rinpoche had changed his name to Topga Yulgyal before the competent court in Bhutan.

On 20 May 1982 a Tibetan Buddhist rinpoche, holding a diplomatic passport, issued by the Royal Government of Bhutan, was apprehended at Calcutta airport for smuggling 150 kg of gold worth Rs. 27.5 million. Tooshar Pandit reported in the 11-17 July, 1982 issue of the Calcutta-based weekly *Sunday* under the column Investigation:

> The rinpoche was driven straight to the customs headquarters at around 9 p.m. where the director of revenue intelligence and other senior officers were waiting to talk to him. They talked for about two hours and finally the rinpoche gave up. Yes, his luggage contained gold. He was carrying it for a businessman with establishments in both Calcutta and Delhi.
>
> The officers then took the rinpoche to the airport where his luggage was kept. Opening the bags they found that they had hit the jackpot. Neatly arranged on grooved thermocole boards were shining yellow bars, 821 pieces in all, each the size of a chocolate bar and weighing 187 gms. The bars were purchased in Hong Kong. For stamp on them was the legend: Chinese Gold and Silver Society, Hong Kong. The purity of the gold too was marked: it was five Tele fine gold and had been cast only recently — in May 1982.

In February 1993, another rinpoche, also carrying a Bhutanese diplomatic passport, was caught smuggling gold at Calcutta airport. In both the cases, the Royal Bhutan Government officers came to the rescue of the apprehended rinpoches. As late as in the last quarter of 1999, the Beru Khyentse Rinpoche, a Bodhgaya (Bihar)-based Kagyu *tulku*, was apprehended by customs officials at Calcutta airport when the rinpoche was found possessing gold. The rinpoche pleaded he was carrying two gold statues of the Buddha, gifted to him by his followers in South-East Asian countries.

Topga Yulgyal took over the reins of general secretary. The state of affairs left behind in Rumtek was, to put it briefly, chaotic. Displaying an aversion to public records, Dhamchoe Youngdu had eluded even the most remote type of accounting and kept all financial matters to himself. When the new general secretary and his team approached his family to take over Rumtek's liquid assets and inspect its financial records, a major scandal came to light. A tiny but expensive looking box, containing only about Rs. 30,000, was handed over to the incumbent by the widow of Dhamchoe Youngdu.

Rumtek was on the verge of bankruptcy. The ambitious project in Delhi (The Karmapa International Buddhist Institute) was just getting off the ground and required a regular inflow of funds. The new secretary launched an investigation into the missing capital. In his burning zeal to serve the Karmapa, Dhamchoe Youngdu had merged his private purse with the public one — to the great disadvantage of the latter. Thus Dhamchoe Youngdu's son, the young reincarnate of Ponlop Rinpoche, and the family of Dhamchoe Youngdu became the subject of an official enquiry. No wonder the inquiry did not suit the family of the late general secretary. They moved heaven and earth to stonewall the investigations and were downright hostile to the whole idea of recovering the Karmapa's money.

The widow of the late general secretary vanished from the scene altogether, to appear later in Woodstock, near New York, and married her old friend and lover, Tenzin Chonyi. The investigations came to a halt. The name of the new general secretary was dragged through the mire, even outside the country. And back in Rumtek, the new general secretary's insistence on managing the Karmapa property and assets on proper lines was declared a heresy.

His opposition to the common practice of swapping *tulku* titles for political and personal loyalty also generated little enthusiasm for him among the powers in Sikkim. He refused to accept the reincarnation of Gyathon Tulku in Rumtek. The XVIth Karmapa had sent Gyathon Tulku to Sikkim in 1954. He died in 1969. Sometime after his death, his servants approached the Karmapa to see if their master had taken rebirth anyway. The Karmapa's answer was unambiguous: "The Gyathon Tulku has not reincarnated; there is no one to be so recognised."

Fourteen years later, in 1983, after the death of the Karmapa, Situ Rinpoche delivered his contribution to the history of the Gyathons. He suddenly introduced the reincarnation of Gyathon to the Sikkimese society. The reincarnate hailed from the powerful Martam family of Sikkim. The new general secretary refused to be involved in what smelt of a conspiracy, and Rumtek's doors were closed on the doubtful reincarnation. Situ Rinpoche became the new guru of choice for the Martam family. Some other Kagyu lamas, unwilling to relinquish their privileges for the sake of modern values such as transparency and accountability, decided to move against the new general secretary.

Topga Yulgyal, even before assuming his duties as general secretary of the Rumtek administration, had proposed in December 1981 in the Kagyu meeting following the Karmapa's cremation that all the four leading disciples of the Karmapa, Kunzig Shamar, Tai Situ, Jamgon Kongtrul and Goshir Gyaltshab, stand together, in the Karmapa's absence, at the helm of the lineage. Each one was to hold responsibility for a period of three years, with Shamar Rinpoche being the first one on account of his seniority in the Kagyu order. The four lineage holders — as they were now popularly called — were also jointly entrusted with the task of finding and delivering the Karmapa's XVIIth reincarnation. From the historical point of view, the new scheme was an innovation. The group regency had never existed in the Kagyu tradition. It was not a setup involving legal documents. The rinpoches, however, accepted the proposal.

Shamar Rinpoche's return to prominence was, at best, a challenge to those around Situ and Gyaltshab Rinpoches who were not in the least disposed to share power with Shamar Rinpoche, 'a newcomer'. Ever since the Karmapa's death, resentful power brokers had tried to pull the rug from under the senior regent's feet. Shamar Rinpoche, the foremost disciple of the successive Gyalwa Karmapas and second in rank in the spiritual hierarchy of the Kagyu order, had been reincarnating at the side of the teacher for centuries. In 1738, Shamar Rinpoche became the object of official curbs and hardships. About a century earlier, due to the notable activity of the VIIIth Tai Situ, another close disciple of the Karmapa, the Kagyu order experienced a revival in Kham, far from Tsurphu, the original seat of the Karmapa in Tibet. Under the patronage of the King of Derge, Palpung (Situ Rinpoche's monastery) in the eastern Tibet flourished.

The then Shamar Rinpoche, brother of the then Panchen Lama — second within the ruling Gelug order — wished to replicate in central Tibet the success Situ Rinpoche had achieved in Kham. However, he was at a disadvantage because his seat was in Yangpa Chen, a day's journey from Lhasa. He therefore teamed up with his brother to achieve his ambitions. The Panchen Lama, who bore a resentment against the Gelug politicians for not being allowed on Tibet's throne, was a perfect ally. Ever since the Chinese emperor had bestowed a rotating monarchy upon the Vth Dalai Lama, the Panchen's successive reincarnations had been waiting in vain for their turn.

The Gelug administration sensed danger from the new alliance. The second in hierarchy of the Kagyu order clubbing together with a claimant to the Gelug throne was a direct challenge to the Gelug rule. The Gelugs decided to act. The Panchen Lama was dispatched with a mission to Beijing where he died under mysterious circumstances. Deprived of his brother's protection, Shamar Rinpoche fled to Nepal. He was immediately accused of plotting against Tibet. Though he later mediated in the dispute between Nepal and Tibet, his days as a prominent *tulku* were numbered. When fighting between the two Himalayan nations broke out, an influential Gelug minister saw an ideal opportunity to permanently rid the government and the 'yellow hat' (Gelug order) of a dangerous rival. Shamar Rinpoche was publicly blamed for Tibet's painful setback in the military confrontation and was proclaimed a traitor. Soon after he was officially prohibited to reincarnate. His monasteries were taken over, and his closest assistants tortured and killed.

A victim of political intrigue, Shamar Rinpoche kept reincarnating secretly for the next 200 years under the protective watch of the Karmapa. The *mantras* spoken against his rebirths had little effect. However, the proclamation banning him from the public eye was strictly enforced. The Tibetan government of Gelug, guarding its political supremacy, made sure that no Shamar *tulkus* were formally recognised.

At the turn of the 20th century, dark clouds began to gather on the Tibetan horizon. The dynamic XIIIth Dalai Lama, however, managed to uphold Tibet's sovereignty despite all odds. He extended a helping hand to the Kagyu and other orders, and, after centuries of exclusion, the XVth Karmapa was welcomed in Lhasa as a partner and friend. For the sake of national unity, the harsh laws targeting the rival orders were relaxed. Shamar Rinpoche also benefited from the new political climate. Though the infamous ban against his rebirth was not lifted, he was tolerated at the Karmapa's side during the tenure of the XIIIth Dalai Lama. However, the hawks among the Gelugs were unrelenting and consistently undermined the Dalai Lama's efforts to form a common Tibetan front.

In 1959, Tibet vanished from the political map of the world and the young XIVth Dalai Lama along with his close circle of attendants fled to India. His departure set off a mass exodus of lamas and monks to the south of the Himalayas. Once in India, representatives of the four orders suddenly found themselves on an equal footing. In India, the power of the Gelugs and the dominance of the central Tibetan government vanished overnight. Past feuds paled before the magnitude of the present catastrophe. Those fortunate lamas who had managed to survive the ordeal of the Chinese invasion and the anguish of crossing the Himalayas on foot in winter were now confronted with the enormous task of rebuilding in exile what they could salvage from the destruction in Tibet.

Influenced by his friendship with the XVIth Karmapa and realising that cooperation was now essential, the XIVth Dalai Lama agreed to lift the 200-year-old ban on Shamar Rinpoche's reincarnation. Shamar Rinpoche was again officially recognised by the Gelug's head. Some in the Kagyu family did not appreciate this development. The Kagyu family itself had witnessed a chequered history over the last millennium. (See Appendix C for more details.)

3

Tremors in Shangrila

About 6.5 million people inhabited Tibet in 1959. Tibet had a total area of 1.3 million sq. km. At least 1,80,000 Tibetans are in exile. India alone accounts for about 1,10,000 while Nepal has about 20,000 and the rest are scattered over Europe, USA, etc. Dharamsala (Himachal Pradesh), Dehra Dun (Uttar Pradesh), Kushalnagar (Karnataka), Darjeeling (West Bengal), Arunachal Pradesh, Sikkim and Ladakh in India have settlements of Tibetan Buddhists. Even the total ruin of Tibet wasn't affliction enough to prevent the collective tendency of the Buddhist lamas to quarrel amongst themselves.

No sooner had the dust from the disaster settled than the old feuds dating back into the past revived with a vengeance. The old Lhasa regime of the Gelugs under a new name, 'Tibetan Government-in-exile', based at Dharamsala in India inherited and resumed the old agenda of hostility towards the other Buddhist orders. The agenda was taken up with all the enthusiasm, prejudices, rivalries and fights of the past.

In 1964, the government-in-exile of the Dalai Lama wanted to introduce social, economic and religious reforms to the recently evicted Tibetans. Gyalo Thondup, the Dalai Lama's brother, dubiously proposed to abolish the old Buddhist orders, and do away with the rich, religious diversity so characteristic of Tibet, and thus bring the high lamas to heel. The new policy in one way or the other sought to curtail the freedom of all Tibetans. The spiritual hierarchies of the Nyingma, Kagyu, Sakya and their corollary sub-orders fell victim to slander and reproach. Gyalo Thondup's Machiavellian programme struck fear into the lamas' hearts. As further details of the elaborate plan surfaced, the lamas realised that a coup against three of the orders was being plotted. The proposed new religious body that would replace the traditional orders would be in the sole control of the Gelug hierarchy. The worried lamas rushed to the Karmapa.

Though the Karmapa resolutely shunned Tibetan politics, he, nevertheless, was a voice to be reckoned with in Tibetan Buddhist affairs. Apprehensive of being swallowed up by the 'big brother' in such a sombre atmosphere, refugees from Kham, in particular, chose the Karmapa as their political leader. Thus, a powerful and opposing power centre to the Dalai Lama and the official line of Dharamsala sprang into existence.

The leaders of 13 large Tibetan settlements created an alliance called 'Thirteen Settlements'. Another large camp from Nepal, led by General Bava Yeshi, joined them, thus becoming 'Fourteen Settlements'. Khamtrul and Chokling Rinpoches were appointed president and general secretary, respectively. Ultimately they prepared to face the Gelug challenge. The stalemate continued for about a decade until the Dharamsala coterie cried it off in 1973. However, for years to come, the Tibetans in exile continued to be polarised into two main groups. Chagrined at not being able to subdue the other orders, the Dharamsala supporters planned to launch a lethal strike. According to the plans, a handful of dissidents were to be eradicated.

On 13 March 1977, dusk was falling in Clement Town, on the outskirts of Dehra Dun in India. Gungtang Tsultrim, a prominent leader of the 'Fourteen Settlements' was strolling in the backyard of his house, oblivious to the threat to his life. Some distance away, behind a tree, an assassin was lurking. The assassin waited for the darkness to deepen. Minutes later, whipping out a gun from a hand-woven sack, he shot Tsultrim several times at point blank range. Simultaneously, the power supply conveniently went off, enabling the assailant to escape.

Horrified relatives and friends rushed out but Tsultrim was beyond all earthly help. They found a sack and a pair of spectacles, presumably belonging to the assassin. A child from the neighbourhood recognised the spectacles as those of his father. The police launched a crackdown on the assailant. Three months later, the Nepalese police arrested a suspect in Kathmandu. Shortly before his extradition to India, where he was wanted in another murder case, the arrested man confessed to murdering Gungtang Tsultrim. Hired for the job, he was paid rupees three hundred thousand by the Tibetan government-in-exile in Dharamsala. The Tibetan government-in-exile had also offered him more money for eliminating the XVIth Karmapa, he confessed.

The Sikkim government immediately provided an armed escort of 11 men to the Karmapa. The assailant was extradited to India, to be lodged in Lucknow prison. There, he repeated his confessional statement. Outraged, representatives of the 'Fourteen Settlements' staged an angry demonstrations at Dharamsala.

Thereafter, matters stayed low-key but the incident was a watershed for many Tibetans. It was obvious that even in exile, the newly installed bureau had brought with it the same old ways of repression, divisive designs and sectarian persecution.

On its part, the Dharamsala coterie would not forgive the Karmapa's uncompromising stance in the dispute and his defiance of the Dalai Lama's authority. Consequently, Kagyus became the targets of unsavoury attacks. The renewed friendship between the Dalai Lama and the Karmapa was strangled by burgeoning hostilities generated by the unsavoury power struggle. And the painful realities made it impossible for either side to forgive or forget.

In the light of the Karmapa's independent position, Dharamsala came to regret the Dalai Lama's change of policy concerning Shamar Tulku. The lifting of the ban was, to a large extent, an empty gesture because neither the Dalai Lama nor his government held jurisdiction in India. Shamar Tulku no longer required permission from the Dalai Lama. The Karmapa and his second-in-command Shamar Tulku were considered a threat to the Gelug's political aims.

The Dalai Lama, as nominal ruler of all Tibetans, was expected to remain above such scheming and unhealthy politics. But, surrounded by players with a serious bent for conspiracy and hamstrung by trying to accommodate all parties, he had only the reputation of his name left at his disposal. In order to check the machinations of the less rational members of his cabinet, he would periodically declare himself to be the last incarnation in the line of the Dalai Lamas. The strategy would work for a time, until his politicians reassumed their scheming tactics against the other three Buddhist orders.

However, clashes among Tibetans were not confined to the harassment of the rivals by the Gelugs. Opposition to Shamar's reinstatement emerged unexpectedly from far more immediate quarters than Dharamsala.

Every *tulku* in Tibet was surrounded and groomed from cradle to grave by a retinue of professional advisers and servants. Life after life, their families held the same functions around their lama. These groups grew in prominence and size until they became de facto courts, strait-jacketing their master. For them, personal ambitions meant a great deal more than one would expect from people in the service of a spiritual teacher.

The reincarnations of the Karmapa and his close disciples maintained such an entourage whose members zealously guarded their place in the hierarchy of the lineage. When Shamar and his household were banned from the public scene, the groups surrounding other eminent Kagyu lamas moved, together with their rinpoches, one notch higher in the pecking order.

Shamar's sudden return brought about an end to that cozy state of affairs. As he reclaimed his place as senior student to the Karmapa, the retinue of Situ Rinpoche was forced one notch down in the power system. Even more displeased were the followers of Gyaltshab Rinpoche. They shared several buildings with the Karmapa's administration in Tsurphu, the traditional seat of the Karmapa in Tibet. On top of that, they had been filing lawsuits for centuries to contest the property rights.

Due to the Shamar's reappearance and after the XVIth Karmapa's insertion of Jamgon Kongtrul Rinpoche as fourth in the lineage, Gyaltshab Rinpoche had to be content with the fifth position. After 200 years of enjoying higher status, the protective families that surrounded Situ and Gyaltshab Rinpoches were unwilling to accept the latest declining twist in their fortunes. In them, Dharamsala found an unforeseen ally in challenging the senior Kagyu lineage holder. It was generally assumed, though not always proven, that the rinpoches themselves were above these Machiavellian calculations.

While the Karmapa was alive, he remained the undisputed leader of the Kagyu lineage. He personally took over the education of his four close disciples who progressed under his supervision, receiving instructions and empowerment into the treasures of the Kagyu transmission. Though growing together under the Karmapa's watch, the four young incarnates did not mix with each other. To cap it, the fact that Shamar and Situ claimed origin from diametrically opposite social backgrounds hardly helped to bridge the differences either. The former enjoyed the lustre of aristocratic descent with links to the Karmapa's family while the latter bore the stigma of the son of a blacksmith.

However, in one respect, Shamar was at a disadvantage. During his two centuries of official banishment, he had lost his loyal retinue of assistants. Therefore, he was more vulnerable to political attacks compared to his three peers.

Before his death in the autumn of 1981, the Karmapa had desired that three vital projects be completed: the Nalanda Institute for Higher Buddhist Studies at Rumtek, the Dharma Chakra Centre in New Delhi, and the printing of 500 sets of *the Tenjyur*, an extensive collection of commentaries on the Buddha's teachings. The first of three projects came under the supervision of the Jamgon Kongtrul Rinpoche, while the project in Delhi, later known as the Karmapa International Buddhist Institute, became the domain of Shamar Rinpoche. The printing of *the Tenjyur*, a tedious and meticulously long process, was also to be finalised in Delhi.

Situ Rinpoche, opting to venture out of the Rumtek monastery in 1976 before the completion of his training, had set up his monastery in Himachal Pradesh in proximity to Dharamsala. Time and again, the Karmapa asked his close disciples of foreign origins to request Situ Rinpoche to return to Rumtek and finish his instructions on *mahamudra* — or the great seal — the ultimate view on the nature of reality. But his appeals fell on deaf ears. When Situ Rinpoche finally came around, the time and terms for the fulfilment of his training were over. In one of his notes to the Karmapa, Situ Rinpoche wondered why the Karmapa refused to answer his many previous letters. Apparently, after years of pleading with his disciple, the frustrated Karmapa had decided against having Situ Rinpoche at his quarters. And, therefore, except for a stay during the Karmapa's cremation ceremony and a few brief visits thereafter, Situ Rinpoche took care to stay away from Rumtek until 1992. But, when he did appear in May 1992, he had a good deal more in his mind than just the desire to perform his religious duties. However, he was with the XVIth Karmapa when the latter breathed his last.

The seeds of confrontation between the two senior regents of the Kagyu order had already been sown earlier. In the summer of 1983, Kalu Rinpoche had agreed to give Rinchen Terdzod empowerment to transmit the main teachings of Guru Rimpoche who was the Indian master who had brought Buddhism to Tibet. The empowerment served as a unique method for preserving the continuity of the teachings in Tibet. During the ceremony, a disciple is introduced to a certain aspect of the Buddha's life and works. An accomplished master would grant it to aspiring students, who would then become holders of the practice with the potential to, one day, fully realise it and pass it on to others. This is not to say that the hundreds that would crowd a monastery's courtyard to receive an initiation were all striving practitioners ready to jump into the regime of a spiritual pursuit. The laity among Tibetans fought fiercely at the completion of each ceremony to get a blessing from the lama, but this was as far as his religious enthusiasm would go during such functions.

Since, in the old days, certain popular empowerments could attract a throng of several thousand people, it was not uncommon that a monastery would encourage its head lama to obtain and later perform the highly sought after initiations. After all, even a few-hundred-strong army of pilgrims was a potent source of income for a cloister. Such practical reasoning was not entirely lost on the masters when Tibetans established themselves on Indian soil. The life of refugees, particularly groups of destitute monks thrown into an environment fraught with unknown hardships depended solely on the spiritual skill of their master for survival.

However, in 1983, nearly 25 years after fleeing Tibet, basic survival was not an issue for most Tibetans anymore. With the sudden and recent arrival on the scene of affluent patrons from the Chinese community in South-East Asia, the high rinpoches and their households sensed big fortunes lying ahead. Not surprisingly, when the rich Chinese devotees showed a penchant for elaborate initiations, a number of lamas and their enterprising assistants went out of their way to satisfy such tastes. An empowerment resurfaced as a hot potato that could buy influence and bring wealth.

Lama Paljur from Palpung, the traditional seat of Situ Rinpoche in eastern Tibet, called Shamar, Situ, Jamgon and Gyaltshab Rinpoches and gave them a dose of what he considered conventional guru wisdom. "Think about the future," he began patronizingly to the rinpoches. "Soon you will need funds to run your monasteries," he dangled the bait. "You should learn the popular empowerment. Consider the thousands that would come when you, the high *tulkus*, grant your initiations. All these people, the whole mass, would become your disciples," Paljur further tempted his listeners. "Kalu Rinpoche is a great master. You must ask him for *rinchen terdzod*, an empowerment in highest demand," Thus, the lama summed up his arguments.

Without delay, Jamgon and Gyaltshab Rinpoches petitioned Kalu Rinpoche, informing him of their desire to receive the invaluable *rinchen terdzod*. When the distinguished lama readily acceded, they engaged the local Kagyu world in energetic preparations for six months of lengthy ceremonies. Shamar Rinpoche himself was lukewarm to the idea because the motivation seemed to be a dubious one. However, since his refusal to join the ceremonies would be construed as an offence to the old Kalu Rinpoche, he reluctantly went along with the others. As usual, Situ Rinpoche stayed at separate quarters.

In the meantime, Lea Terhune — dismissed from the services of the Rumtek administration and later made the secretary of Situ Rinpoche — came out with a paper accusing Shamar Rinpoche of usurping the Delhi land of the Karmapa. The three other rinpoches, without pursuing a fair inquiry into the allegation, decided to take the senior regent, Shamar Rinpoche, to court.

And so, as lamas and students gathered at Sonada, Kalu Rinpoche's seat that lay seven kilometres from Darjeeling, to receive the empowerment, the three venerable rinpoches readied to deliver a masterstroke of their own making. One misty morning, nearly halfway through initiations, Shamar Rinpoche received a startling legal notice from lawyers representing the three lineage holders. Three of the Karmapa's 'heart sons' — as they were called because the Karmapa had accepted them as his sons — intended to officially charge their senior peer with stealing the Karmapa's property in Delhi.

Adding insult to injury, the three Eminences had schemed to counter-coup a notch higher. Shamar Rinpoche discovered that they had approached Kalu Rinpoche with an intricate request: At the completion of the ceremonies, the eminent lama was to publicly ask the four regents to place the future XVIIth Karmapa in Tsurphu in occupied Tibet, rather than at his new seat at Rumtek. Thrangu Rinpoche, the chief abbot of Tsurphu, was already pressing the point for the sake of the old cloister. To Shamar Rinpoche, the whole idea behind the benevolent desire to rebuild Tsurphu was nothing less than a manoeuvre to seize control of the Kagyu order. Were the reincarnation of the Karmapa to fall into the communists' grip, the allies of China, the powerful lamas could remain at the helm of the lineage and rule the roost. If caught unawares, Kalu Rinpoche would have to come down after the empowerment with this peculiar announcement. Shamar Rinpoche then would be left with no other option but to agree to his appeal. After receiving the precious initiations from Kalu Rinpoche, Tibetan etiquette would leave Shamar Rinpoche with no choice but to concede the teacher's wish — no matter how wilful this was.

Disgusted with such intrigues but bent on avoiding a showdown during the ceremonies as well as the prospect of the XVIIth Karmapa becoming a citizen of China, Shamar Rinpoche decided to leave Sonada. Taking leave of Kalu Rinpoche, he rushed to Delhi. In Sonada, his seat remained conspicuously vacant during the second half of ceremonies. The senior regent's departure was a bolt from the blue for the naive Tibetans. To avoid further embarrassment, Beru Khyentse Rinpoche, another prominent Kagyu lama, was rushed in as his replacement for getting empowerment.

Despite their attempts to sully Shamar Rinpoche's image, his three rival lineage-holders failed to carry the day in court. Lawyers hired by the general secretary of the Rumtek administration proved the absurdity of the charge. The plot of land in question had been donated to the XVIth Karmapa by the then Prime Minister of India, Mrs. Indira Gandhi. The land was given on a 99-year lease on a token lease rent of rupee one per annum. This meant that the real owner of the land was the Government of India and not the Karmapa. The whole allegation that the Karmapa's land had been transferred in someone else's name was, therefore, ludicrous.

Replying to a query by Shamar Rinpoche, Mr. Samar Roy Choudhury, a Calcutta-based advocate, in September 1983, said:

> By virtue of, and under a registered perpetual lease, the President of India transferred the Delhi land in the name of the Karmapa as the supreme head of the Dharma Chakra Centre. You can rest assured that there is no way in law to remove the name of the Karmapa with regard to the said land. Unfortunately some errors and mistakes have been found in the said deed and, as such, the same are required to be rectified immediately. As per the provision in the law, the proposed rectification can only be done by executing

> another document named 'Deed of Rectification', and such document like another deed can only be executed by and between the original lessor, that is to say, the President of India, and the original lessee, that is to say, the Karmapa. But since the Karmapa is no more, the proposed deed should be registered by and between the President of India and the successor of the Karmapa. Execution of the said deed of rectification in the aforesaid manner, that is to say, by and between the President of India and yourself as the sole executor to the Karmapa, shall not be treated as transfer of the said land. Your role in the said deed will be to represent the Karmapa since deceased.
>
> The deed of rectification can easily be executed in the aforesaid manner which will be the part and parcel of the original deed of perpetual lease and both should be treated as a part of each other and as such the Karmapa's name as the original transferee of the said land will be unaffected.

A legal signatory that represented the Karmapa was required. All this happened after the group regency of four rinpoches had been established and, during his tenure, Shamar Rinpoche acted on behalf of the group. This amended document was what Lea Terhune, the dismissed clerk of the Rumtek administration, had unearthed.

Now, it was the turn of Shamar Rinpoche to deliver his masterstroke. Threatening his peers with legal action, he stated that he had lost trust in the three Eminences' integrity to stand for the lineage. He, however, proposed to drop his proposed lawsuit against them if they, in return, agreed to dissolve the group regency. Caught between the devil and the deep sea, Jamgon Kongtrul and Gyaltshab Rinpoches chose not to walk the plank and signed the corresponding declaration. And so, after merely a few years of its unsteady course, the group leadership ceased to exist.

Under the Karmapa's administration, Kunzig Shamar Rinpoche, according to tradition, assumed the role of the representative of the Karmapa till the reincarnation was found but his role was restricted only to officiating and attending formal ceremonies on the Karmapa's behalf. The four rinpoches still remained, as agreed beforehand, in joint control of the process of recognition of the reincarnation. Meanwhile, Topga Yulgyal, General Secretary of Rumtek administration, became a thorn in the flesh of the three Eminences, Situ, Jamgon Kongtrul and Gyaltshab Rinpoches.

At this stage, in contrast to the other two rinpoches, Jamgon Kongtrul Rinpoche tried to mend fences and establish a new relationship with Shamar Rinpoche based on mutual trust and respect for the main regent's position.

4

Monks with Daggers

The subject of finding the XVIIth reincarnation of the Karmapa had fuelled the imagination of his students from the very first moment after the cremation of the XVIth Karmapa. Tibetans are said to excel at fanning outlandish ideas as to the whereabouts and identity of the reincarnation of the Karmapa. And this ability is matched by a credulousness that's truly incredible. With each passing year the proposed theories grew more outrageous and the public had to put up with an exotic selection, ranging from a Bhutanese royal to a Tibetan born in America, for aspirants to the Karmapa's throne. The rumour mills kept on grinding with a vengeance.

One candidate was spotted by Drupon Dechen Rinpoche, a resident of Tsurphu. He was interested only in rebuilding the Tsurphu monastery. Once, when he was travelling in Bata (Tibet), a boy came up to him. Pointing to the protection cord which the rinpoche had received from the Karmapa, the boy said, "I have given you this". Intrigued, the rinpoche tested further by putting two black pills in the palm of his hands, one being a real Karmapa's black pill and the other made by him. The boy immediately pointed out to the real one and again said that he had given it to the rinpoche. The boy also mentioned that his monastery was in India. In 1984, the rinpoche visited Rumtek and disclosed the matter. Though confidential, the news spread far and wide. Many people believed the boy to be the reincarnation of the Karmapa.

Another claimant was born in 1983 in Bodh Gaya. The parents were Tibetans who had just come out of Tibet. The boy was brought to Situ Rinpoche's monastery at Sherab Ling, where the boy stayed. Sangye Rinpoche, an important Kagyu teacher, would perform a bathing ceremony for the boy everyday, which was seen as a sign that the boy was very special. Many believed that he might be the new Karmapa. Now, he is said to be the reincarnation of Gongkar Rinpoche. This lama was famous in Tibet and became the main teacher of many Chinese people. While breathing his last, he gathered his disciples and told them to leave China and settle in Taiwan. These settlers invited Tibetan rinpoches and other lamas. They also established monasteries for Gongkar Rinpoche.

Then there were several pregnancies which many expected to bring about the Karmapa. Around 1982, the sister of one of Situ Rinpoche's secretaries was pregnant. She reportedly claimed she had received from Situ Rinpoche a special ceremonial scarf apparently indicating that the child in her womb was the reincarnation of the XVIth Karmapa. Her husband shot off letters to his friends informing them that the Karmapa would appear as his son. Sadly for them, however, it was a girl and not a boy born later that year. Later in a publication, *Karmapa Khenno*, he described the incident as a blatant lie and a motivated allegation.

Much the same happened in the case of the daughter of Lama Donchen. She had also been told by Situ Rinpoche that she was carrying a special child but she too gave birth to a girl.

A rumour once spread related to the royal family of Bhutan. The king has several sons and one of them was born around 1983. At a certain time people started saying that he was a very special child. They said that he liked to use a drum and bell and that he always wanted to wear yellow clothes. When people started saying that he might be the Karmapa, the king issued a warning, saying that whomsoever spread this rumour would be punished. Thereafter, all fell silent in Bhutan and nothing more was heard of the matter.

Regarding the allegation that Topga Rinpoche wanted to establish a prince of Bhutan as the Karmapa, Shamar Rinpoche says:

> It originated in 1983 or 84, when everybody was really waiting for some indication of the reincarnation of the Karmapa. At that time I was in Bhutan. One day there was a very clear sky and beautiful weather. There was incredibly clear rainbow around the sun. This is one of the auspicious signs that can indicate the birth of a great being. I thought that it meant that the Karmapa had been born.
>
> Actually such auspicious sign is interpreted as portending that a great being has passed away or has been born. I thought then that it could mean that His Holiness (the Karmapa) had been born. I was very happy about it. Therefore, I wrote a letter to Rumtek, rejoicing in a way that may be the Karmapa's reincarnation had now been born, and I suggested that it might be appropriate to celebrate and offer prayers.
>
> As regards the rainbow, I do not think it was necessarily related to a person in Bhutan. Probably everybody could see it, even in Sikkim. It had no connection with Bhutan as a country. If at that moment a Bhutanese prince was born — who knows — then it would just have been a coincidence, and who is to blame for that? I cannot ask the rainbow, 'Why did you appear?' Seriously, though, the point is that they knew very well I was not fabricating a Karmapa — you cannot fabricate a Karmapa.

In 1987, a man on the Indo-Bhutan border claimed that his son was the Karmapa and many people believed him. The Bhutanese government tried to apprehend him, but he escaped. A picture of the boy was even brought to the Rumtek office.

In 1990, a Bhutanese princess had a vision. Shamar Rinpoche recalled this incident and admitted his mistake. In 1988, Dingo Khyentse Rinpoche had been informed by one of the sisters of the King of Bhutan, Princess Sonam Chodron, that she had a vision in which she had been given information concerning the reincarnation of the Karmapa. She had spoken of a lake in To region as the birthplace of the Karmapa's reincarnation. She wrote about it to all the four Eminences and the Dalai Lama.

Shamar Rinpoche confirmed that the princess was gifted with quite remarkable qualities. It was well known that she was a clairvoyant. Once during a summit meeting attended by the then President of Egypt, Mr Anwar Sadat, the princess had a vision pointing to Mr Sadat's assassination. Subsequently, the vision proved to be true. During his visit to Tibet, Shamar Rinpoche shared it casually with one of the secretaries of his seat, the Yangpachen monastery. Apparently, the secretary later passed this information to the Tsurphu monastery and it triggered several subsequent events. Shamar Rinpoche visited Tibet but clarified that he had not gone to Tibet merely on account of the vision of Princess Sonam Chodron but his visit was to investigate another child.

Bardo Tulku, a lama from Woodstock, a Kagyu monastery north of New York, amid great pomp and flair, blessed the general public with a pretentious announcement that the fortunate woman who was carrying the future Karmapa happened to be his wife. He succeeded in drumming up some support for his fanciful claim. Sensation, flourish, climax... then anticlimax when his wife gave birth to a girl. Traditionally, all Karmapas incarnate in a male body. Way back in 1982, a prominent British newspaper had predicted that the Karmapa would be born in Hong Kong.

On New Year's day in 1998, Dawa Sangpo Dorji, then 21-year-old, from Mangen in Sikkim, came to the Rumtek monastery in a cavalcade of cars claiming he was the XVIIth Karmapa. He says though he was born before the XVIth Karmapa died, he lived in a body without a soul, waiting for the Karmapa's passing away for his soul to enter the body. He was not allowed to enter Rumtek. In January 2000 he reiterated his claim.

On 9 February 1986, Shamar Rinpoche in an open letter to all Kagyu lamas and *tulkus* forewarned, "Many rumours are being circulated in these degenerated times. Therefore, the issue of the Karmapa's reincarnation needs to be approached with utmost care." He further cautioned that various individuals would make false claims to have received instructions and prophecies as to finding the reincarnation and requested lamas and *tulkus* not to trust any such claim. He added that he would not put his faith behind such frivolous claims.

Increasingly from 1984 onward, the regents found themselves more and more pressed by individuals demanding an announcement about the next Karmapa. Tibetans are masters at applying pressure to their beloved rinpoches. Humbly begging, praising and pleading, they will not stop until a besieged and badgered lama caves in, defeated.

And deliver the lamas did. In 1986, to the joy, merriment and applause of Kagyu followers all over the world, the Eminences declared that the prediction letter left by the XVIth Karmapa had finally been located. But the exalted announcement had a rider. The prediction letter had 'inner' and 'outer' layers of instructions. The outer layer contained instructions for removing obstacles and the inner layer contained the instructions for finding and identifying the reincarnation.

In the 'testament', the XVIth Karmapa had asked his disciples to perform numerous rituals and recite *mantras* before the content of the real letter containing the details of his XVIIth rebirth could be revealed. Though the number of *mantras* mentioned ran into billions, Kagyus everywhere rolled up their sleeves and set to perform rituals. Before long, the task was completed.

In May 1988, the Rumtek staff confirmed that all rituals specified in the additional letter had been performed. Thus, the obstacles to opening the final testament had been removed. While jubilant disciples celebrated their achievement, the regents kept dragging their feet and the long awaited announcement was nowhere in sight. With great determination, they tried to avoid, for some inexplicable reason, the whole subject altogether.

With equal determination, they also kept avoiding each other. After their inspiring communiqué in 1986, the four met officially only three times in the course of the next four years. Most meetings fell through because the Eminences were unable to agree on the time and place of the gatherings; Situ and the Shamar Rinpoches would under no circumstance accept each other's proposals for the talks. Situ Rinpoche just would not turn up at a gathering endorsed by Topga Yulgyal, while Shamar Rinpoche equally pointedly ignored his rival. Not only were their gatherings scarce but also largely inconclusive. Moreover, the consultations did not seem to get to the core of the issue.

After 1990, the pressure to deliver the Karmapa grew stronger. Demands turned more insolent, even as the contacts between the regents became even more sporadic. Rumours spread and one wild theory chased another. A whole array of seasoned groups cropped up on the scene. Some accused the senior regent Shamar Rinpoche with purposefully obstructing the process of recognition. The general secretary, too, was accused of draining the Rumtek's coffers. Word spread that Shamar Rinpoche, allegedly in league with the general secretary, was about to enthrone a Bhutanese prince as the XVIIth Karmapa. Tirades against them were well orchestrated. A torrent of proclamations and appeals went flashing out to monasteries and politicians. With each consecutive wave, the invectives unleashed grew more virulent and poisonous. Shamar Rinpoche and Topga Yulgyal found themselves under siege and constant fire from enraged 'defenders' of the Karmapa's legacy. Characteristically, the 'incensed citizens of Tibet' reserved their praise for Situ Rinpoche, describing him as the only one among the regents to advocate swift action on the vexing issue of reincarnation of the Karmapa. The pattern in the mischievous campaign was clear. It was Situ Rinpoche behind the veil. The Tibetan rumour mill ground on, merrily and noisily, while the besieged clasped their hands to the ears and waited helplessly for the tirades to end.

In fact, the top of the lineage had already split. The attempt to seize the Karmapa's heart after the cremation ceremony in Rumtek, the ill-fated motion to take Shamar Rinpoche to court, and the slander campaign were all part of a concerted move to oust the senior regent from his seat. These moves were but pointers only to the extent of the conspiracy. Shamar Rinpoche failed to realise that the ground was shifting under his feet and that behind the lies and quarrels a more serious intrigue was being hatched. The vilification campaign did not remain confined to India and Tibet. It spread to Samye Ling and Woodstock monasteries in Scotland and upstate New York, respectively. The monks in these monasteries too added their own contributions to spread the rumours.

Lama Ole, a distinguished foreign disciple of the XVIth Karmapa, kept advising Shamar, Jamgon Kongtrul and Gyaltshab Rinpoches: "There must be no public announcement before the child (reincarnation of the Karmapa) is safe in Rumtek. We cannot work with the Chinese breathing down our backs." He even suggested a scheme to quickly slip the child out of China's reach and into India. Shamar Rinpoche, smuggled his candidate from Tibet in 1994 while his rival, Situ Rinpoche succeeded in bringing his choice in January 2000. His detractors allege that Situ Rinpoche staged a coup of sorts in connivance with the Chinese authorities.

Early in 1992, the general atmosphere concerning the XVIIth Karmapa became one of growing anticipation. Two of the Eminences, Jamgon Kongtrul and Gyaltshab Rinpoches, broke their traditional silence and timidly hinted that a proclamation might be close at hand. But the grand hopes were quickly dispelled by Jamgon Kongtrul Rinpoche who recanted and excused himself for having raised false hopes and quickly got back to the now quite familiar pledge that an announcement would follow soon. He was just back from the three-month, arduous journey in Tibet and, maybe, he had come back with a different point of view from the one expressed earlier.

In the meantime, Situ Rinpoche's supporters trumpeted around Rumtek that Situ Rinpoche had just found the reincarnation of the Trungpa Tulku in eastern Tibet. The claim seemed dubious as the last Trungpa had predicted that he would reincarnate as an ordinary Japanese worker.

Trungpa, along with the Akong Tulku, was the member of a four-member contingent from a high-profile school for reincarnates in Himachal Pradesh. The team arrived in England in the mid-sixties. The idea to send the young hopefuls to Europe came from Gelongma Pag-Mo, a traditional and well-connected

Buddhist nun (mother of Indian movie star Kabir Bedi) who used her influence and power of persuasion to convince the Karmapa that the entry of a group of educated Tibetans into Europe would create a lasting bridge between Tibet and the West. In that party, only Ato Rinpoche avoided controversy and settled down to a quiet life in southern England. He commands respect and serves as a living example of the virtues of Buddhism. The rest contrived to wreak much havoc on Buddhism both in the West as well as in India and Tibet, and the bridges they created were mainly those of confusion or shock, or simply over troubled waters.

Trungpa and Akong Tulkus were not only the most forceful but also the most questionable individuals in the group. Puffed with grand ambitions, they perceived themselves as spokesmen for Buddhism and propped themselves up as future leaders of the lineage in the West. However, the harmony between the two was short-lived. In his book *Born in Tibet*, Trungpa called Akong paranoid and scheming. Trungpa, in trouble in any case, decided to try his luck in America. The British police were hunting him for drug abuse at Samye Ling, the retreat centre he had founded with Akong in Scotland. After hiding in a stable, he ventured across Atlantic to America where, with the help of others, he founded the Dharmadhatu organisation. In a short time the Buddha's teachings were distorted into a pyramidal institution that adopted the features of a small feudal kingdom from the old Tibet.

The lama-king with a court responding to his every whim ruled undisputed while most disciples were moulded into an obedient, sheep-like crowd. Having befriended a group of celebrated intellectuals in the sixties, Trungpa began basking in his newfound role of 'crazy wisdom' guru. He flourished financially and otherwise. A series of books adapted from his lectures and bearing the guru's signature appeared in the market. The highest principles of Buddhism were thus made accessible to the Western mind. For a while Dharmadhatu achieved nation-wide acclaim, and Trungpa himself became the model for aspiring Tibetan lamas on how to succeed in the West.

The system, however, was rotten to the core. The spiritual leader and his close circles of favourites lived the lives of spoiled princes, indulging in drunken orgies and flagellation that rivalled those of the decadent emperors of ancient Rome. On the other hand, hundreds of ordinary members had to go through a regimen of years-long and robot-like sitting practices that not only drained their brains but also emptied their pockets. Trungpa died an alcoholic, and his regent, Ozel Tenzin, was accused by his male lovers of knowingly infecting them with HIV from 1983 to 1988. Tenzin himself died of AIDS in 1990. However, *thankas* (Tibetan religious scroll paintings) depicting the venerable Trungpa Tulku, comfortably stretched out on a sofa, looking more like an eastern prince than a hard-working lama, and surrounded by an array of holy icons and auspicious symbols were easily available in Rumtek. In the corner of the painting, humbly squatting at the feet of his guru, appeared Trungpa's regent Ozel Tenzin.

Kalu Rinpoche, the old lama of the Kagyu school, having his monastery at Sonada on way to Darjeeling had already earned an unsavoury reputation owing to his uncompromising stance on monastic vows and stubborn insistence on celibacy, which looked distinctly hollow if not downright dishonest. In the autumn of 1996, June Campbell, one-time translator and close disciple of Kalu Rinpoche, shocked the Buddhist community by revealing that she was, in fact, the rinpoche's lover during the years she travelled as part of his entourage. In her book *Traveller in Space*, she paints a highly critical picture of the Tibetan monastic system and confides that how she was sexually exploited and deceived by the illustrious lama when he had been sent on a trip to Europe in early and mid-seventies by the Karmapa.

Akong Tulku was made of sterner stuff than his rival, Trungpa. He clearly lacked Trungpa's charisma and attracted neither glamour nor attention. Small, but powerfully built, head set atop a corpulent body, he possessed one quality that eclipsed all other streaks in his stolid character: patience and perseverance to achieve his long-term objectives. Soon after arriving in England, the young *tulku* set his ambitious goals. He first sent his brother — married to the same woman as himself — into closed retreat. Then came the time to act. Having little disposition for the lavish style of living that would bring the Trungpa's downfall in England, Akong's aim was less extravagant and more concrete: control over the growing Kagyu followings in Europe. But he was not welcomed there. During the first visit of the XVIth Karmapa to Europe in 1974, the French centres refused to receive him as part of the Karmapa's entourage. In the end, the Karmapa himself had to curb his ambitions. Having only the Belgians on his side, Akong Tulku had no other choice but to return to Samye Ling where, for the next few years, he remained forgotten but unable to forget.

In fact, Akong does not belong to the Kagyu order. The first Akong had been a black magician and caretaker of a temple in a village in eastern Tibet. When he died, the villagers requested a visiting lama to recognise his successor. He recognised a child and declared him the incarnation of Akong, i.e. the second Akong. In exile in India, the child was patronised by Chogyam Trungpa Rinpoche. Trungpa Rinpoche is a Kagyu *tulku*, and that is how Akong came close to the Kagyu tradition.

With the sharp eye of a tactician, Akong saw his moment coming after the Karmapa's death when the division between the two senior regents, Shamar and Situ Rinpoches, began to manifest. Around the early eighties he decided to throw his weight and his centre in Scotland behind Situ. Having signed Samye Ling over to Situ, Akong assumed the role of advisor, gray eminence, and finally emissary to China. Soon after appearing at Situ's side, he was rubbing shoulders with the top hierarchy in Beijing. He organised the Situ Rinpoche's visits to eastern Tibet — that came only a few years after the Dalai Lama's brother went in 1979 on a historic mission to Lhasa in an attempt to open a dialogue and win concessions from Red China.

However, little had come of the Dalai Lama's overtures. For, in Akong and his peer Situ Rinpoche, China found prospective allies to further its interests in occupied Tibet. Situ Rinpoche visited China in 1982 and 1984. Tibet's locked doors were generously opened for him. In 1985, Situ was allowed to enter the off-limits Kham and, for a time, basked in the newfound role of protector of Buddhism in his occupied country. His journeys through eastern Tibet, the first such venture by a high Tibetan lama since the Chinese occupation of Tibet, were perceived as an enormous success. They were glorified as the first step in restoring Buddhism in the land of snows. The picture of the rinpoche's meeting and blessing hundreds of Khampas and recognising just as many *tulkus* in his native Kham was indeed touching. High expectations aroused among Tibetans-in-exile at a time when lama activity was all but forbidden in their ruined country.

The regent's emergence in his oppressed land was a consequence of a new and greatly refined policy adopted by China after Mao's death. With the rise of Deng Xiaoping, pragmatism became the official line. The Communist leadership concluded that the only way to control the unruly Tibetan nation was to restore some of the monasteries and at the same time place them under strict government rule. To ensure this, the heads of the cloisters would have to be chosen directly by Beijing, as was decreed long back by the VIIth Ching Lu, the ruler of China. The Dalai Lama was unwilling to grant more concessions to China.

The Chinese hunt for a suitable target that could be exploited to tame the Tibetans coupled opportunely with Situ Rinpoche's lust for power leading him into the Chinese camp. His sudden tremendous fecundity in recognising *tuluks* in an area around his old seat in eastern Tibet helped him in creating a power base for the future. And, in him, China found an unusually flexible negotiator, a loyal partner, and also a dutiful messenger.

At the same time, Dabsang Rinpoche, a high Kagyu lama from Nepal, suddenly died in Hong Kong under bizarre circumstances. The rinpoche's Chinese students had arranged a heart surgery for him. Dabsang — just as every Tibetan of his age who was addicted to butter tea — suffered from high blood pressure, but an operation was not quite necessary. However, his disciples insisted. To dispel any doubts, Situ Rinpoche, Dabsang's closest disciple, was also consulted. The young regent came down with a clear-cut divination: "Lama Dabsang should go under knife." The result was that Dabsang Rinpoche ended up in the operating theatre, undergoing a heart surgery he did not really need.

The operation appeared to have gone well — except for a crucial detail. The surgeon, in his zeal to quickly complete the task, left a pair of scissors inside Dabsang's chest. And so, merely hours after the strenuous surgery, the entire procedure had to be repeated. The rinpoche's chest was once again cut open to remove the doctor's instrument. The additional dissection proved a bit too strenuous for his, by then, weakened heart, and by the time the surgeon finished, stiching the lama up for the second time, the patient was dead. Situ Rinpoche failed to reach Kathmandu for the last rites. The lengthy rituals then fell on the frail shoulders of Jamgon Kongtrul, who was not well at that time.

Jamgon Kongtrul, shocked and almost in despair, kept muttering that this death should never have happened and that the loss was an enormous catastrophe. To the others, his reaction seemed quite out of proportion. After all, a high lama was expected to master the process of death. Or, was it a premonition about his death?

The four regents were to meet in Rumtek on 16 March 1992. Though they had last met in 1990, it was back in 1986 that they had converged on Rumtek, when a declaration about the Karmapa's prediction letter had been made. The important and fortunate events seemed to be on the way. In 1989 Situ Rinpoche informed the other three regents that he was in possession of "good news similar to the joyful cries of peacocks". It was indeed a most optimistic claim. Later, however, Situ Rinpoche concluded that the news was too joyful for his peers to appreciate, and he simply held it back from the regents at their meeting in Delhi, another inconclusive gathering, in 1990.

The proposed March reunion did not materialise. Situ Rinpoche postponed his arrival in Rumtek. The new date for the meeting was set after three days. Two days before the date of the meeting, the Kagyu centres worldwide were flooded with copies of a mysterious letter. A group of Tibetan traders from Nepal, operating under the name of Derge Association, called upon the Karmapa's students to de facto rebel against the collective leadership of the four regents and to ignore Shamar Rinpoche. The harshest words in the letter were reserved for

Shamar Rinpoche and Topga Yulgyal, who were blamed for purposefully delaying the process of recognition. In sharp contrast, Situ Rinpoche was described as the only one capable of bringing forth the Karmapa's XVIIth reincarnation. Most of the European centres responded in a novel way. Scores of neatly folded scraps of toilet paper, of course unused, inscribed with a sharp rebuff were sent to the Derge Association.

When in the early morning of 19 March 1992, the four regents got together for their meeting in Rumtek, they found a large and noisy congregation of Khampas (erstwhile residents of Kham) positioned outside the room as if trying to exert pressure on them. Some Khampas had arrived from Kathmandu. Akong had flown from Scotland to be in the crowd. Somebody had obviously been busy extending invitation to all such notables. The mood was restive and increasingly aggressive. "You must decide now!"— was the collective demand.

Situ Rinpoche began, first by asking each regent if he was in possession, or had knowledge, of the Karmapa's holy instructions. When he satisfied himself that nobody could produce anything, he took a white scarf, bowed down to the altar, and solemnly announced the long awaited news that he had the Karmapa's prediction letter. The rest three regents were shown an envelope scribbled with red ink on it. Gyaltshab and Jamgon Kongtrul Rinpoches lost no time in expressing their approval. Gyaltshab Rinpoche, eyes brimming with tears, even prostrated himself full-length on the ground. Shamar Rinpoche was the only regent who remained unimpressed and eyed the whole show with doubt. When the letter was fished out of the envelope, he examined it and stood his ground. "What has been placed on the table in front of me looks very much like a forgery," he challenged in a firm voice.

First the handwriting — it seemed unstable and spread all over the page as if coming from a shaky and insecure hand. It was in sharp contrast to the elegant, firm and very tasteful presentations of the XVIth Karmapa. Second, the text bore no resemblance to the Karmapa's literary style. Being familiar with the character of the Karmapa's poems, Shamar Rinpoche could not hide his chagrin. The sentences were clumsily put together;

they lacked the warmth and insight that one so much admired. Moreover, there were several striking contradictions.

In his speech at Rumtek on 12 June 1992, Situ Rinpoche said that at the time of writing the 'peacock letter', he possessed a testimonial letter which should be opened in the Iron Horse year (1990). It meant that the Tibetan New Year (26 February 1990) was the first opportunity to do so. But it was not before March 1992 that Situ Rinpoche disclosed the existence of the letter.

Moreover, the seventh sentence in the letter read: "He will be born in the Earth-Ox year." The National Tibetan Radio and Lhasa Radio described it as a 'good year' instead of 'Earth-Ox year'. It was a sheer impossibility. Had the child (the reincarnation of the Karmapa), as per the letter, been born in the Earth-Ox year, he would have been either 32-year-old when the Karmapa died in 1981 or he would be born 26 years after the Karmapa's death in 2007 AD. These were only two such striking possibilities with Earth-Ox year (See Appendix B for a note on Tibetan calendar).

Finally, the signature! It was clear that somebody had tried to imitate the Karmapa's distinctive inscription, but the imitation came out rather poorly. It was covered by a large red blurred end that pretended to define the Karmapa's name, a far cry from the Karmapa's swift and nearly vibrant personal signing. It was as though in his most important document, the distinguished lama had all but forgotten about calligraphy and good taste, and just casually scribbled the crucial words, totally indifferent to form and not clear about the content.

Shamar Rinpoche refused to acknowledge the document as the Karmapa's genuine testament and demanded to know how Situ Rinpoche had got hold of such a 'dubious' document. At this stage, Jamgon Kongtrul Rinpoche also began to express some doubts. The fuzzy signature and awkward handwriting seemed to have overcome even his goodwill and conciliatory nature. Only Gyaltshab Rinpoche embraced unconditionally the weighty news and, hardly glancing at the letter, nodded his head in full agreement with Situ Rinpoche.

Situ Rinpoche brazenly went on to recount the story. He had received the letter concealed in a protection amulet from the Karmapa at Calcutta, a few months before the Karmapa passed away in 1981, with no indication whatsoever of its historic content. He claimed that the Karmapa had told him that this would be of immense help to all in the future. He did not even know there was a letter, wrapped in silk inside the locket. For the next few years, he had devoutly worn it around his neck, totally unaware he was walking around with the details of the lineage's future hanging on his chest. One hot summer evening in 1989, he decided to change the worn out string that had supported the amulet. In the process, the amulet fell open and a letter dropped out of the amulet. "Open in the Iron Horse Year" was the solemn command that greeted his hopeful eyes, he recounted.

Situ Rinpoche said he waited for the prescribed year to break the letter's seal but did not invite other regents to join him in the procedure. Once acquainted with the document's significant content, he dutifully informed his peers that he was in possession of news similar to the "joyful cries of peacocks" but somehow failed to spell out the reasons why the peacocks were suddenly so joyful. At the same time, for the next two years he painstakingly avoided meeting the other regents though he seemed to have taken Gyaltshab Rinpoche into confidence. Even during their meetings twice in Delhi in 1990, he kept the matter close to his chest. Now he calmly announced that to show the letter in Delhi would have been inappropriate.

Unconvinced, Shamar Rinpoche questioned why the envelope looked less used than its contents. He demanded that the letter be put to a forensic test. Situ Rinpoche said that such a test would cost too much and take years for the results to come in. However, Shamar Rinpoche managed to secure a photocopy of the 'prediction letter'.

Topga Yulgyal was called in. After examining the text of the letter, he voiced his concern. He became convinced that the regents had penned it themselves. Having found a candidate but unable to find the written instructions, they simply composed a suitable document. He announced that these were not the

Karmapa's authentic instructions. He appealed to the regents to come forward with the real reincarnation and pointed out to Jamgon Kongtrul Rinpoche that there was little wisdom in pursuing a clearly false lead.

The regents settled down to the monotonous task of analyzing the intricate text word by word. It turned out that the content was just as elusive as the form was unrefined. Although the names of the child and parents and other details were all there, it felt as if somebody had forced these particulars into an unrelated wording. Hours of tedious reading and torturous interpretations brought no conclusive result, and as the day wore on, the four lamas struck a compromise. Due to visit Tibet soon, Jamgon Kongtrul Rinpoche would try to sniff things out by himself. He would make contact with the child on the basis of description from the letter. As matters stood, he seemed the ideal choice because he was acceptable to both the warring factions.

The meeting ended early in the evening. The four regents agreed to keep their discord confidential and not to rush out with any disclosures. They were to meet again in June after Kongtrul's return from Tibet. The agreement, however, lasted a few minutes. In fact, it had perhaps been made to be breached. As soon as the regents stepped out of the room, Gyaltshab Rinpoche seized the occasion and flashed the envelope from a distance, calmly pointing out that there were the Karmapa's holy words. Situ Rinpoche whipped out the letter and held it up for all to admire. The restive audience, mostly brought for a pre-arranged drama, cheered. The volatile Tibetans began shouting approval of Situ Rinpoche's gesture while demanding quicker results from the others.

The next day, as if the agreement he had sealed with his brethren meant nothing, Situ Rinpoche sped off to Dharamsala to disclose all the developments to the Dalai Lama. A few days later, he defiantly informed all Dharma centres in Nepal that the search party for the reincarnate of the Karmapa was being formed.

In the meeting of the regents on 19 March it had been agreed that Jamgon Kongtrul Rinpoche would travel to Tibet on 'a highly sensitive assignment'. A week before his departure, an extravagant gift for him was received from his brother in USA:

a brand new BMW 525. The rinpoche, at once, was besotted with his new toy and, without giving the whole thing much thought, came upon the rather eccentric idea of going to Tibet in his state-of-the-art car. It was a ridiculous endeavour to drive such a vehicle in the extreme and inhospitable conditions of the high Tibetan plateau. Moreover, going to Tibet on a secret mission and choosing a latest BMW 525 as his means of transportation was at best an imprudent, if not a totally foolhardy, move. To perform anything remotely secret under such conditions would have been nothing less than a miracle. It is difficult to imagine that he was so naive and inexperienced as not to notice the absurdity of his venture. He never got a chance to show what his clandestine business was to have been. He did not get a chance to test his BMW in Tibet either.

On 25 April he went to meet his mother at Kalimpong. The BMW mechanic was scheduled to arrive by air from Delhi to perform a final check on the vehicle. Next day, Jamgon Kongtrul Rinpoche received a message that the flight from Delhi was delayed and might even be cancelled. Impatient to hit the road with his new possession, the Jamgon Kongtrul Rinpoche decided to leave without the mechanic. His two attendants occupied the back seat.

According to the story, recounted later by Tenzin Dorje, secretary of the rinpoche and the lone survivor, Kongtrul's BMW roared along the slightly wet asphalt road towards Siliguri, the second city in West Bengal after Calcutta. Suddenly some black birds appeared on the road, right in front of the car. The driver, in a desperate attempt to save the birds, swerved violently, throwing the vehicle into a wild skid. Whether he ever had the time or skill to steer it back on course remains a mystery. The heavy car fishtailed at full speed for 30 to 40 yards until it hit, with tremendous force, a huge tree beside the road. It all took only seconds, but the impact was devastating. The sheer force of the collision threw everyone out of the car. The rinpoche died instantly. One of his assistants and the driver succumbed to their injuries in a hospital. Tenzin Dorje, Kongtrul's secretary, was thrown out of the rear window and landed in the paddy fields beside the road. He suffered only minor injuries. The needle of the speedometer had stuck at 110 mph.

Shamar Rinpoche immediately rushed to the scene of the accident and took care of the rinpoche's body. Gyaltshab Rinpoche, struck with extreme grief, was said to have suffered a mild heart attack. It was decided that there would be no immediate cremation and Jamgon Kongtrul's body would be preserved for 45 days for the last rites. The traditional rituals began that very evening.

His death set the Kagyu on an immediate collision course. A struggle for power that had been ripening for years was now, with Kongtrul's passing away, ready to come to full light and explode. In fact, Jamgon Kongtrul Rinpoche was a sort of mediator between the two warring factions of the regents. Now even that facade of unity would evaporate, giving way to a somewhat less idyllic image of power-hungry lamas and dishonest monks.

The general secretary and the senior regent were accused of having planted a bomb in Jamgon's car. There was a rumour that Jamgon Kongtrul Rinpoche stood in their way to crowning a puppet as XVIIth Karmapa, and the malicious pair had simply decided to eliminate him. Another rumour had it that the two villains secretly sneaked in under the cover of the night and poured salt or sugar into the BMW's petrol tank, thus causing the engine to seize and catapult itself out of the car at high speed.

Anybody with even a remote understanding of mechanics and a fair dose of common sense would refuse to accept such obvious nonsense. A car's engine tainted with sugar would simply slow down and eventually bring a vehicle to a complete and unquestionable halt; it would under no circumstances accelerate the car to the rather extraordinary velocity of 110 mph, and would certainly not defy the laws of gravity to suddenly eject itself out of the body of the car. The lone survivor's detailed account of the dramatic event contradicted this grotesque claim. Finally, a BMW expert was called in to put a decisive end to the ongoing tongue wagging. His clear-cut testimony supporting Tenzin Dorje's account should have closed the issue once and for all. But 'there are none so blind as those who will not see', and despite scientific evidence and witnesses' statements to the contrary, the slander against Shamar Rinpoche and Topga Yulgyal continued unabated, drawing increasingly wider circles.

5

The Wrathful Buddhas

In April 1992, amidst the last rites of Jamgon Kongtrul Rinpoche, Shamar Rinpoche left for America. Situ and Gyaltshab Rinpoches usurped the positions of full-time regents at Rumtek. They were calling the shots. On 17 May they publicly announced that Akong Tulku, the famous eminence from Scotland, representing Situ Rinpoche and Sherab Tharchin, representing Gyaltshab Rinpoche, were on their way to Tibet to look for the reincarnation. The representatives turned out to be shadowy.

Three days later, Situ Rinpoche swung into more action. He staged his coup. The prediction letter was shown to Sakya Tridzin, the head of Sakya order. He asked Sakya Tridzin to compose a prayer for the Karmapa, which the latter did instantaneously. Though just a gesture, it was depicted by Situ Rinpoche as support for his action. Traditionally, the Sakya Lama had no role whatsoever in the process of the Karmapa's recognition. Conspicuously absent from the event were two key figures in the delicate procedure: the senior regent Kunzig Shamar Rinpoche and the General Secretary Topga Yulgyal. None of the eminent lamas who assembled in the Rumtek courtyard seemed to recognise, let alone protest, their exclusion. It was as if the two had ceased to exist. Nobody defended Shamar Rinpoche and Topga Yulgyal as their rivals spread canards and lies about them. They were accused of obstructing the XVIIth Karmapa's way to Tsurphu.

Shamar Rinpoche, who had left the last rites ceremony of Jamgon Kongtrul Rinpoche midway on the pretext of delivering pre-arranged lectures in America, was carrying the copy of the 'prediction letter' for a forensic test. Confident that Situ Rinpoche would find it inappropriate to make a move during the holy observances, his hopes were crushed when his efforts to get the letter tested forensically proved futile. He was told that a copy, no matter how good, was definitely not enough for a reliable and scientific inspection of any document.

Events had definitely run ahead of him. The senior regent began to suspect that his venerable peers had cast him aside. If he was ever to have a say in the recognition of the XVIIth Karmapa and in the future of the lineage, Shamar Rinpoche realised, he had better hurry home. On his way back to Gangtok, he ran into the then Chief Minister of Sikkim, Nar Bahadur Bhandari, at the Bagdogra airport, about 115 km from Rumtek. He confided his problem to the chief minister. Earlier while leaving for America, he had sought the chief minister's help to guard the prediction letter. The request had been granted, and policemen were posted outside the room where the document had been kept. Now, the senior regent admitted, he was unable to accept the letter as genuine and asked for assistance from the ruling politician to get the original text for forensic examination. Bhandari forced a smile and politely explained that he had assigned this matter to Karma Topden, Member of Parliament. The Topden family was already under the total influence of Situ Rinpoche.

On 7 June, Shamar Rinpoche returned to Rumtek. He intended to question the two regents, but inexplicably the pair had vanished. That very morning they had left the monastery in haste to seek an audience with the Dalai Lama at Dharamsala. Shamar Rinpoche had the smug optismism that the Dalai Lama and half of his government-in-exile were in Brazil to attend an environmental conference. Confident that the visit of the two regents would not bear fruit, Shamar Rinpoche convened a meeting of all Tibetans in the Nalanda Institute in Rumtek. The time had come to speak out, he felt.

Recounting the events since the March meeting, and the agreement between the regents to keep the discord secret, he also recalled the happenings during his absence in Rumtek. There was also another letter, he stressed — the one the four rinpoches had found in the Karmapa's relic box in 1986. This letter was difficult to interpret, but when the time was right, its meaning would become clear. He placed his trust in the people of Rumtek, in the lamas, monks and others. He urged them to look for truth, to insist on the verification of the 'prediction' letter.

Next day, he assembled all the foreign disciples of the Karmapa and repeated his speech in English. He also disclosed a few more things. There was a close disciple of the late Karmapa, a most trustworthy person, who had approached him with the news that he possessed direct instructions from the last Karmapa. This man, highly respected by all, would not come forward publicly. Not yet! He had been told by the Karmapa himself when to reveal his possessions, and the time was not ripe yet. Shamar Rinpoche was fully confident that the man carried the right information and that he would offer himself when the time was suitable. The senior regent finished, stating rather sombrely that he would resign his seat and title if his trust in the man proved wrong. He requested the audience not to speculate about who the real Karmapa was but to show confidence in *dharma* and to practise the same instead.

Shamar Rinpoche opted for a session with questions. As hands went up and later down, he proceeded with details from the turbulent years that followed the XVIth Karmapa's cremation. The atmosphere in Rumtek was strained. Although the prayer ceremonies proceeded according to schedule, everyone had his eyes set somewhere else. The Tibetans from that otherwise sleepy village were quick to make up their minds and began to cast their lot with one or the other regent. The Rumtek administration was getting exasperated. Meanwhile, the supporters of Situ Rinpoche started letting everybody know how many days were left for the XVIIth Karmapa to arrive in Tsurphu.

On 11 June, Shamar Rinpoche issued an official statement where he made public his doubts about the authenticity of the letter. He distanced himself from the two other regents' present manoeuvres in Tibet and from Akong's and Sherab's efforts to find the reincarnation on the basis of the information from the disputed letter. As long as the document in question remained unchecked, he would not advise anybody to "rush into any kind of action." The statement was without any rancour against the other two regents.

The following afternoon, horns resounded from the roof of the temple, signalling the return of Situ and Gyaltshab Rinpoches from their five-day travels. Thrones were erected and loudspeakers installed in the monastery's courtyard; the regents' servants and assistants were busy ushering people in and out. Everybody was told that the two lineage holders were going to make an important announcement. Pointedly, no seat was put up for Shamar Rinpoche, as if to drive home the point that the senior regent did not count anymore.

Situ and Gyaltshab Rinpoches emerged through a side door. Without mentioning the absence of the senior regent and the reason behind it, Situ Rinpoche cleared his throat and launched into an hour-long speech in Tibetan. When he finished, a disorderly round of hearty applause greeted his words. The noisy acclaim came especially from the numerous guests that kept popping up from nowhere. Gyaltshab Rinpoche too added a few sentences of his own. Then Situ Rinpoche grabbed the centre-stage again with a microphone in hand, this time talking in English.

He began that both of them — Gyaltshab and himself — had seriously considered whether or not they should disclose this, but since Shamar Rinpoche had already done so, they felt that they were breaking no vows by saying it again now. Ever since the Karmapa passed away in 1981, the four rinpoches had been devotedly searching for their guru's written instructions about his incarnation. They firmly believed that the Karmapa had left such a letter. So they had tirelessly looked for it in all possible places. As the years were going by and the letter was still elusive, they had become anxious as to what to tell the people. One day they found a special *gau* (relic box) that belonged to the Karmapa. They fixed it on the altar and calmly stated that they had found the prediction letter inside it. Feeling somewhat guilty that people would have to prostrate to an empty box, they decided to place one of the Karmapa's texts, a poem or something spiritual in the *gau*. Well, the Gyaltshab Rinpoche knew a four-verse meditation prayer that the Karmapa had composed at his request. And so, Jamgon Kongtrul Rinpoche wrote it down and the four regents unitedly put the paper in the relic box. All for the best, beamed Situ Rinpoche.

He paused to allow for the implications of his words to sink in. The listeners gaped at each other with disbelief. So this was the Karmapa's famous letter that, with much pomp, the regents announced they had located in 1986! What they had done was to simply recall a poem, copy it, and place it in a relic box! The listeners clearly remembered. The lineage holders had claimed to have discovered two letters, one inside the other, a "pregnant creation", as Situ had smartly called it at that time. Subsequently, they had engaged the followers of the XVIth Karmapa all over the world in scrupulous rites and infinite *mantras* to allow for the second letter to be opened. However, it was all a product of their fantasy. The first and the second letter did not exist at all. Situ Rinpoche brushed it off as a motivated, if slightly irresponsible, act, a result of their frustration with the search for the real text and of their desire to calm Karmapa's devotees.

Seemingly indifferent to the baffled faces around him, Situ ploughed on with his speech. He went on to describe the days in 1989 when he realised that for eight long years he had been carrying the Karmapa's genuine instructions close to his body. He recollected his unceasing efforts in trying to organise a meeting with the other three regents and how he finally secured their presence in Delhi. But the Indian capital seemed so unsuitable a location. Alas, he felt, he had to remain silent. He trusted, however, that Rumtek was the proper place to reveal such important news and had thus embarked on a plan to bring the four of them together at the Karmapa's seat. He informed the other three regents that he would arrive in Sikkim on 19 March and requested them to be ready at his side. He then shared with the audience the details from the March meeting. The regents also decided to remove the four-line prayer that they had secretly placed in the relic box six years before. Since Gyaltshab Rinpoche had come up with the verses, he was then to have the paper back.

Not only was there no mention of the senior regent Shamar Rinpoche, but the eminent speaker also seemed to be giving himself the entire credit for the great success he thought he was achieving. His account of their March meeting was totally different from that of Shamar Rinpoche a few days before. Situ Rinpoche gave not so much as the tiniest hint that two of the regents and the general secretary had, in fact, objected to the prediction letter. Undeterred by any such contradictions, Situ Rinpoche droned on. He had arrived in Rumtek to pray for the late Jamgon Kongtrul Rinpoche on 5 May. His plan was to confer with the two rinpoches — Shamar and Gyaltshab — about their future course of action. Situ Rinpoche added that Shamar Rinpoche's "*dharma* obligations overseas" presented a setback to his plan, but he respected his peer's call of duty and, together with Gyaltshab Rinpoche, shouldered the responsibility of bringing forward the XVIIth Karmapa upon his already burdened shoulders. Their inability to wait for the senior regent's return had forced them to move on without him. Now, due to his and Gyaltsab's heroic efforts, their representatives, Akong Tulku and Sherab Tharchin, were about to bring the reincarnation to Tsurphu. However, he preferred not to disclose why he could not call up Shamar Rinpoche on phone before taking such an important decision. All through his speech, Situ Rinpoche had an oily smile pasted on his face.

Suddenly, a servant laden with a chair appeared in the yard. Sweating profusely, he elbowed his way through the throng. Once he reached the rinpoches' thrones, he placed, with relief, the piece of furniture on the ground and whispered into the ear of Situ Rinpoche. Situ Rinpoche turned pale. But he immediately gained his composure and stared nonchalantly at the gathering.

Gathering momentum, he reached the core of his address. He said that having completed their duties, Situ and Gyaltshab Rinpoches had decided the time was ripe to pay their respects to the Dalai Lama and to petition the Tibetan leader for the recognition of the XVIIth Karmapa. And so, on the morning of 7 May, the two had set out on the long journey to Dharamsala. But to their disappointment, the Dalai Lama was away in Brazil. With the help of his secretary, they settled down to the lengthy process of phoning Brazil from India. It was late in the night when they got the Tibetan leader on the phone. They informed the Dalai Lama of how they had located the genuine letter left by the late Karmapa and that with devotion all Kagyu rinpoches, lamas and monks agreed with the enclosed instructions. The Dalai Lama expressed a wish to see the letter, so the rinpoches faxed him the document. They also included all other details they thought were necessary.

Speaking on the phone a few hours later, the Dalai Lama stated that since the information they had relayed to him matched the instructions in the letter of prediction he had received by fax, and since all rinpoches and lamas had agreed with unanimous faith and aspiration, he would confirm the reincarnation as that of the XVIIth Karmapa. The next day the Dalai Lama's office in Dharamsala issued a document verifying his words.

The two regents hurried back to Rumtek. Right after their arrival and without breaking for a single moment of rest, they called a meeting to show all disciples the Dalai Lama's letter of approval. Situ Rinpoche emphatically took a pause to stress the fact that the two had not slept for nearly a day. He was about to roll out a document he had kept all this time on his lap when a commotion resounded at the entrance to the monastery's yard. With his head defiantly up, Shamar Rinpoche briskly strode into the square. A monk running ahead of him kept clearing a passage in the thick crowd. Also, suddenly, a jeep full of Indian Army soldiers drove in at high speed through the gates of the courtyard and came to a screeching halt right before the gathering. Six armed men jumped out and, ignoring the vociferous protests of the spectators, followed Shamar Rinpoche into the throng.

When Situ and Gyaltshab Rinpoches noticed the senior regent with conscripts trotting obediently behind him as bodyguards, they turned white, hopped off their thrones, and unceremoniously scuttled off towards the monastery. The unusual sight of the obviously terrified high eminences holding up the skirts of their robes and running away from their senior regent and the party of Indian soldiers was indeed amusing, but nobody felt like laughing. The Khampas, who had come to Rumtek only a few hours before, began to yell at Shamar Rinpoche.

Reaching the safety of the cloister, the two rinpoches zipped past their bewildered attendants at an astounding pace. Without a word of clarification, they made for their respective rooms and bolted themselves in. Shamar Rinpoche followed them, at a more dignified step, into the building and, arriving at their doors, loudly called their names. The rooms remained solidly locked, and utter silence answered Shamar Rinpoche. One could almost hear a pin drop. By now the supporters of Situ Rinpoche had congregated to block the way to the rinpoches' quarters. Even as more and more hostile characters kept pouring into the corridors, and their mood seemed to be hostile, Shamar Rinpoche prudently opted for the exit. Loyally, the soldiers strode out after him.

In the meantime, the atmosphere outside was turning volatile. The tension building up over the last few days had finally ignited. People screamed and ran in all directions. Scuffles between the monks of warring factions erupted. Tsultrim Namgyal, the XVIth Karmapa's loyal servant, received a head injury, bleeding profusely. The policemen began to restore order. For a while, an ominous silence prevailed.

Situ Rinpoche's supporters launched a virulent verbal attack. Their hysterical outbursts portrayed a mad Shamar Rinpoche heading a division of the Indian Army in a brutal assault on the monastery. 'Witnesses' swore they saw the senior regent wildly charging at the two rinpoches and giving orders to the soldiers to raze the monastery to the ground. They added that it was only due to the calm but firm response of Situ and Gyaltshab Rinpoches that a tragedy was averted. Shamar Rinpoche was portrayed as a bully determined to chase everybody out of Rumtek.

Situ Rinpoche alleged:

> Shamar Rinpoche arrived with a group of fully armed soldiers purporting to be of (the) Kumaon Regiment of the Indian Army, to intimidate Gyaltshab Rinpoche and me and those present there. Some senior officials of the Sikkim government, such as the Resident Commissioner of Sikkim at New Delhi, even reasoned with these soldiers and requested them not to enter the shrine hall of the monastery with their shoes and arms, but they ignored these pleas, and stormed a place of worship against a completely unarmed public, without any provocation or reason. This resulted in a serious breach of peace, and severe injuries to the innocent public. The Sikkim government had to post police and the CRPF (a para-military force) at the monastery in order to maintain law and order. It is incomprehensible that Shamar Rinpoche, a foreigner, was being allowed to lead armed troops into a monastery, without the sanction and/or the knowledge of the concerned state government, and that too in Sikkim.

In fact, sensing trouble, Topga Yulgyal had told his wife (aunt of the King of Bhutan) about the eventuality of threat to the life of Shamar Rinpoche in the wake of presence of aggressive Khampas, who had been called in a sizable number from Nepal. Topga's wife requested her nephew (the King of Bhutan) to help. The King, with a history of the Karmapa-supporting ancestors, in turn, made a request to the Indian Ambassador in Bhutan. The Government of India conceded the request of the King of Bhutan. Due to paucity of time, however, the nearest Army contingent was ordered to rush to help Shamar Rinpoche. The Sikkim government was not taken into confidence because it was blatantly taking sides in the dispute.

Moreover, the Government of India could not remain a mere spectator to the sordid drama taking place at the behest of China which way back in 1962 had occupied Indian territories in army action.

Over the next few days, Rumtek settled down to an uneasy stalemate. The strength of Sikkim policemen was increased. The monastery's monks continued with the rituals for Jamgon Kongtrul Rinpoche. The administrators of the Rumtek monastery and Tsultrim Namgyal, the personal servant of the XVIth Karmapa, stood firmly behind the senior regent. Topga Yulgyal, having received threats to his life, left Sikkim as the Sikkim government headed by Nar Bahadur Bhandari refused to guarantee his safety. The Rumtek village and the capital city of Gangtok resonated with wild gossip and absurd rumours. Shamar Rinpoche was the talk of the town.

Bhandari's ruling party called for a general strike protesting the army's intervention in Sikkim without permission from the state government. Shamar Rinpoche's camp clumsily failed to brief the press whereas the rivals, with the help of the state government, went all out to spread canards and speculation in the guise of press statements. Expectedly, the headlines in local newspapers next day screamed, 'Rumtek high cleric and Indian Army take over monastery'. It was a classic case of bad press for Shamar Rinpoche.

On 15 June, Jamgon Kongtrul's *kudung* (mummified body) was brought from the monastery to the main hall in the Nalanda Institute in Rumtek amid pushing and pulling, the usual Tibetan way. The last rites began. The next day, Situ and Gyaltshab Rinpoches again went on the offensive.

During the *pujas* on 16 June, while all the rinpoches were seated in long rows reciting their prayers, two letters were sent down the aisles. The first one, addressed to all lamas and followers of the lineage, was a demand for unconditional acceptance of the prediction letter. It stressed that the XVIIth Karmapa had been recognised in accordance with the instructions from the sacred testament. This had been confirmed by the Dalai Lama. The Karmapa would be brought to Tsurphu and some time later installed on his throne in Rumtek. The letter also referred to some holy vision that the Dalai Lama had had — a further proof of the authenticity of the choice.

The second letter was an expression of deepest gratitude to the supreme Tibetan leader for having confirmed the Karmapa's

XVIIth reincarnation. After having placed their signatures on both documents, Situ and Gyaltshab Rinpoches passed them over to the other rinpoches. Every one of the eminent lamas signed without so much as a blink as no Tibetan ever dares to go against his or her highest political leader. Moreover, collecting the signatures during the main *pujas* for the late Jamgon Kongtrul was a sort of collective pressure on the assembled rinpoches. One after the other, they obediently put their signatures on the circulating set of papers. After all, these most venerable monks were no men-at-arms and would much rather trot behind power and titles than fight for some uncertain principles.

The unprecedented act of collecting signatures in order to certify the Karmapa's authenticity was also a dubious innovation. So far the procedures to identify a reincarnation had never called for any signature-drive to determine the accuracy of a given choice. But the two regents felt themselves standing on a shaky ground and, as such, needed the long titles to lend credence and support to their claim. Once the letters had been crowned with the distinguished names, Situ's attendant pocketed the documents and vanished from the shrine room. The eminent Kagyu teachers' autographs were neatly lined up at the bottom of each page: Situ Rinpoche, Gyaltshab Rinpoche, Beru Khyentse Rinpoche, Bokar Tulku, Thrangu Rinpoche, Ponlop Rinpoche, Sangye Nyenpa Rinpoche, Chokyi Nyima Rinpoche and many others. Conspicuously absent were two signatures. They were of the senior regent Shamar Rinpoche and General Secretary Topga Yulgyal.

In his eagerness, Situ Rinpoche forgot that the zealously promoted acceptance from the Dalai Lama was in fact no more than just an informal recollection of his words spoken on phone from Brazil and hurriedly put on paper late at night in Dharamsala by his secretary. It fell short of a formal recognition, which would not happen until 29 June, when the Dalai Lama would return to Dharamsala. A corresponding document would eventually be issued on 3 July by the foreign office of the Tibetan government-in-exile. The rinpoches were bowing down to a useless piece of paper, the statement by Dharamsala.

Moreover, the document issued on 3 July by the Dharamsala foreign office read as if the three regents, Shamar, Situ and Gyaltshab Rinpoches, had been together on 29 June in the audience with the Dalai Lama and apprised the Tibetan leader of the details concerning the reincarnation. The Dalai Lama had then issued the formal confirmation letter. His words were quoted in full. The document was signed by Tashi Wangdi, a minister in the Tibetan government-in-exile.

In fact, the two regents — Situ and Gyaltshab Rinpoches — had called on the Dalai Lama in the morning, and Shamar Rinpoche had done so in the afternoon of the same day. They also probably had very different things to say. Shamar Rinpoche later disclosed that he had apprised the Dalai Lama other clues as to the identity of the XVIIth Karmapa and had requested him to examine all these clues when the time was ripe. According to an interview published in *the Tibetan Review* in the following August, the senior regent Shamar Rinpoche claimed that the Dalai Lama had consented to his request.

In fact, the issue of recognition had never rested in the hands of the Tibetan government or the Dalai Lama. In the past, when the supreme political authority in Lhasa validated the reincarnation of the Karmapa, it was purely a political, and in no way a spiritual, decision which merely certified that the matter had been decided within the Kagyu order. It did not determine the eligibility of a candidate. The Karmapa was not approved or chosen but proved and presented, sometimes by a testimony left by the predecessor and always by the virtue of his deeds. The Karmapa's line went back to the 12th century, whereas the Dalai Lama's incarnations started three hundred years later. How then could he have approved the first four Karmapas?

Together with the official document issued in Dharamsala, a 'brief advice' from the Dalai Lama to Situ and Goshir Gyaltshab Rinpoches was also released. It is not clear who added this extra sheet of paper. It bore no official stamp or signature but claimed to be a transcription of the Dalai Lama's words. In his short message, the Tibetan leader was said to disclose tactfully that it was mainly Situ and Gyaltshab Rinpoches and those closely connected with them who were responsible for finding the reincarnation of the Gyalwa Karmapa. How the Dalai Lama had arrived at this conclusion is also shrouded in mystery.

Traditionally, the process of recognising the Karmapa had never been restricted to one particular lama or a given group of lamas, certainly not to just Situ and Gyaltshab Rinpoches as the Dalai Lama was maintaining. Looking back in history and quoting the clearly impartial written records left by the VIIIth Situ Rinpoche, *Choskyi Jungne* (the Garland of Moon Water Crystal) one discovers that until the time of the XIIIth Karmapa, the main person to have brought forward the successive Karmapas was, in fact, Shamar Rinpoche. He had recognised five reincarnations of his teacher. Situ Rinpoche was responsible for three recognitions, including his contribution in locating the XVIth Karmapa. But, most of the findings happened during the period of Shamar's official banishment. Gyaltshab Rinpoche's sole claim to fame was his backing of the wrong candidate during the search for the XIIIth Karmapa.

That evening, Situ and Gyaltshab Rinpoches announced that Ugyen Trinley (their candidate as reincarnation of the XVIth Karmapa) had arrived the previous day in Tsurphu. The Rumtek monks and ritual masters were ordered to sound the horns and get ready for an official ceremony the next morning. Everybody else was told to be present at sunrise to offer *khada* (scarf) on the Karmapa's throne. Late that night, the monastery's senior staff secretly fled Rumtek. Afraid of being party to the dispute, they took shelter in Gangtok.

A day before the *pujas*, Ugyen Tulku (not to be confused with Ugyen Trinley Dorji) and Lopen Chechoo, the highly respected Kagyu lamas, arrived from Kathmandu to mediate in the dispute between the regents. They were highly regarded by all concerned, both having been very close to the XVIth Karmapa. Ugyen Tulku was also teacher to the four lineage holders. The high lamas sitting in Rumtek wanted at all costs to patch up the disagreement.

Ugyen Tulku conferred first with the two lineage holders, Situ and Gyaltshab Rinpoches. Several hours elapsed before he emerged from their quarters and at once directed his steps to Shamar's house. He then proceeded to press the senior regent to surrender. "Rinpoche must accept the letter and withdraw his insistence on a forensic test," he pleaded. The elderly lama painted a gruesome picture of blood being spilled in Tibet and Kathmandu if the senior regent stuck to his guns. Besides, the Dalai Lama had already given his recognition. They could not oppose the Dalai Lama. Eventually, the distinguished *tulku*, with tears in his eyes, fully prostrated himself in front of the senior regent, imploring him to see reason. Shamar Rinpoche could hardly bear the sight. After all, Ugyen Tulku was his senior and his teacher. The apprehension of trouble to his followers in Tibet too lurked in the mind of Shamar Rinpoche.

The next day the venerable lama returned — armed with the ammunition of emotional blackmail. Situ Rinpoche, he disclosed, was sitting in his room distressed, crying his eyes out. He also feared that if the letter were put to a forensic test, Situ Rinpoche would end up in prison for forgery. Shamar Rinpoche then finally gave in and agreed to the Ugyen Tulku's supplications.

Ugyen Tulku brokered a meeting between the two on 17 June in the Karmapa's private quarters on the first floor of the monastery. Shamar Rinpoche insisted that Gyaltshab Rinpoche stay away. The senior regent recalled the distasteful epithets Gyaltshab Rinpoche had hurled at the Dalai Lama at the time when a division between the Tibetan political leader and the XVIth Karmapa had manifested. The young Gyaltshab Rinpoche had become those days the Dalai Lama's loudest and most passionate critic, but his insolence had done Rumtek little good. Everyone just wished that Gyaltshab Rinpoche would keep his vile and slanderous mouth shut. Now, in an abrupt change of heart, the same Gyaltshab was very conveniently hiding behind the Dalai Lama's holy name.

As Shamar Rinpoche ascended the steps of the temple, he noticed a large gathering of Khampas and monks from the monastery of Situ Rinpoche in Himachal Pradesh defiantly lined up in the corridor. Their aggressive postures and unpleasant remarks were by then becoming a common occurrence in Rumtek. Hastily, he forced his way through groups of hostile individuals and arrived, unmolested, in the Karmapa's room. Situ

Rinpoche was already in place. The two lineage holders locked themselves inside, but the windows were left open. Shamar Rinpoche let it all hang out: the eleven years of rumour mongering and defamation, the campaign of hatred against him and Topga Yulgyal, the aborted attempt to take him to court, and the recent illegal proceedings. Surprisingly, Situ Rinpoche meekly accepted his peer's accusations.

Eventually, after Shamar Rinpoche had exhausted his litany of woes, the time had come to sign. Ugyen Tulku was called in as witness. However, when the senior regent was about to give his written acceptance of Ugyen Trinley (Situ's candidate as the reincarnation of the Karmapa), suddenly a former Dharamsala minister burst inside. In the old days, when the XVIth Karmapa was still alive, the same person had made himself famous for opposing the Karmapa. Now, in a new role, he came to lecture Shamar Rinpoche on the senior regent's lukewarm devotion to his guru and on the consequences of his 'foolish' acts. Whatever the minister intended to achieve, his words at once achieved the opposite. Shamar Rinpoche put away his pen, grabbed the document, and was about to tear it up when he met Ugyen Tulku's eyes. The old lama pleaded with him to stop. Also Situ Rinpoche, his hands folded in supplication, pleaded humbly, "Please, rinpoche, don't." The senior regent paused. Then, as if trying to put an end to the embarrassing scene, with one frenzied stroke of his pen, recognised — in accordance with the Dalai Lama's decision — Ugyen Trinley as the XVIIth Karmapa. However, he did add a rider. The shrewd politician in him led him to include, "Hence I suspend my demand such as having the handwritten prediction letter being subjected to a (forensic) test."

Hours later, Situ Rinpoche and his supporters let the world know that the senior regent had unequivocally offered his willing approval and would therefore no longer pursue the matter of examining the sacred testament. The Situ group deliberately distorted the letter. In a letter to Situ Rinpoche on 18 July 1992, Shamar Rinpoche said the translation of his letter on behalf of Situ Rinpoche was a distorted one. He enclosed the English translation and asked Situ Rinpoche to see that the distorted version was not circulated anymore. Situ Rinpoche said that once you accepted a cow, you could not say that you would not have the tail.

Ugyen Tulku announced in his speech on 18 June, "The regents had reached a compromise and the Situ group submitted the statement signed by Shamar Rinpoche accepting the verdict of the Dalai Lama to the chief minister of Sikkim on 29 June. Obstacles had been overcome."

Of course, there was Topga Yulgyal who had not recognised Situ's candidate as the XVIIth Karmapa as he was away from the scene, at his home in Bhutan.

6

The Red Shadow

Amidst all the drama, on 15 June, Ugyen Trinley, the candidate of Situ Rinpoche, reached Tsurphu. Escorted by a convoy of seven cars, the child looked rather disorientated. There had been an accident en route and two people had been killed. Chinese officials were calling the shots. About 2000 Tibetans paraded before the *tulku* to receive his blessing. A couple of days later, the boy's public appearances were abruptly cancelled. Now one could only get a blessing through a glass panel. Akong Tulku admitted that he had given the order to shield the reincarnation. No representative from Rumtek had joined the celebrations.

Drupon Dechen Rinpoche was the head lama in Tsurphu and one of the main figures in bringing Ugyen Trinley to the Karmapa's seat. Years before, he had approached the XVIth Karmapa with an offer to travel secretly to Tibet and help rebuild the old monastery. Notwithstanding the lama's fervour, the idea failed to enthuse the Karmapa. Without opposing him, the Karmapa had dissuaded him, saying frankly that he saw no future for the place. But after the death of the Karmapa, Drupon Dechen Rinpoche went to Tibet on orders from Situ Rinpoche. Now, he was claiming that the XVIth Karmapa had sent him to Tsurphu.

He disclosed that the search party for the XVIIth Karmapa, headed by his assistant, Lama Dholmo, and armed with a copy of the prediction letter, had actually left Tsurphu as early as 8 April. The group was dispatched despite the prior agreement among the four rinpoches that no such mission should take place before Jamgon Kongtrul Rinpoche reported his initial contacts. The four regents had decided that Jamgon Kongtrul Rinpoche, and not Lama Dholmo, was to make the first approach. How a local lama got hold of a copy of the then top-secret document and why he was usurping Kongtrul's place more than two weeks before Kongtrul's tragic death was a mystery. Drupon Dechen Rinpoche admitted that Akong and Sherab, the two regents' emissaries, had personally handed over the copy of the letter to him. At that time, they had no business in Tsurphu and were hardly supposed to be roaming the distant stretches of Tibet, certainly not with a copy of the prediction letter in their pockets.

Drupon Dechen Rinpoche described the different wonders that had occurred during the time of the child's birth: among others, the sound of musical instruments had been heard for two hours in the valley and four suns had appeared in the sky. (In his address in Tibetan at Rumtek, Situ Rinpoche had mentioned only three suns though while addressing the foreigners in English, he forgot the suns altogether.)

He acknowledged that in 1991 Situ Rinpoche had visited the monastery where Ugyen Trinley (the candidate) was a monk. Interestingly, Situ Rinpoche, who in 1991 alone had recognised the rather extravagant number of about a hundred and sixty reincarnations in eastern Tibet, had been unaware of a boy whose birth had been accompanied by such miraculous signs. Furthermore, the boy was believed to have taken part in one-and-a-half months of initiations that Situ Rinpoche had given in Palpung, the headquarters of his monastery in Tibet, that same year. To the discerning eye, it all looked like Situ Rinpoche had fixed his eyes on the child long before he sat with his peers to interpret the instructions concerning the whereabouts of this child.

On 24 April, a picture of the boy was taken, and a pick-up party was being organised to bring the *tulku* to Tsurphu — all this prior to Jamgon Kongtrul's death. On 17 May, the two regents declared publicly in Rumtek that, since Shamar Rinpoche was away, they had to act alone and were therefore sending Akong and Sherab on a search mission to Tibet. The two emissaries arrived in Tsurphu in the second half of May, and a group of sixteen was promptly sent to Kham. It was also announced that Ugyen Trinley, the XVIIth Karmapa, would arrive in Tsurphu on 20 June. He arrived on the fifteenth instead.

If this group of sixteen had indeed been the initial discovery team, then these men had been given at the most 20 days to complete a round-trip journey from central to eastern Tibet. Their task: to locate the boy in the large, nomad area of Kham, and to negotiate with the parents for his delivery to Tsurphu. All travel was to be taken on the one-lane, treacherous, gravel roads of the high Tibetan plateau. It was a physically impossible task. Although the interpretation of the prediction letter was clear as to the name of the family and the general region in the east of the country, there was, of course, no address. There must have existed at least one earlier search team, which was exactly what Drupon Dechen Rinpoche had carelessly disclosed. More than that, Lama Dholmo's group, which had set off on 8 April, was probably looking for somebody Situ Rinpoche knew fairly well, as he seemed to have met the child at least in 1991, if not before. The group that was dispatched from Tsurphu at the end of May was merely a reception committee. They were well aware of where to go to collect the boy.

Apparently, Situ, Gyaltshab, Akong Rinpoches and others were going hand-in-glove with the Chinese. Secretly, they had planned to exclude Shamar Rinpoche and install their candidate in Tsurphu without his knowledge. But this was never a secret to Beijing. They could not have accomplished such a mission without official Communist blessing and active help; in fact, the two eminences had a lot to thank the Politburo of the Communist Party of China for.

In the meantime, Situ Rinpoche recognised the reincarnation of Kalu Rinpoche. The mother of the reincarnation was said to have been a few months pregnant, carrying the new Kalu, at the time when the old Kalu passed away. In April 1999, Situ Rinpoche sought special permission from the Government of India to visit Sonada, the seat of Kalu Rinpoche, as the father of the reincarnation of the rinpoche had expired. In his request, he mentioned that the deceased was his relative.

Ever since Situ Rinpoche had announced his discovery of the reincarnation of the XVIIth Karmapa, he had been promising his followers that the Karmapa would be, in no time, officially installed in Rumtek. The departure of the reincarnation for India was said to be only a matter of days, maybe, weeks. Later, however, with no sign of Ugyen Trinley outside Tibet, the weeks stretched into months and the months became years. Situ Rinpoche and his followers staged a coup by 'smuggling' Ugyen Trinley to India in the first week of January 2000.

In an earlier communication, Lama Ole, a European Buddhist monk, had demanded to know what would happen if the officially chosen Karmapa would request, of his own free will or prodded by the Chinese, that the 'black crown' and other relics be returned to Tibet. How could we delay or refuse such a request, he asked.

On 27 September 1992, when Ugyen Trinley was ordained in Tsurphu as the XVIIth Karmapa, the Rumtek monastery, members of the Karmapa Charitable Trust, and the majority of the representatives of the Kagyu centres in the West did not approve of the procedure. Shamar Rinpoche, historically second after the Karmapa in the Kagyu spiritual hierarchy, did not attend the ceremonies.

Beijing had officially recognised the Karmapa two months ago, on 29 June bestowing the title of the 'Living Buddha' on him. The Chinese recognition coincided with the Dalai Lama's formal approval, which was given in Dharamsala on the same day. The title itself was a Communist synonym for a cooperating lama. Akong Tulku of Scotland monastery had already joined the ranks of the Living Buddha. He had also been appointed to the government of the Tibetan Autonomous Region (TAR). The Communist propaganda machine did not fail to mention that the XVIIth Karmapa would become an individual loyal to his socialist motherland.

The high profile of the Chinese officials punctuated the installation ceremony. The enthronement was preceded by their speeches, a presentation of a letter from Beijing — the government's seal of approval on the reincarnation and the enthronement — and by the exchanges of the traditional scarves and gifts. The shrine room overflowed with visitors from all over Tibet. The Tibetans working for the Chinese-backed government in Lhasa arrived in full force. There were also many Kagyu rinpoches from Nepal and India and some westerners.

The child looked quite distressed, just as a seven-year-old would under such circumstances. He could not sit still for more than a moment, had no clue as to what was happening — as he was constantly being whispered to whenever the ceremony required even a minimal level of his participation — and towards the end got clearly irritated. Probably it was nothing unusual for a boy of his age coming from a nomad family.

Looking rather out of place on his throne and in his gold brocades, clearly uncomfortable with the rituals being performed around him, he also displayed an intolerant streak. Easily angered, he constantly threw things at anyone entering the room. His grimaces were those of anger and not of mischief as generated by a boyish desire to tease his elders. The happy family reunion on the terrace of the monastery came to an abrupt end as the young boy dismissed his parents and siblings with a proud gesture.

China's Tibet, a quarterly review magazine from Beijing, claimed that 40,000 people filed by in an orderly fashion to receive blessings from the XVIIth Karmapa. In the meantime, a two-page release signed by Lobsang Deleg Rinpoche reached the Kagyu centres overseas. He had a lot of interesting things to say. According to his statement, the important ceremony in Tsurphu was, in fact, preceded by rather inauspicious events both in Rumtek and in Tibet. When Ugyen Trinley was officially brought to his seat, a golden banner fell down from the protector's shrine in Rumtek. Also one of his cars in the entourage skidded and overturned on the dangerous road, killing two passengers. At the enthronement ceremony itself, some people waiting outside were injured by a boulder that rolled down a mountain slope beside the monastery. Situ Rinpoche's younger brother started a scuffle with the police, and was arrested and held for several hours. Finally, the monks, in an attempt to manage the crowd, had fought with the other participants and a chaotic atmosphere had set in.

Meanwhile, a pamphlet bearing the name of J.P. Smith from Dharamsala landed at Kagyu centres all over the world. It stated that the dispute in the lineage was an integral part of Asian politics. Power and money were behind it. The next year (1993), the American Congress was to review China's most-favoured-nation status. Beijing was earning billions of dollars in trade with the United States of America; the American trade deficit with the Communist nation was, in fact, topped only by its deficit with Japan. With the Democrats in the White House, the passage of the Bill in Congress was not expected to be such a smooth ride as it had been during Bush's tenure. China needed to show the world, and especially the Congressmen in Capitol Hill, that she was treating her minorities well.

The pamphlet added that Beijing had managed to split the Tibetans between the Dalai and Panchen Lamas so as to suppress the occupied country, but in 1989, when the Panchen Lama had died, Tibetans began to rebel. Demonstrations had been held in Lhasa and in the big monasteries around the capital. The inevitable clamp-down followed. Western television showed scenes of Chinese soldiers beating, even torturing Buddhist monks. The Chinese Politburo needed somebody to calm the rebellious Himalayan nation, and so they fixed their gaze — not for the first time — on the Karmapa. The Chinese leaders had rightly concluded that the best way to control the Chinese Tibetans would be to manipulate their *tulkus*. A policy of Politburo's official involvement in the recognition of reincarnates had been, in actual fact, confidentially adopted a few years before. The old Maoists had become experts in the delicate process of locating famous lamas. The Communists, who did not even admit to the mind's existence, had suddenly become an authority in recognising a mind's reincarnation.

After the happenings in June '92, Situ and Gyaltshab Rinpoches ruled the roost at Rumtek. It seemed that they were bracing to assume full control of the Kagyu order. Shamar Rinpoche left the scene of the battle altogether and stayed in France for some time.

The Rumtek monks' main concern was to carry out the instruction of their lama, the XVIth Karmapa. They pledged to continue with their duties in the monastery and made a strong commitment not to let the place fall into the hands of outsiders. Consequently, in order to prevent the possible removal of the Karmapa's possessions, they locked up and sealed all the Karmapa's belongings. Confronted with the sharp division at the top, they decided neither to follow nor to oppose any of the regents. No wonder, the cloister's legitimate inhabitants fell victim to insults, followed by intimidation, and finally physical violence for their tepid support to Situ Rinpoche. The monks brought from other monasteries during the last rites for the late Jamgon Kongtrul Rinpoche began to interfere systematically in the monastic administration and harass the legitimate caretakers. Topga had already been forced to leave the monastery for Bhutan for want of adequate security from the Sikkim government.

Early November 1992, Shamar Rinpoche and Rumtek monks together with members of the Rumtek administration and a group of trustees held a meeting at the Karmapa's headquarters. The room was jampacked. Everybody sensed that a significant decision was to follow. Shamar Rinpoche began by repeating his assertion in June and also narrated the following developments. He iterated that he had knowledge of a trustworthy person who had been holding the XVIth Karmapa's instructions concerning the XVIIth reincarnation. The time had come for him to devote his full attention to the fulfillment of these instructions. He solemnly declared that until the Karmapa was found in accordance with such a genuine mandate, he would be unable to perform his duties at Rumtek. He was, for the moment, giving up his commitments in the monastery. His words were greeted with uncomfortable silence.

It was an unexpected about-turn. The Rumtek monastery and the Nalanda Institute would be left exclusively in the custody of the monks and the Karmapa Charitable Trust. Situ Rinpoche had, of course, no business at the Kagyu headquarters. His seat, Sherab Ling, lay in the west Himalayas, more than 1800 km from Rumtek. During the years after the death of the Karmapa in 1981, he had shown scant interest in the Rumtek affairs and had not contributed a rupee to its coffers. His present bid for the leadership of the Kagyu order's headquarters had no legitimate basis whatsoever except that he was one of the trustees of the Karmapa Charitable Trust. His ally, Gyaltshab Rinpoche, although a resident of Sikkim, had not offered much support either. He was devoted to his own monastery, Ralang, in Sikkim.

The Karmapa's main seat had been, in fact, managed and financially supported by Topga and his administration. He was actively assisted in this task by Shamar and Jamgon Kongtrul Rinpoches. Since Topga was away, the management would come to rest on the monks' shoulders. The trustees, two of them based in Gangtok, remained the legal caretakers, but they were hardly in a position to travel daily to Rumtek and share the duties with the monks. In any eventuality, the monks would have no one to help them to confront the intruders. The Sikkim government, headed by Nar Bahadur Bhandari, was least expected to intervene impartially.

On 17 November, Shamar Rinpoche issued an official statement. He declared that he would not object to the Chinese government's decision to recognise Ugyen Trinley as the Karmapa. He had no jurisdiction in China and was completely unable to stop their action. Disclosing that his agreement to the Dalai Lama's recognition was delivered out of respect to the Tibetan leader, he pledged that he would hold firmly to the tradition of the Gyalwa Karmapa by following only his genuine instructions.

Tension escalated in Rumtek. Gyaltshab Rinpoche had convened an assembly of Kagyu monasteries from India and Nepal on 30 November. Ten days earlier (on 20 November), Shamar Rinpoche held an emergency meeting with the monks. They realised that they themselves had no power to stop the rabble from getting into Sikkim and staging their gathering at the Karmapa's seat. Some of the younger monks, getting restless, called for confrontation but, in the end, the idea of violence was abjured. Instead, the participants decided to ask Chief Minister Nar Bahadur Bhandari for protection. Sitting in the chief minister's office later in the afternoon, Khenpo Chodrag

Thenphel, the head abbot, Nendo Tulku, *vajra master*, and a few others expressed their apprehensions about the planned conference. They stated their position and asked the chief minister to prevent an illegal occupation of the monastery. Before leaving, they submitted an appeal to the chief minister.

The appeal was made on behalf of the entire monastic community at Rumtek. The signatories unanimously declared that until a genuine Karmapa was accepted by all, the monks, together with the trustees of the Karmapa Charitable Trust, would hold full responsibility for the management of the monastery. They insisted that the prediction letter presented by Situ Rinpoche be scrutinised by scientific methods. They asserted that they would react to any attempt at interference with their duties. No spiritual or political authority other than the Karmapa Charitable Trust would be welcome in Rumtek. The chief minister assured them of his unyielding efforts to keep peace at Rumtek and, with a reassuring smile, shooed his guests out.

The next day, the caretakers at Rumtek reached a decision. They would lock the monastery to prevent the gathering convened by Gyaltshab Rinpoche from taking place. If the visitors managed to make it across the Sikkim border from Nepal via West Bengal and arrived at the monastery's doors, they would find the portals bolted. The majority of the monks were to leave for Nepal to participate in another ceremony for the late Jamgon Kongtrul Rinpoche. Shamar Rinpoche was already on his way to Nepal. The students from the Nalanda Institute were also departing for winter vacation. Major activity in the cloister would cease. There were only a few staff members and monks left. Situ Rinpoche assailed the decision of the senior regent to close all the shrines of the monastery abruptly.

On 25 November, the Sikkim police entered Rumtek and took up positions around the monastery. They came to ensure that no fighting broke out when the other party arrived for their planned assembly.

The next day, Tsechokling Rinpoche, a government official from Gangtok, appeared outside the nearly deserted Rumtek. Armed with the chief minister's orders to make the place accessible for the planned conference, he demanded that the doors of the monastery be opened instantly. "Make haste," he thundered at the lone staff member who showed up to receive him. Confronted with a Sikkim government official waving a bunch of documents in his face, the stupefied man quietly extracted the keys from his pocket and quickly unlocked the gates. Hectic preparations for the planned conference continued for the next three days, and the monastery's legitimate custodians were ignored. The handful of administrators present travelled daily to Gangtok to petition the chief minister for action against this act of trespassing of their cloister. They were informed that the chief minister was in Delhi and his office had no power to act. Unable to stop the aggression, the monk and nun community, the Nalanda Institute, and the Rumtek administration resorted to the last weapon available. On 29 November, their representatives issued one more written statement.

They declared that they did not refuse to accept Situ and Gyaltshab Rinpoches' claim to have located the Karmapa's true reincarnation on the basis of authentic instructions. Neither did they decline to accept Shamar Rinpoche's assertion of the existence of genuine instructions indicating a true reincarnation. However, they could only follow decisions made by the Karmapa Charitable Trust and under no circumstances would they accept resolutions made by lamas, their administrations and other political groups.

Despite the protests, the state government backed the 'Kagyu International Assembly', as the meeting was called by the organisers. It began with a bang.

The Karmapa Charitable Trust was a painful thorn in the flesh of Situ and Gyaltshab Rinpoches. Although a trustee himself, Situ Rinpoche stood as a single minority within the trust. The other trustees were not rushing into an endorsement of Situ's candidate. To complicate matters, Topga did not seem to exercise his fellow trustees' restraint and was, in fact, moving ahead full steam against the two regents. Situ Rinpoche feared that Topga's bellicose mood was having a contagious influence on the other trustees who might soon catch the infection and contemplate a more aggressive course of action. The dangerous situation had to be dealt with immediately.

Hence, in his opening address, Situ Rinpoche proposed that the present board of trustees be dismissed and a new group of individuals be appointed trustees. He alleged that the trust had come under the negative authority of Topga and, as such, was exerting an undesirable influence on Rumtek and other Kagyu places in the world. Its present trustees had to be discharged. He argued that the monastery and all of the Karmapa's property was not safe until they had a new and healthy trust. The rag-tag assembly convened by the two eminences seemed to fully agree with the reasoning.

A few voices of dissent piped up unexpectedly. These dissidents argued that the trustees had been personally selected by the XVIth Karmapa, and to dismiss them would be to go against the wishes of the late Karmapa. This point did not appear to faze the venerable regents presiding over the meeting. Situ Rinpoche casually remarked that they could do that, they could fire the notorious troublemakers and appoint good trustees in their place. They could also establish a new trust. Unexpectedly this state of affairs did not appeal to a couple of delegates from Gangtok, and feeling they were skating on thin ice, the two delegates suddenly left the room. Surprisingly, one of them was Tsechokling Rinpoche, the Sikkim government official who had brought the order of the chief minister to unlock the portals of the monastery for the assembly.

The proceedings were promptly restored, and the rest of the gathering, in utter disregard of the legality of their action, went ahead with the controversial resolution, undisturbed by the fact that they were going against the XVIth Karmapa's legacy. The existing Board of Trustees of the Karmapa Charitable Trust was dissolved with immediate effect and seven persons appointed as new trustees. In addition, Topga was relieved of his function as general secretary of the trust with immediate effect, and Tenzin Namgyal was unanimously elected in his place. The supporters of Situ Rinpoche conveniently forgot that altering a country's laws was more difficult than adjusting a historic tradition or forging a religious document. The trust was operating as per Indian laws in a democratic and modern society. Another resolution adopted in the meeting said, "The trust does not have any jurisdiction over the recognition of the Karmapa or any other reincarnate lama."

Firing Topga from his post within the trust apparently did not fully satisfy the organisers' thirst for vengeance. And so the assembly was also invited to denounce, in most severe terms, the 'ex-general secretary'. The delegates of the Kagyu International Assembly were only too happy to comply with the diktat. Having listed all "his malicious deeds", the participants unanimously stated that Topga Yulgyal "had been causing destruction to the *dharma* and therefore the assembly condemns his actions." In the lengthy resolution, Topga was accused of having sold the Karmapa's property in eastern Bhutan, of having caused friction between *dharma* teachers and disciples of the Karmapa at Karmapa's main institutions, and of having led armed soldiers into the seat of the Karmapa. The assembly then proceeded to dismiss him from his post of treasurer and general secretary of the Karma Kagyu institutions, meaning, in this case, Rumtek itself.

Behind the allegation about the Bhutan property hangs an interesting tale. Tashicholing is a palace located in the eastern Bhutan. It belonged to the mother of the IIIrd Bhutanese King, Jigme Dorje, Puntsog Chodron. During a visit to Bhutan, the Karmapa was offered Tashicholing, including all the land and buildings on it. The queen mother desired that the Karmapa make a *shedra* (institute) or *drubdra* (retreat centre) there. The Karmapa accepted the gift and decided to construct a *shedra*. Many people suggested the use of the existing buildings instead of constructing a new one. They also pointed out that political changes could occur in the country. The Karmapa answered, "I am a *dharma* practitioner, and whatever is beneficial for Buddhism, I will do. Even if I built a monastery today and it were dismantled tomorrow, I would not regret it."

The *shedra* was constructed. It could accommodate 300 students. It took quite a while to build, but could not start functioning immediately because of the political changes in the country.

In 1983, everybody was trying to carry out those activities that the Karmapa had wanted. One of the projects was the *shedra* at Tashicholing. Efforts were made to complete the painting of the *shedra*. After completion of the work, Shamar Rinpoche, the official representative of the Karmapa at that time, as per an arrangement between the four rinpoches, wrote to the King, Jigme Senge, a disciple of the Karmapa, but in vain. He then wrote to the home minister. Silence reigned on that front too. At that time restrictions were in force against foreigners establishing any kind of institution within Bhutan. A request was again sent to the home minister that the *shedra* would be a purely Bhutanese one. Another one was sent to the newly established religious department. Still no reply came.

Then the Rumtek administration asked for an unequivocal answer: either to give it permission to open the *shedra*, or say so otherwise. This time, a reply came. It quoted a resolution that no foreigner was allowed to establish any kind of institution in Bhutan, religious or non-religious. Therefore, permission could not be granted. The letter added, "If you wish to sell the property, the land, the old building and the newly built *shedra*, the government will buy it." The trust convened a meeting and decided to accept the Bhutanese government offer. Shamar, Situ and Jamgon Kongtrul Rinpoches were present in the meeting. They endorsed the resolution. Since there is a strong *dharma* link between the Kagyu order and the successive Bhutan kings, the trust asked the Bhutanese government to assess the valuation of the property and give whatever would be appropriate, and added that this would be acceptable to it. In the meantime, Je Khenpo, the highest ranking monk in Bhutan, called up Topga and offered to buy the building for the monastic community. But the trust had already decided to transfer the property to the Bhutanese government. The payment was not received in cash. It came in the form of bank demand drafts as this was not a private transaction. The amount was rupees four million.

On 3 December, the last day of the conference, the last resolution was passed. Neatly printed on the Rumtek's official stationery, the text read: "We, the followers of the Kagyu order, pledge with one pointed faith and reverence to confront anyone who may plan negative and destructive actions concerning this non-controversial issue. We pledge never to acknowledge any other person who may be falsely given this title." In a letter to the chief minister of Sikkim, the delegates went one notch further and dramatically stated, "We take oath that we can never accept and will fully confront if there is any other candidate for the Karmapa."

The signatories on each paper of the documents included, besides Situ, Gyaltshab, Ponlop and Bokar Rinpoches, Bardo Tulku, and Kunga Trinley, signing on behalf of the Dalai Lama, and Trakel Rinpoche, a representative of Tenga Rinpoche. Another resolution passed on the last day of the conference denounced *The Karmapa Papers,* a publication from Paris on developments in respect of the vexing issue of reincarnation of the Karmapa, as a heap of "fabrications, misinformation, and outright lies, and not even a paragraph of truth to be found in this corrupted and false publication."

Later, talking to his European disciples, Shamar Rinpoche presented the situation in allegorical terms. He quoted the Tibetan fable of the lion and the elephant, which vividly illustrated Situ's machination to usurp the seat of the Karmapa. The story goes: The lion and the elephant both wanted to be king of the animals. The lion declared that the elephant's eyes were too small for such a serious task. He roared and showed his big teeth, claiming only he could protect the animals. Obviously, they needed witnesses to settle the issue. They then summoned the tiger, who at once agreed that the lion was by far the best suited for the job. But then somebody had to be witness for the tiger. And so the buffalo was called in and he witnessed for the tiger, then the pig witnessed for the buffalo, and so on until in this fashion it boiled down to the tiniest flea. The flea voted for the lion. And thus it happened that the lion was crowned king of the animals by a flea.

He told them of the volte-face of several rinpoches and *tulkus*. They had to act in accordance with the political status quo of the region. Having monasteries in Tibet, they were responsible for their people in the occupied country. If they wanted to visit their old places and preserve their positions, they had no choice but to follow the Chinese line. Such points might be difficult to accept for people with a free, democratic background, Shamar Rinpoche admitted, but added that the lamas were bound by the traditional rules and current political realities.

Probably aware that the dissolution of the trust might pose some legal complications, the 'new trustees' began to consider other means to exert pressure on the 'dismissed trustees'. They opted for direct confrontation.

Tenzin Chonyi, the freshly appointed member of the trust, presented himself at the Gangtok residences of two of the legitimate trustees, Jigdral Tashi Densapa and Sherab Gyaltshen. In an aggressive and loud manner, he demanded that the two trustees sign an acceptance of the assembly's resolutions. The two trustees let the agitated Tenzin know that they had been entrusted by the XVIth Karmapa to assume, with five others, the administrative authority of the order from the time of his death until his XVIIth reincarnation became 21 years old. They told him that in no way did they intend to ignore their duty and so, under no circumstances, would they consider handing over their responsibility to anyone other than the XVIIth Karmapa himself. In particular, they refused to accept the illegal and disrespectful way things had been managed lately.

Seeing that he was getting nowhere with his threats, Tenzin Chonyi decided to apply more concrete pressure. He warned the two trustees that if they did not deliver their agreement to the resolution, they would be immediately forced to resign from the trust. Sherab Gyaltshen and Jigdral Tashi Densapa, in a restrained manner, simply asked their uninvited guest to leave.

A group of settlers, coming from Tibet, had collected a sum of about Rs. 2.51 lakh. This amount formed the corpus of the Karmapa Charitable Trust in 1961. The income, profit or any reasonable portion of it was meant to be spent for the benefit of the Karmapa's followers.

Sikkim had not merged with India at that time. Therefore, the deed of the trust was signed in the Indian residency, i.e. office of the political officer for India at Gangtok in Sikkim. At that time, the registered office of the trust was at 142, Rashbehari Avenue, Calcutta (India), which was perhaps the residence of Ashok Chand Burman, an Indian industrialist and a close confidant of the XVIth Karmapa. Burman had also been named as one of the trustees by the XVIth Karmapa.

The XVIth Karmapa was the sole trustee. The deed of the trust specifically mentioned:

> And it is hereby declared that in case of the *mahanirvana* (death) of the trustee, i.e. His Holiness the 16th Gyalwa Karmapa, as stated hereinabove, his successors in office, i.e. His Holiness the next Karmapa, i.e. the 17th Karmapa, shall become the trustee. During the intervening period of the *mahanirvana* of H.H. the 16th Karmapa and the reincarnation of the next Karmapa, i.e. the 17th Karmapa when reincarnated, and if he is below the age of 21 years, then till the time when His Holiness the 17th Karmapa attains the age of 21 years, the seven persons named below and, in case of their death or refusal to act as trustees, their heirs, legal representatives or successors in office, as the case may be and as provided hereinafter, shall become the trustees for the management of the 'Karmapa Charitable Trust' with all the power of the trustees as vested by this deed of trust.

The seven persons in the trust were: Rai Bahadur Tashi Dadul Densapa, Ashok Chand Burman, Gyan Jyoti Kansakar, Sherab Gyaltshen, Dhamchoe Youngdu, Jewon Takpoo (Dragpa) Yulgyal (Topga Rinpoche) and Gyonpu Namgyal.

The deed of the trust further specified:

> It is also provided that in case of the death of any of the future trustees No. 1 to 4 named hereinabove dying before or after the *mahanirvana* of His Holiness, i.e. the 16th Karmapa, and before His Holiness the next Karmapa, i.e. His Holiness the 17th Karmapa is reincarnated and attains the age of 21 years, then their legal male heirs by the principle of primogeniture shall hereditarily become the trustees in place of the deceased trustees. And it is also declared that in case of any of the heirs of the future trustees Nos. 1 to 4 refusing to act as trustees, the other trustees

will be entitled to nominate a competent male member of the family of the deceased future trustee as aforesaid as one of the trustees, and if no such person is available, then anybody else that the other future trustees as aforesaid may think fit and proper to act as trustee, in place of the trustees so dying or refusing to act.

If is further declared hereby that in the case of the death of any of the trustees named from Nos. 5 to 7 hereinabove representing the Karmapa sect (order), before or after *mahanirvana* of His Holiness the 16th Karmapa and/or before His Holiness the next Karmapa, i.e. His Holiness the 17th Karmapa is reincarnated and takes charge of the 'Karmapa Charitable Trust' after attaining the age of 21 years, the members of the Karmapa sect of Tibetan Buddhism will elect the required member or members of their sect as vacancy may arise (amongst the trustees Nos. 5 to 7) to act as trustees in place of the deceased trustees.

Provided that the trustee or trustees so appointed in place of any or all of the future trustees named hereinafter from 1 to 7 will have the same power or rights as if he or they was or were originally appointed the trustee or trustees under these presents.

The original deed said, "His Holiness the Gyalwa Karmapa Lama Dharm Chakra Centre Trust Runtak (sic) Sikkim." In the rectified version "Dharm Chakra Centre Trust Runtek" was replaced by the words: "Supreme Head of the Dharma Chakra Centre of Rumtek in the state of Sikkim."

Rai Bahadur Tashi Dadul Densapa has been succeeded by his son Jigdral Tashi Densapa (he resigned but his resignation letter was not accepted); Ashok Chand Burman resigned; Shamar Rinpoche was adopted by the rest of trustees to replace him; Gyan Jyoti is living in Nepal and Sherab Gyaltshen is living at Gangtok. After the death of Dhamchoe Youngdu in December 1982, Jamgon Kongtrul Rinpoche was adopted as trustee. In 1993, Jamgon Kongtrul too died in an accident. Jewon Takpoo Yulgyal, son of the sister of the XVI Karmapa, and general secretary of the Rumtek administration as well as the trust, died in 1997. Gyonpu Namgyal died. He was replaced by Situ Rinpoche.

The present composition of the trust is: Gyan Jyoti Kansakar (Nepal), Sherab Gyaltshen (Gangtok), Shamar Rinpoche and Situ Rinpoche. Three seats (Nos. 5 to 7) are vacant.

At present, Situ Rinpoche is banned from entering Sikkim and Darjeeling in West Bengal while the Sikkim government has imposed restrictions on the visit of Shamar Rinpoche to the Rumtek monastery.

Topga Rinpoche admitted in 1996 that during the lifetime of the XVIth Karmapa and for the immediate years after his death, the trust had remained inactive and widely forgotten. The Karmapa was the sole trustee. Therefore, there was no need to activate the trust. It was only after the death of Dhamchoe Youngdu, the old General Secretary, in 1983, with the financial crisis looming over Rumtek that the new administration had dug out the corresponding documents, and consequently, the trust's seven-member board, as per the deed of the trust, came to life.

In April 1984, the first meeting of the trust after the death of the XVIth Karmapa was held at the Rumtek monastery. The meeting resolved that the Rumtek monastery affairs would be conducted on the basis of the deed of the Karmapa Charitable Trust. Generally, the trustees were to meet twice a year. Funds were provided liberally by Shamar Rinpoche. He and Jamgon Kongtrul Rinpoche contributed greatly to accomplish the intentions of the XVIth Karmapa. During the same period, Situ and Gyaltshab Rinpoches devoted themselves to construct their own monasteries.

"When the dragon's thunder is heard, peacocks cry out in joy", Situ Rinpoche wrote in a letter in 1992 to three other regents, the Rumtek Monks' Association, Topga Rinpoche and others in Rumtek village. The trustees took note of it and convened an emergency meeting. They concluded that letters of this kind were not acceptable as a lot of expectations were generated. Previously there had been excitement over the inner and outer letters. If Situ Rinpoche had substantial material to communicate, everyone would be overjoyed. But if not, letters of this kind would not do much good. The trustees asked Topga

Rinpoche to convey these sentiments to Situ Rinpoche, which he did.

In his capacity as general secretary, Topga Rinpoche wrote a letter to the trustees as the situation was a pressing one. He stated:

> Ever since the meeting on 19 March 1992, Situ and Gyaltshab Rinpoches have chosen to ignore the Karmapa Charitable Trust. Situ Rinpoche, being a trustee himself, has consistently failed to inform the general secretary and the fellow trustees of the historical steps he was taking and has acted as though the governing body did not exist. Legally, however, nothing could be undertaken on behalf of the Kagyu order without the trust's formal consent.

The letter was later made public. The general secretary recalled that the trust had always been under the impression that the XVIth Karmapa's testimonial letter was found in 1986 in his relic box, as declared by the four regents. However, now this letter had become invalid because of another letter produced by Situ Rinpoche. The trust, however, was not informed about this latest document. In order to satisfy the international following of the Gyalwa Karmapa, the general secretary added, Situ Rinpoche's letter needed to be tested by reliable methods. Since this was not being done, the trustees had to find an alternative to prove the authenticity of the XVIIth Karmapa so recognised.

Topga Rinpoche also stressed that the trust had to take measures to safeguard all the valuable articles that the XVIth Karmapa had brought from Tibet with such great effort. It was extremely important that those treasures be prevented from falling into the wrong hands. "As the Gyalwa Karmapa trustees, we must see to it that the real Karmapa be enthroned," the general secretary concluded. He also counselled that at this juncture it was not advisable to make any changes either in the policies of the trust or the composition of the board of trustees.

In November 92, the trustees assembled in New Delhi. Sherab Gyaltshen was the sole absentee. In the meeting, Topga Rinpoche remarked that many letters about the Karmapa's reincarnation were sent out. Surprisingly, the contents of these letters always added up to the same, even though they were said to be sent by different organisations and individuals. And coincidentally, or perhaps deliberately they all seemed to be about the proceedings of reincarnation of the Karmapa. All the letters demanded "that the proceedings be speeded up and led by Situ Rinpoche in collaboration with the Dalai Lama as had been done in the past."

Topga Rinpoche said:

> Before the meeting I had written to Shamar Rinpoche to convey what I just said. Copies of my communique were also sent to three other rinpoches. In my letter I had asked if the four rinpoches were no longer willing to shoulder the responsibility for the proceedings together. During the meeting I also told the others that we must be clear about this. I had pointed out that the letters implied that the reincarnation proceedings were not being speeded up because of a certain individual who attempted to obstruct the proceedings. If there were such an individual, he would be an enemy of the *dharma*. Therefore, we must know who this person is.

The four rinpoches responded in writing. They wrote that they still collectively shouldered the responsibility for finding the Karmapa's reincarnation and that there was no individual who tried to obstruct the proceedings.

As matters stand today, the trust, according to the supporters of Situ Rinpoche, is a defunct body 'as its purpose has already been served'. They assert that it was formed by settlers, who were entitled to take back the money invested in the trust. According to Situ's supporters, majority of them had retracted their contribution in the late XVIth Karmapa's lifetime. Prominent among the contributors was the Tsurphu *labrang*, the main administrative body formed by the founder of the order, the First Karmapa. The late XVIth Karmapa had signed on behalf of this body in the deed of the trust.

They prefer to forget the other purpose of the trust, i.e. management during the intervening period between the death of the XVIth Karmapa and his reincarnation, which has been specifically given in the deed of the trust. Shamar Rinpoche insists that the aim of the trust is to maintain all the movable and immovable properties left by the late Karmapa, which languish under the illegal occupation of usurpers aided by the Sikkim state government. Ironically, the Situ group wanted to infuse its men in this trust even though it described the trust as a dead horse.

Shortly after the Karmapa's death, there was a proposal to establish a new trust. According to Topga Rinpoche:

> Some aspects of the administrative work changed. The tax-laws and so on were not the same. It became necessary to create a new trust as the administration was not able to locate the legal documents of the old trust. Thus the members in the administration travelled to Delhi for this work. This trust was to include the four regents, ten other persons and myself. But just as we were about to register the trust with the Indian authorities, the documents of the old trust were found.

The late Karmapa had also constituted another trust in April 1967 to purchase the land for the present monastery. It was named Karmai Sheydup Chho-Khor-Ling Trust (Dharma Chakra Centre Trust). Only two out of the nine trustees are alive. They are Dungche Dr Ugyen Jigmee and Dungche Tenzin, Personal Secretary to the late XVIth Karmapa. *Dungche* is a Tibetan word which means *secretary*. Tenzin, previously the deputy general secretary of the main administrative body, has been elevated as the general secretary by the Situ Rinpoche and his supporters. Though there is a provision for the election of trustees by the religious followers of the Karmapa, the vacancies have not been filled so far.

The deed of this trust specifically mentioned:

> After the passing away of the present Holiness Gyalwa Karmapa, and until the next *avatar* (reincarnation) attains the age of 18, the powers exercisable by his Holiness under this trust will devolve upon the successive '*Karmai choo-ghar theipa*' or the occupant of the Karmapa sect (order) and the private secretary of His Holiness Karmapa jointly.

An extraordinary meeting of the 'Settlers of the Karmapa Charitable Trust' held on Saturday, 12 December 1992, at the registered office of the trust at Rumtek was presided over by Lodro Tharchin, teacher of Situ Rinpoche. No-confidence was expressed in Jewon Takpoo Yulgyal, a trustee and general secretary of the trust for not recognising the candidate (of Situ Rinpoche) as the reincarnation of the Karmapa. It was also decided to reconstitute the board of trustees. A resolution said:

> Resolved that the present board of trustees be and is hereby dissolved with immediate effect and the following persons are appointed as the new trustees with immediate effect: 1. Kunzig Shamar Rinpoche, 2. Kenting Tai Situ Rinpoche 3. The Goshir Gyaltshab Rinpoche, 4. Bokar Rinpoche, 5.Tenzin Namgyal, 6.Tenzin Chonyi and 7.Kunzang Sherab.

It was also resolved that the reconstituted board of trustees would have the same powers and duties and would be governed by the same deed of trust dated 23 August 1961 as the outgoing board. Through a resolution, the assembly treated a letter from Topga Rinpoche to Situ Rinpoche refusing to recognise the latter's candidate as the Karmapa as the former's resignation letter.

Another resolution said:

> Resolved that Jewon Takpoo Yulgyal ceases to remain general secretary of the trust with immediate effect and that Tenzin Namgyal has been unanimously elected general secretary of the Karmapa Charitable Trust with immediate effect.

The third and the last resolution stated:

> Resolved that all the bank accounts of the Karmapa Charitable Trust shall hereinafter be operated by (any two of) the trustees as under: (1) Tenzin Namgyal, (2) Kunzang Sherab and (3) Goshir Gyaltshab Rinpoche. If any of the above have to go out of station for any period of time, he may authorise any of the other trustees to operate the bank accounts on his behalf during the period of his absence.

After two days, on 14 December the copy of the said resolutions was sent to the secretary, land revenue department of the government of Sikkim for the purpose of record-keeping.

Meanwhile, letters of query about the new trust started pouring from various towns in Europe in the office of the government of Sikkim as well as to the trustees, as per the deed of the trust.

Panic swept the Buddhist world. On 18 January 1993, the said Lodro Tharchin, wrote another letter to the land revenue department, withdrawing his earlier letter and the copy of the resolutions. He further requested for the return of the submitted papers. The government decided not to process the case for registration but pleaded its inability to return the submitted papers as they were now part of the official records.

On 1 March 1993, the commissioner-cum-secretary of the land revenue department wrote to Herbert Giller of West Germany and admitted that a request had been made by certain parties for a change in the existing trust. But the parties concerned subsequently withdrew their request for registration of change of the trust. "In view of the withdrawal, the state government has not registered any new trust nor recognised any change in the original trust existing as the Karmapa Charitable Trust," the government official added.

The chief secretary to the Sikkim government in 1997 in his confidential report to three senior functionaries of the Government of India wrote:

> While the regents are responsible for the religious affairs of Rumtek, these are the trustees who are really the inheritors

> of the trust, constituted by the sixteenth Gyalwa Karmapa. Three of the regents were members of the trust. One of them died in an accident. After the so-called discovery of the reincarnate in Tibet, Situ Rinpoche has been avoiding attending the trust meetings and in any case after 1993 his entry to India has been banned. He, therefore, seems to operate through Gyaltshab Rinpoche who continues to be in Rumtek. For some strange reasons though he is also a Tibetan refugee like Shamar and Situ Rinpoches, Gyaltshab's permit to remain in Sikkim is renewed by the state government year after year whereas Shamar Rinpoche has not been allowed to enter Sikkim for some time now.
> ....the legally established trust exists and was functioning in a normal fashion until the controversy erupted in 1992. Even thereafter, in spite of the trust being, for all practical purposes, boycotted by Situ Rinpoche, it continued to meet right until 1995. The resolutions taken by the trust from time to time have appealed for moderation, for settlement of dispute by adopting the middle path and dialogue. The efforts of the trust for bringing about a rapprochement have been dismissed somewhat derisively by the joint action committee, possibly inspired by Situ Rinpoche. In fact, the joint action committee seems to have organised something called Kagyu International Conference and had gone to the extent of calling for the resignation of the trustees. They also made an effort to replace the present trustees with a set of their own but this was not successful. Because of the possession of the monastery by Situ group the trustees have not been able to occupy their official position within the monastery nor have they been able to perform their functions in a proper manner.

The chief secretary added:

> Kunzang Sherab, an ex-bureaucrat not particularly known for integrity or efficiency and who for some time was the secretary of the ecclesiastical department of the government of Sikkim; Namkha Gyaltsen, an MLA who represents the

Sangha constituency, Sonam Topden, younger brother of Karma Topden, Congress Member of Parliament (Rajya Sabha) and a few others formed the joint action committee.

Kunzang Sherab is the chairman of the joint action committee of all Sikkim Buddhist organisations. In the campaign to install the 'Chinese' nominee as the Karmapa, head of the Kagyu order of Tibetan Buddhism, the Congress member of the Rajya Sabha from Sikkim, Karma Topden, has also reportedly joined hands with Kunzang Sherab. Sonam Topden, younger brother of the Congress MP is the general secretary of the joint action committee. The Topden family reportedly nurses a grudge because a child of the family was not recognised as reincarnation of one rinpoche despite efforts by Situ Rinpoche, the leader of the group campaigning to install the 'Chinese' nominee.

Three prominent families in Sikkim, namely, Lharipa, Topden and Pasang Namgyal, are also allegedly hand in glove with him. It is alleged that this body (JAC) is involved in unleashing a virulent campaign against the group, which has refused to recognise the 'Chinese' nominee as reincarnation of the Karmapa.

In March 1992, during a meeting of Situ and Gyaltshab Rinpoches with the then Sikkim government headed by Nar Bahadur Bhandari, the representatives of the so-called 'joint action committee' were also present. After the meeting, the secretary of Gyaltshab Rinpoche commented, "the joint action committee has especially been formed to protect the interests of the Sikkim government, the Tibetan government-in-exile of the Dalai Lama and the government of China. That is why it is called joint action committee."

It was on behalf of the joint action committee that the monks attacked the Rumtek monastery on 2 August 1993. It is in the name of the committee that the monastery has been occupied. In 1994, when Nar Bahadur Bhandari lost the elections, the joint action committee shifted its allegiance to the Sikkim Democratic Front of Pawan Kumar Chamling but the latter did not welcome its office bearers. The joint action committee later switched its allegiance to the Congress.

The chief secretary said:

> The joint action committee has been keeping the (reincarnation) issue alive and influencing the local population in Sikkim to subscribe to the view that the reincarnated Karmapa in Tibet is the only real reincarnate. The group has been able to capture the loyalty of the local Bhutia-Lepcha population to a large extent because of the fact that its members do not hesitate to use strong-arm tactics whenever necessary.
>
> They are also supported by some local politicians such as Thuckchuk Lachungpa who is currently with the Congress but was earlier with the Sikkim Sangram Parishad (of Bhandari) and who specialises in agitational politics.
>
> It is due primarily to the joint action committee that an ugly situation was created in the monastery itself, as a consequence of which two groups fought each other and the group of lamas owing allegiance to Shamar Rinpoche was physically thrown out of the Rumtek monastery. This group of lamas has been given shelter near the monastery but not allowed to enter it.
>
> The presence of Gyaltshab Rinpoche and the fact that the group owing allegiance to Situ Rinpoche is in physical possession of the monastery has enabled them to claim that the monastery already belongs to the reincarnate of the XVIth Gyalwa Karmapa from Tibet and that he be brought from Tibet and enthroned in Rumtek. The joint action committee keeps issuing pamphlets, monograms, cassettes — all calculated to establish that the Tibetan reincarnation is the only correct reincarnation. The propaganda has no doubt had an impact on the local population. Attempts by Shamar Rinpoche's followers to enter the monastery even for the purpose of worship have been beaten back by use of force by the group in occupation of the monastery. It needs to be highlighted that the local bureaucracy and the police have also been heavily influenced by this strong propaganda.

Discussing the role of the state government, the chief secretary said:

> It has been reported that the then Chief Minister Nar Bahadur Bhandari had developed links with Situ Rinpoche and his attitude towards the Rumtek controversy was, to a large extent, influenced by the Situ group. Reports also indicate that his election campaign was financed by Situ Rinpoche. It is possible that Bhandari wanted to keep his hold over the Bhutia/Lepcha voters who he thought were inclined towards Tai Situ group. Bhandari's own political history indicates that he was opposed to the merger of Sikkim with India and he has not hesitated from taking anti-India stances whenever it suits his political convenience.
>
> What needs to be highlighted is that when the controversy erupted and developed into a law and order problem, the Sikkim government officers, who went to the monastery to control what was basically a law and order situation, seem to have exceeded their authority. Whether they did this because of express instructions by Bhandari or not is unclear but having arrived at the site to control the situation, created by warring groups of lamas, aided generously by outside elements reportedly gathered by the members of the joint action committee, the then home secretary and the inspector general of police seem to have also got hold of the keys of the monastery. They did not care to make an inventory of the articles in the monastery. What is more important is that the keys were handed over not to the duly constituted trust or any of its trustees but to Tai Situ group. By this act of the state government, intentionally or otherwise, the possession of the monastery was handed over to Situ Rinpoche group which since then is prohibiting the other group from entering the monastery.
>
> The trustees have not been able to enter the monastery either and perform their duties and have been writing to the state government to take corrective action in the matter and Shamar Rinpoche has been trying to impress upon the government that they should also be given access to the

> monastery. An attempt was no doubt made to get the monks of Shamar group back into the monastery but in the face of violent opposition from Situ group from within the monastery, it was given up. The trustees have not met since 1995 but the Shamar group is now attempting to take recourse to legal remedies. The state government has received a notice from a legal firm, on behalf of the majority of the trustees, asking for restoration of possession of the monastery and its properties along with a list of articles that are supposed to be a part of the monastery.

The Bhutia and Lepcha communities comprise different clannish groups in Sikkim. Top on the social rung are the Kazis, or landowners, traditionally the noble families of the state. The Kazis, for centuries, have exerted a great deal of influence in the region during the centuries-old dynasty of the Chogyals. Leaning on the middle rung stand the Babus, a clan of usually educated members but traditionally subordinate to the Kazis. The lowest rung is of commoners. They are usually the uneducated segment of the Bhutia-Lepcha community and more often than not exploited by politicians.

Interestingly, successive Chief Ministers, Nar Bahadur Bhandari and Pawan Kumar Chamling, are supporting the group headed by Situ Rinpoche. In the 32-member state assembly, 12 seats are reserved for the Buddhist Bhutia-Lepcha communities, besides one seat for the *sangha*. Therefore, every political leader in the state continues to meddle in all affairs, including religious affairs of the Buddhists.

Over the past 15 years, the Babus have garnered support from the commoners and pushed Kazis to the side. In the beginning, The Topden family of Karma Topden and Kunzang Sherab threw their weight behind Nar Bahadur Bhandari against L.D. Kazi, the first chief minister of the state, who was instrumental in bringing about the accession of Sikkim to India.

Similar is the role of the Derge Association based in Kathmandu. The steering committee of this group comprises Dhonyod Gyago, Kelsang Chimi and Dontsay Karge, all associated with the monastery of Situ Rinpoche situated in Himachal Pradesh.

7

God's Abode Under Siege

The situation in Rumtek was incredibly complex. The immediate consequence of the Kagyu International Assembly's resolutions for the monastery was the removal by Situ's party of the old team that had run Rumtek since 1982. The new management comprised persons dismissed from the Karmapa's seat either by Topga Rinpoche or by the Karmapa himself. The new secretary, Tenzin Namgyal, had been relieved from his official duties in 1988. And as for the newly appointed assistant secretary, Lodro Tharchin, the late Karmapa in 1971 had personally asked him to leave Rumtek. He had then taken up a job with the Dharamsala government where he did not hide his animosity towards his former benefactors. The new, though illegal, administration began to take over Rumtek's good name and its resources.

The Rumtek monks, however, were unmoved and refused to accept the Topga's dismissal. Since the resolutions had not been approved by the Karmapa Charitable Trust, they did not hand over the keys to the monastery's office. As a result, Rumtek settled into the reality of having two administrations. The one composed of Topga's team kept on performing the daily duties and the task of running the place. It lacked a head though, as the general secretary had lately been turned away from Sikkim border by the government and sent back to

Bhutan. And then the new group, without any legal sanctity, consisted of the appointed secretary and his two assistants who kept themselves busy holding meetings and shooting off petitions — in short, trying their best to obstruct the work of the lawful custodians.

It turned out, though, that the Karmapa's seat was not to enjoy a long spell of peace. The monks had regained control of the monastery and had, in fact, stopped the two regents — Situ and Gyaltshab Rinpoches — from performing any rituals in the shrine room. They had also requested that Shamar Rinpoche preside over the lama dances for Losar (the Tibetan New Year). Shortly before the event, Situ Rinpoche turned up at Rumtek. This was an ominous sign. Each time Situ Rinpoche appeared in Sikkim, trouble erupted. Now, his people insisted that he was to offer a religious ceremony. The legal caretakers of the Karmapa's place, fearing another onslaught by strangers on the monastery's grounds, would have none of that. They made it quite clear they had no desire to host any of the lama's offerings. The rinpoche was left with little choice but to remain in his room during his entire stay in Rumtek.

Before the dances began, rumours spread that a gang of Tibetans from Gangtok was coming to take part in the ceremony, presumably to disrupt it. Fearing trouble, the monks decided to cancel the event altogether. It was announced that, as an expression of respect for the late Jamgon Kongtrul Rinpoche, the lama dances would not take place this year. Shamar Rinpoche would instead be only conducting the *Mahakala* rituals.

Eight cars, packed with young Tibetans carrying iron rods and cycle-chains, arrived in Rumtek. They were looking for an excuse to pick up a fight. It did not take long before they found their first victims, two of Shamar Rinpoche's attendants. Acting in a partisan manner, the police detained and sent the victims to jail in Gangtok. The aggressors were allowed to go scot-free. It was later explained that the arrests were a 'protective' measure. To keep peace, 60 Sikkim policemen were deployed in Rumtek.

The Beijing Government did not wait any longer to let the Tibetans and the rest of the world know about the big plans they had in store for their 'Living Buddhas'. Around mid-June, at a United Nations conference on human rights in Vienna, the Chinese delegate announced "that the Karmapa, the future successor of the Dalai Lama, was prepared for his tasks in Tibet."

Throughout the first half of 1993, the atmosphere in Rumtek remained tense. The state government drew up an order prohibiting General Secretary Topga from entering the East district of Sikkim. Supporters of Situ and Gyaltshab Rinpoches grew bolder and more aggressive by the day. Acts of violence became the norm. In May, a vehicle owned by the monastery was vandalized. In June 1993, Trinley Dorje, a student from Sonada monastery, stabbed Sonam Tsaring, a junior *khenpo* who had reprimanded the former. A FIR was lodged with the police. Trinlay Dorje was released on bail. The surety was furnished by Kunzang Sherab, President of the Joint Action Committee.

Alarmed by such incidents, the monks approached the police for help. The authorities, however, took no action to expel the intruders, leave aside arrest the delinquents. Officers and civil servants in Gangtok showed not only utter indifference to the victims' plight, but also left little doubt where their sympathies lay.

Having failed to garner help from the state administration, the monks themselves decided to enforce strict control over the monastery and prevent interference by outsiders. At that time, monk students at the Institute and the Rumtek monastic community had split into two groups. Some of the newly enrolled students from Bhutan were staunch supporters of Situ Rinpoche and as such felt they had to voice their preference in an increasingly militant way.

The traditional *yarney* (rainy season six-week retreat) was drawing near. The custom dated back to the Buddha Himself, who used to spend a period in meditation with his disciples each year during the monsoon. The annual observance had been held at Rumtek ever since the monastery was established, and the monks and students would normally perform a ceremony as a preparation for the long period of study and meditation. On 22 August 1993, the ceremony of *yarney* was being held. Throughout this ceremony, four monks at a time took the oath from the abbot and the ceremony must be completed by mid-day. During *yarney* only those taking the monk's oath are allowed to be present in the monastery, as this is a sacred event. Now, it became clear that if the two groups were to continue the *yarney*, or even the preparatory puja, clashes would inevitably follow.

To defuse the charged situation, Shamar Rinpoche, as director of Nalanda Institute, and the Khenpo Chodrag Thenphel Rinpoche, the chief abbot at Rumtek, decided to give the school a holiday. Situ Rinpoche alleged that Shamar Rinpoche cancelled all the traditional ceremonies without any reasons. An unscheduled vacation of one month was announced for the Pal Karmae Shri Nalanda Institute for Higher Buddhist Studies at Rumtek, forcing students to leave for homes. However, some remained behind and got ready for a showdown with the Rumtek monastic community.

On 22 July, Shamar Rinpoche left for Europe to visit his ailing mother. A few days later, as if following a familiar sinister pattern, Situ Rinpoche arrived in Rumtek and joined Gyaltshab Rinpoche who was already there. He declared that he was taking over as principal of the Nalanda Institute. The decision, he said, was in accordance with the arrangements made by the four rinpoches. He also claimed that it was his turn now as all four rinpoches had completed their one cycle each while Shamar Rinpoche had also served his term in the second cycle. The chief abbot of the Pal Karmae Shri Nalanda Institute, Thrangu Rinpoche, had sent him a letter in this regard, he claimed. He conveniently forgot that Shamar Rinpoche had already dissolved the group regency in 1983 with the consent of the late Jamgon Kongtrul and Gyaltshab Rinpoches.

After five days, on 31 July, he had a letter delivered to Shamar's residence below the monastery. The letter said that Situ Rinpoche was assuming control of the school and requested the return of all Rumtek's files and records.

Meanwhile, a small section of monks in the institute insisted on taking part in the *pujas* planned for 2 August. Fearing a confrontation, the monks decided to boycott the ceremony and informed Situ Rinpoche of the escalating tensions and of their desire to stay away from the function. The rinpoche was inflexible. The monks had to perform the rituals together with the students from the school. Nobody could be excluded. It was an order.

With no one else to turn to for advice, late at night on 1 August, the monastery's residents preferred to lock the doors to the main shrine room. Being Rumtek's legitimate caretakers, they felt responsible for the cloister. Neither would they allow outsiders to create a disturbance nor would they open the monastery under such threatening conditions.

The next morning, the party from the institute, led by Situ and Gyaltshab Rinpoches, came to attend the *puja*. Finding the doors to the shrine room and the hall locked, they sat down on the ground outside. Just then, a large cavalcade of cars drove into the courtyard, while a large crowd too began to assemble. The regents, gazing at the locked portals, began to recite *mantras*, while the devout stared curiously at the spectacle of two high rinpoches flopping down on the ground in front of the bolted doors. Later, it transpired that Situ Rinpoche had sent word to Gangtok that he would be making the special initiation open to the public. This was a ploy to gather participants and pose as though the monks were denying the venerable rinpoches access to the shrine and thus preventing them from delivering the promised empowerment. The visitors were unaware that no initiations or public meetings were scheduled to take place during the monsoon retreat. According to custom, the opening ceremony and the *yarney* itself were an exclusively monastic practice.

Seeing the two regents humbly squatting on the ground, and ignorant of the reason for the locked shrine room, people became agitated. Everyone concluded that the insensitive monks were harassing their holy rinpoches. Obviously, as long as the shrine room remained solidly locked, the empowerment was out of the question. This was precisely what Situ Rinpoche wanted. Angry shouts were heard demanding the keys from the monks. The mood began turning increasingly violent. At the same time, it also became clear that not all the guests were regular visitors eager to attend a religious ceremony. In fact, a sizeable number of them were hoodlums hired by Situ Rinpoche.

Also, as if by coincidence, the chief minister of Sikkim dispatched a massive police force to the monastery. Senior government officials started to arrive as well. The home secretary, accompanied by the district police chief and some cabinet ministers, summoned the monks' representative and in loud and menacing tones demanded that the shrine room be immediately opened to the public and the ceremonies commence without further delay. The officials refused to listen to the monks' explanation or reasons. Buckling to pressure, Omze Ngedon, the senior chant master, came outside the main building. He disclosed that the keys were with the monks who had gathered in the dining hall. The officials ordered him to fetch the keys at once. But the problem was that he would have to make his way through the crowd to get back to the dining hall. By now, the gathering had become openly hostile and threatened to beat him. Enraged yells demanding punishment for the impertinent monks rent the air. Omze fettered and stepped back but two policemen pretended to offer protection. Insisting that he should go, they shoved him out.

As Omze stepped out, some men and, in particular, women began pushing and hitting him. They wrapped his yellow ceremonial robe around his neck, and dragged him like a dog across the courtyard towards the monastery. While police stood as mute spectators, the mob punched and kicked him. Four monks rushed out of the dining hall and somehow managed to rescue Omze from the mob. Carrying the injured man back into their hall, they barricaded themselves in along with the other monks. The crowd charged at their quarters, throwing bricks and stones. Some from the crowd flashed their knives, windows were smashed, and five others from the monastery were seriously injured. The monks too returned the brickbats with energy. The two rinpoches — Situ and

Gyaltshab — all the while remained passively seated in meditation.

At last, the policemen put an end to the violent scuffle. The home secretary and other senior officials gave the besieged monks five minutes to deliver the keys. They threatened the monastery's inhabitants with prison terms if they refused to cooperate. The monks had no other option. The shrine room was opened, and Situ Rinpoche was free to proceed with his initiation. Police volunteered to take the injured men to hospital for treatment. Instead they were driven straight to prison.

In the midst of the intimidation and violence, some of the monks escaped. Left with little alternative but to flee the monastery, they knew they were running for their lives. The situation was very alarming but somehow they escaped into the nearby forest.

The following day, while the remaining monks were dining in the hall, followers of Situ and Gyaltshab Rinpoches, escorted by the policemen, burst in and installed a portrait of Ugyen Trinley, the candidate of Situ Rinpoche as the XVIIth Karmapa, high on a shelf. Senior lamas such as Bokar Rinpoche and Ugyen Tulku pleaded their inability to do anything when approached by the senior monks.

The monks were ordered at gunpoint to bow before the portrait and swear an oath that the boy was the true Karmapa. They were threatened with dire consequences if they defied the order. Thereafter, the policemen collected a wide assortment of kitchen knives and wood cutting tools and laying them on a table, ordered the monks to stand next to it. An officer proceeded to take photographs of the scene. This and other contrived evidence would later be used against the legitimate caretakers of the monastery as proof of their 'aggressive' schemes.

Other residents of the monastery were also chased away from their quarters, which were either locked or taken over by outsiders. Some of them even lost their belongings. Having no other place to go to, they took shelter at Shamar's residence, about 1 km. from the monastery.

Over 170 monks, nearly the whole of the Rumtek monastic community at that time, fled to Shamar Rinpoche's house. Conditions were tough. The house obviously was too small for so many people. Therefore, the basic facilities fell far short. In such cramped situation, there was little hope of continuing with their studies and monastic duties. Their long ordeal as outcasts from their own monastery had begun.

Situ and Gyaltshab Rinpoches had again managed to stage a coup to instal the picture of the Chinese-backed candidate in the coveted seat of the Karmapa. Interestingly, during the next few days, Situ and his group launched a full-scale campaign to portray themselves as the victims of the monks' aggression and the sole defenders of the Karmapa's legacy. Shamar Rinpoche was depicted as the villain and instigator of violence. Situ Rinpoche had the full backing of the state government. A letter addressed to the senior regent, Shamar Rinpoche, ostensibly endorsed by a large number of individuals from all walks of life in Sikkim, accused him of bringing disgrace to everything from Buddhist robes to the holy Buddhist scriptures.

The Gangtok press, too, went along with the assailants. 'Cops Quell Querulous Clergy' yelled a headline in a local newspaper. *The Hindustan Times*, a prominent paper of India published from New Delhi, carried a story the next day under the headline 'Pro-China Coup in Gangtok Monastery'. To buttress Situ's propaganda, Kunga T. Tamotsang, an MP of the Dharamsala government-in-exile, complained to the then Indian External Affairs Minister, Salman Khurshid, alleging involvement of Indian officials in the campaign against Situ Rinpoche in the Indian press.

To legitimize their occupation of Rumtek, the regents enlisted the help of various organisations from Gangtok. According to a document signed jointly by eight groups, "a large number of devotees" had been prevented on 2 August by a small 'gang' of monks from performing religious rites at Rumtek. It condemned what it defined as a "sabotage of religious functions" by a "handful of monks". It claimed that the law enforcement agencies too had discovered a stash of lethal weapons which the handful of monks had stored with the intention of causing harm to the devotees.

The outraged activists were, of course, strongly condemning such actions as "being mischievous, unwarranted, and with ulterior motive". They also disclosed that the above acts were inspired by "foreign elements" with "vested interests" and called upon the state government to confiscate all property of the foreigners involved. This was seen as pointing to Topga Rinpoche who held a Bhutanese passport. The protestors, however, were blissfully unaware that Situ, Gyaltshab, Shamar Rinpoches and other high lamas too were carrying diplomatic passports issued by the same country. In fact, it is a facility, extended by the Buddhist country to Buddhist monks and lamas as a matter of reverence. The activists later formed the joint action committee to further the interests of Situ Rinpoche.

Soon after its formation, the joint action committee staged a noisy protest in front of Sikkim High Court against a petition filed by Karma Gonpo and Dugo Bhutia, two former legislators of the Sikkim Assembly, in July 1993. They had prayed for forensic examination of the prediction letter. The petitioners could not appear in court and requested for adjournment of the case. Their advocate Moulick also refused to represent his clients. The crowd attacked the house of Sherab Gyaltshen, one of the trustees of the Karmapa Charitable Trust, broke the windows and abused the family. The windowpanes of Hotel Dewachen in Gangtok, owned by a cousin of Shamar Rinpoche, were smashed.

On the way to Rumtek, the aroused protestors called on the home of one of the signatories to the petition. More slogan shouting and stone pelting followed. An advocate went to the extent of saying, "All the judges put together cannot give a decision on the Karmapa. Although the judges are wise, they are not enlightened. Only an enlightened Buddha like the Dalai Lama will be obeyed by people". Following these developments, the petitioners withdrew the writ petition on 19 August 1994. A division bench of Sikkim High Court comprising Chief Justice S.N. Bhargava and Justice R. Dayal dismissed the petition as withdrawn but added that the court had not gone into the merit of the case at all.

Then Ngedon Tenzing (Omze) filed a case in the Supreme Court of India. The case ended at the preliminary hearing stage in the court on 11 March, 1996. The order said, "Counsel for the petitioner applies for leave to withdraw the writ petition and states that the petitioner shall adopt an appropriate remedy other than a writ petition before the High Court. The writ petition is dismissed as withdrawn." The initiative for withdrawal came from the court.

Cases for the possession of the land owned by the XVIth Karmapa and withdrawal of prohibitory orders too were contested in the courts. Situ Rinpoche also filed a case for dislodging Shamar Rinpoche from the Karmapa International Buddhist Institute (KIBI) in Delhi but he lost.

Earlier, Karma Gonpo and Dugo Bhutia, the two former legislators, along with two other residents of Rumtek, had sent a memorandum on 21 December, 1992 to Situ and Gyaltshab Rinpoches, with a copy to the Dalai Lama, to reconsider the matter.

On 24 March, 1997, Narain Singh, a resident of Munger in Bihar, and a disciple of the XVIth Karmapa, filed a writ petition in Patna High Court. It was dismissed after a week. The High Court observed that if the petitioner felt concerned about the matter, he ought to move the appropriate authority of the Union Government. Narain Singh filed a civil suit in the court of Munsif II, Munger, Bihar. He also filed a criminal complaint on 18 September, 1998 in the court of the chief metropolitan magistrate, Delhi.

Shamar Rinpoche cut short his programme in Europe and flew to India on 5 August, 1993. He found the situation hapless as the state government was completely hostile to him. He then sent an open letter to Situ Rinpoche. The copies of the letter were also sent to Gyaltshab Rinpoche and some of his supporters. In the letter, dated 12 September, the senior regent listed the many actions Situ Rinpoche, as a trustee of the Karmapa Charitable Trust, had undertaken without the approval of the board of trustees and often against the interests of the trust itself. In particular, Situ Rinpoche had promoted and helped set up an illegal trust with the aim of gaining control of the Karmapa's assets. Shamar Rinpoche denounced Situ Rinpoche for having taken over the Rumtek monastery by force and expelling the resident monks, and causing their imprisonment. Situ Rinpoche said that Shamar Rinpoche had caused great concern for the Government of India, their host. Shamar Rinpoche believed that his peer's actions had laid the Kagyu order vulnerable to international intrigue. The senior regent declared that, as a consequence, he had requested that the members of the Karmapa Charitable Trust join him "to reverse by legal means all the latest changes that the Situ had made to the status and peace of the Rumtek monastery." He declared he would never accept the use of force against monks in order to assume control of a monastery in the name of religion.

Shamar officially charged Situ Rinpoche with unlawful acts at Rumtek and with involving the Kagyu order in the power politics of the region. He also pledged to initiate court proceedings to regain the Karmapa's seat.

As for Situ, his secret involvement with China was no secret in India anymore. The regent's alliance with Beijing and his aggressive campaign to bring Ugyen Trinley to Sikkim were viewed with a great deal of concern at the highest government level in Delhi. Probably at Situ's urging, the successive chief ministers of Sikkim took up the matter of the Tsurphu boy with the central ministers, but their repeated requests to allow the child to enter Sikkim, even for a brief visit, were firmly turned down by New Delhi.

China is the only country that has not recognised India's sovereignty over Sikkim, and the mere thought of having a Communist-appointed Karmapa, a Chinese citizen, residing in Rumtek or shuttling between Tsurphu and Gangtok, made the Indian government shudder. Given such licence, the Chinese candidate would be drawing dangerously close to claiming the Karmapa's property in Sikkim as Chinese. Situ's amateurish overtures with Beijing and his dabbling in the delicate Sikkimese politics had raised eyebrows more than once in New Delhi, which was getting rather tired of their restless guest, Situ Rinpoche, enjoying the status of a Tibetan refugee and holding only residential certificates.

The Communists lost interest in Situ Rinpoche. On his part, Situ Rinpoche was soon to discover that the once-friendly doors in the Chinese capital were closed to him. Blind to political realities, the regent, however, would not give up.

Rumtek had changed beyond recognition under Situ and Gyaltshab Rinpoches. Hiding in Shamar's house, the resident monks-turned-refugees were banned from entering the monastery's premises. A number of suspicious characters dressed in monks' robes were brought to the cloister to take their place. The ritual, chant and discipline masters were all dismissed. New appointees were brought in. People in the village were forced to sign pledges of loyalty, petitions and denunciations. Those who tried to resist were blacklisted and harassed by the conniving police. Police saw it as their holy duty to re-educate the less enthusiastic supporters of the Chinese candidate. The families who stayed loyal to Shamar Rinpoche were persecuted.

Towards the end of August 1993, a German film crew turned up in the village for some major shooting. The filmmakers announced that they were seeking official permission to film inside a sealed room that supposedly contained certain sacred and precious relics. This was the room where the lineage's relics, together with the 'black crown' and the disputed letter, had been kept. Ever since the drama in June 1992, the room had been locked and sealed, and a posse of the Sikkimese police stayed posted round-the-clock.

The in-charge of the filming project was warmly greeted by Situ and Gyaltshab Rinpoches who filed a petition with the chief minister requesting him to open the sealed room. The two Rinpoches were determined to gain access to the area. Had it been just for Bhandari to decide, he would have happily given the regents the required permission. But New Delhi was not so generous. The whole controversy had achieved international dimensions, and the Government of India could not afford to have the lineage's most important items disappearing into China to be later used as a claim on Rumtek. The petition was rejected and Bhandari was firmly instructed to keep the place shielded.

On 4 May 1994, a group of people was engaged in damaging the garden of the late Karmapa. Benza Guru, the caretaker of the Karmapa's residence and a close attendant for more than a quarter of a century, challenged the miscreants. The group left the place shouting that the reprimand would be retaliated.

Early next morning the mangled body of Benza Guru was found on one of the pathways leading to the Karmapa's residence. He had died under mysterious circumstances. Gyaltsab Rinpoche said that he had fallen from the roof while the body was found about 30 metres from the building.

Ten days later the grand-nephew of Benza Guru, Sherab Mangyal, was beaten up by miscreants at the main gate of the monastery. After a few days, Apa Tswang, an elderly attendant of the former general secretary, was severely beaten up and left unconscious.

A year-and-a-half later, after the crisis had begun full blast in the latter half of 1993, Shamar Rinpoche seemed to be getting ready to execute a historic move. So far, he had just been responding to the escalating events, the initiative being fully in Situ's hands. He had helplessly watched the coups against his position unfolded with unexpected success. He had seen his influence and reputation gradually evaporating among the exiled Tibetans. His status as second-in-command within the hierarchy of the Kagyu order depended, to a large extent, on his Tibetan brethren lending their support. But the words of endorsement pouring in from his kinsmen were scarce. He was drawing fire virtually from all quarters in Asia for his official rejection of the candidate in Tsurphu. The time had come to retaliate and to give credence to his claims and carry out the Karmapa's authentic instructions that Shamar Rinpoche insisted were in the custody of a trustworthy person.

The most potent weapon against the presumed forgery, the analysis of the disputed testament, was obviously not going to be used. Rumtek was in Situ's clutches and the letter was out of Shamar's reach, in danger of being destroyed altogether. It was crucial that Shamar Rinpoche present his own choice for the XVIIth Karmapa. This was, of course, a terribly risky enterprise. Any mistake would have repercussions too widespread to control

China would certainly not remain idle, or passively watch while a rival to her Karmapa was installed in India.

Everyone assumed that Shamar's candidate was somewhere in occupied Tibet — an anonymous child happily living a normal life, unknown, at the moment, to Tibetans and Chinese alike. The senior regent had been reiterating that he knew a man who had been guarding such explosive details.

In January 1994, the candidate of Shamar Rinpoche reached Delhi. He had been smuggled out of occupied Tibet. Years later in 1996, at an international Karma Kagyu conference in New Delhi, Shamar Rinpoche would disclose the events that led to the finding and recognition of the XVIIth Karmapa. He recounted the turbulent years that followed the XVIth Karmapa's death in 1981 and also clarified that the instructions about reincarnation were not analogous with, say, a will that parents leave to regulate the distribution of their property among their heirs. Instructions left by high spiritual masters such as the Karmapa are very different. Buddhas and *bodhisattvas* do not think in terms of just one person and one short life; they have the constant good of each and every sentient being in mind. They take the past, the present and the future into consideration. The circumstances of their reincarnations are related to specific purposes. What is more, the process of identifying a reincarnation is a spiritual practice. This process is not comparable with the way in which, for instance, a king leaves instructions for his country's crown prince. Thus, the process of identifying the reincarnation of the late Karmapa is fraught with difficulties.

Mistrust and animosity ultimately got the better of the rinpoches responsible for the future of the Kagyu order. During that unstable period, the process of identifying the next Karmapa, a solely spiritual task, became hostage to mundane gains. A number of lamas went after money and power. Forced to operate in a worldly-minded environment, and probably convinced that his rival, Situ Rinpoche, was pursuing an agenda over the head of the Karmapa's interests, Shamar Rinpoche chose to go it alone.

In 1986, Shamar Rinpoche had received an unexpected visitor in New Delhi — Chobgye Tri Rinpoche, a highly qualified Sakya lama who had been held in greatest esteem by the XVIth Karmapa. He had an urgent message to convey to the senior Kagyu regent.

Chobaye Tri Rinpoche stated enigmatically:

> Shortly before the late Karmapa passed away, I had had a dream that the Karmapa went around a stupa wearing his usual *dharma* robes. He appeared to be sad. In my dream, I too felt sad and shed tears. Soon after my dream, the Karmapa died. Then, just a few days before coming here, I had yet another dream. This time, the Karmapa was clad in a yellow robe, while again he walked around a stupa. The colour of his vestment was radiant. He also wore the Gampopa hat, and his mood was cheerful. At noon the same day, a relative who had arrived from Lhasa visited me. He brought a photograph of a young child who was well known in the area my relative came from. People there knew that the child had on several occasions said that he was the Karmapa.

When he heard this, Chobgye Tri Rinpoche said, he felt he had to communicate the news to Shamar Rinpoche. And so, cutting short a visit to a monastery in Mussoorie (Uttar Pradesh), he presented himself without delay in Delhi. "You must not make a decision on the basis of what I have told you," Chobgye Tri Rinpoche concluded gravely. "Your judgment must be based on the instructions left behind by the late Karmapa as well as on the visions and experiences of qualified spiritual masters in the order. Since you are the Shamar reincarnation, I wanted to convey to you what I have just told you. Historically, in the Kagyu order of Tibetan Buddhism, Shamar and Karmapa lamas are regarded as inseparable."

The child in the photograph looked very young. Shamar Rinpoche guessed he was barely three years old. The Kagyu senior regent decided to keep the information to himself. He too concluded that the matter was well worth further investigation. An opportunity came soon in his hands in early

1987 when the Lopen Chechoo Rinpoche, representing the Nepal Buddhist Association, was sent to Lhasa. Shamar Rinpoche asked him to discreetly approach the child and ensure that nobody discovered the real purpose of his mission. The child's family was living at that time in the *bakhor* of Jokhang temple in Lhasa. He was one of the sons of Mipham Rinpoche, a well-known Nyingma master.

Lopen Chechoo Rinpoche returned to Nepal with plenty of information. He learned the parents' names, their history, and the birth dates and places of birth of their two sons. Chechoo Rinpoche also discovered that the father of the child was in possession of a good number of religious objects and letters that belonged to the previous Mipham. One such letter caught the Lopen Chechoo's attention. The document stated that in his next incarnation, the Mipham would beget a son by the name of Rigpe Yeshey Dorje. The late Karmapa's own name was Ranjung Rigpe Dorje. The clue was very encouraging.

Seeking further details, Shamar Rinpoche sent yet another emissary to Tibet. This second person came back with more exciting news. One account, in particular, must have put the Kagyu regent on the alert.

One day, the young child went to the Jokhang temple of Lhasa accompanied by his father's friend. While the two walked around the building, they noticed a large crowd that had gathered at the entrance. Following the group inside, they saw a heavy-set lama applying gold paint to the face of a Buddha statue. When the child spotted the lama, he ran up to him and asked, "Do you recognise me?" The lama nodded in the negative. Later, the father's friend recounted the incident to the parents. Curious, they decided to talk to the lama. After making inquiries, they found out that it was Gyaltshab Rinpoche. However, as they were getting ready to meet the prominent rinpoche, their son stopped them. "I do not want to see him because he does not recognise me," the child exclaimed and refused to see the lama.

In his letter to Shamar Rinpoche, the secretary to the Dalai Lama pointed out:

> During earlier audiences you had informed His Holiness the Dalai Lama repeatedly that the late Karmapa Rinpoche had

> told about his reincarnation to an old and pure monk and that when the time became ripe the identity would be revealed. His Holiness had said that if this was true then it could be one of the body, speech or mind manifestations of the Karmapa Rinpoche. However, during your last audience, you informed His Holiness that Chobgye Tri Rinpoche had recognised your candidate as the reincarnation of the Karmapa. This implies that the old and pure monk you have been referring to is Chobgye Tri Rinpoche.
>
> On 18 January 1997, in a letter addressed to Your Eminence and which was sent through the Bureau of H.H. the Dalai Lama, New Delhi, we mentioned about the enquiry made about this issue from Chobgye Tri Rinpoche last year through our office in Kathmandu. We had enclosed in the letter to you the copy of Chobgye Tri Rinpoche's response which clearly stated that he had not bestowed such a recognition. Therefore, because of the lack of convincing and satisfactory evidences, recognition of the different manifestations of the previous lama's body, speech or mind is not possible.

Shamar Rinpoche denies disclosing the name to the Dalai Lama though the Dalai Lama had told him that he was entitled to this information. In an interview to Eva Blach Jespersen from Sweden, who was working on this controversy for her doctoral dissertation, Chobgye Tri Rinpoche would not say anything about whom he considered to be the right Karmapa. He was of the opinion that this was something the Kagyus had to find out. Shamar Rinpoche holds Chobgye Tri Rinpoche in high esteem as the previous Chobgye Tri Rinpoche was a direct disciple of the XVth Karmapa. The late XVIth Karmapa always respected him as a great *bodhisattva*. He is the guru of Sakya Trichen Rinpoche, the Dalai Lama and many other lamas.

Around that time, a well-respected person, a devotee of the XVIth Karmapa, approached the senior regent with a momentous disclosure. The highly regarded individual claimed to be in possession of the Karmapa's instructions that indicated the Karmapa's succeeding reincarnation. He claimed to have obtained the information directly from the Karmapa but, bound by his guru's command, was unable to reveal until now.

The more signals Shamar Rinpoche received about the Karmapa's next rebirth, the less he seemed inclined to share these reports with the other three rinpoches. Secretly pursuing his investigation, Shamar Rinpoche decided to send a third courier to Lhasa. The child's father, a known lama, was in a special position. He would frequently be asked to assist people in spiritual and worldly matters. The family kept their home open; anybody could drop in to request for a blessing or advice from the lama. Shamar's directives to his envoy were to contact the family on the pretext of seeking business guidance. The emissary was then to return daily with the hidden purpose of observing the child. The clandestine plan though did not quite work as expected. No sooner had Shamar's man entered the house than he thought it prudent to withdraw in haste. A child of fair complexion met him inside and calmly declared, "You've come to look for me." That was enough. The man stayed for a few more days in Lhasa and quickly returned to Nepal. But the story he brought was further proof of the child's exceptional qualities. The research was gathering pace.

Now Shamar Rinpoche chose to do a meditation retreat. This was a method traditionally used by lamas to verify their choice of reincarnation. In the absence of authentic instructions, the only reliable signs could be obtained through meditation. On the morning of the seventh day of the retreat, Shamar Rinpoche had a singular dream. The XVIth Karmapa was performing a ritual on behalf of a deceased person. Upon completing his prayers, the Karmapa declared, "I have liberated the person I set out to liberate. Now I can come to wherever you want me to come." The next day, yet another dream followed. In his dream Shamar Rinpoche saw a golden Buddha statue of enormous proportions. As he started to throw rice grains towards the Buddha, the rice turned into rain that fell on the statue. Light started radiating in all directions from a very large butter lamp that was filled to the brim with nectar. In the centre of the butter lamp, where the flame should have been, there was a luminous ball from which light radiated. Of course, this was just a dream.

It was an indication of the authenticity about the young child in Lhasa as a reincarnation.

At this stage, the Kagyu senior regent made arrangements to travel to Tibet in order to examine the child secretly. His design was to appear in the Tibetan capital disguised as a businessman, enter the family's house with an excuse to consult the father, and then check the young boy. He secured a tourist visa from Hong Kong, using his contacts among the native Chinese. The plot, such as it was, seemed easy enough, and so Shamar Rinpoche embarked on his covert mission, probably confident that soon he would set his eyes on the young Karmapa.

As it happened, the exquisite plan backfired badly. Since he had never been to Lhasa before, Shamar Rinpoche had imagined that the *bakhor* where the family lived was a large area where one could move undetected. In fact, the *bakhor* turned out to be a crowded, tiny locality — a few narrow streets that led to the Jokhang temple — a lot like the enclosure of a small monastery. Much to his disappointment, the regent realised that he could not mingle incognito with the people. On top of this, the streets were filled with Tibetan merchants from Nepal — some of them his neighbours in Kathmandu — who might find it peculiar if not totally bizarre to see the Kagyu senior regent running around Lhasa in a business suit. Chances were that if he ventured anywhere near the family's home, he would be exposed at once.

The Chinese authorities were no fools either and had probably sniffed out the fact that Shamar Rinpoche had entered Tibet and was at the moment playing tourist in the Tibetan capital. Confined to the security of his hotel room, Shamar Rinpoche understood that he was under surveillance. Any attempt to enter the family's house under such inhospitable conditions might have had grave consequences. He had no choice but to abort the mission. To confuse the Chinese police, the regent opted for an excursion to Namtso, a tourist area in northern Tibet. When he returned to Lhasa, he quickly took the next flight back to Kathmandu.

Back in Kathmandu, Shamar Rinpoche resorted to another method to confirm his presumption. In Tibet, a person looking for signs about a reincarnation would traditionally write down the various possibilities on paper, then roll the pieces of paper into balls of dough, and throw them into a vessel. He would therefore journey to a holy site and pray that the paper with the correct indication would fall out when the vessel was turned over. Determined to verify what, by that time, must have been a near certainty that he was on the right track, Shamar Rinpoche sent his senior adviser, Lama Tsultrim Dawa, to the sacred places in and around Kathmandu with directions to perform the customary ritual. The learned emissary went to Pharping, outside Kathmandu, which was highly popular with pilgrims. There is a spontaneously arisen image of Tara at Pharping.

Two scraps of paper were put in a basket: one read that Mipham Rinpoche's son was the reincarnation of the XVIth Karmapa; the other stated that he wasn't. Lama Tsultrim Dawa repeated the ritual four times, besides Pharping, at a place near Kathmandu where there is a sacred Mahakala image, another spot in Kathmandu where there is a painting of Mahakala by the Xth Karmapa, Chos Ying Dorje, and in the last at a Kathmandu sacred place called the World's Noble White Buddha. Each time the paper asserting that the boy in question was the XVIIth Karmapa fell out.

In the senior regent's eyes, the evidence was overwhelming. Having amassed the proof, Shamar Rinpoche contacted the person who had confessed to be in possession of the late Karmapa's directions. The man stressed that he could not, at this point, reveal his information. The time to do so had not come yet.

Shamar Rinpoche kept his mouth shut despite obtaining a set of assurances in respect to the identity of the reincarnation. He wished to bring the boy out of Tibet in the first instance. Even when in a meeting of the four regents in March 1992, Situ Rinpoche had come out with the prediction letter and Shamar Rinpoche had refused to accept the authenticity of the letter, the latter had not mentioned his own breakthrough either.

After Situ and Gyaltshab Rinpoches swiftly executed their scheme and, with the Dalai Lama's formal approval and Chinese support, brought forward and recognised their choice for the Karmapa, Shamar Rinpoche was left helpless. He once again sought the advice of the person guarding the XVIth Karmapa's mandate. Shamar Rinpoche wanted to know if the letter was genuine and how to proceed in the light of the latest incidents. Without wavering, the man declared that the Situ's 'prediction letter' was a forged one, but as nothing else could be done at that moment, he recommended that the senior regent let the others finish what they had so deviously started. Thus, for the next year-and-a-half, the Kagyu regent waited patiently for his hour, sometimes confused, sometimes discouraged but always staying in touch with this mysterious person.

Towards the end of 1993, Shamar Rinpoche, in confidence of the mysterious person holding the prediction letter, planned to smuggle the boy from Lhasa. But the man would not reveal the Karmapa's instructions. He insisted on doing things exactly as he had been told, and the time was not ripe yet to disclose the message he had been entrusted to protect.

Meanwhile, in Tibet, the clock was ticking on. The child and his relatives had lately become the objects of official harassment. The hardships imposed bore no relation to the still hidden fact that Shamar Rinpoche had his gaze fixed on the family's junior offspring. But the senior regent knew very well that it was only a matter of months, perhaps even weeks, before the Chinese connected the boy's growing fame within his community with the Kagyu regent's clandestine research in Lhasa. So, in January 1994, the young boy and his parents applied for a permission to visit Kathmandu and upon receiving their passports, immediately set out on the overland journey to Nepal. It was a legal coup. The Communists did not realise until it was too late that they had allowed the candidate for the coveted seat of the Karmapa out of occupied Tibet. The Mipham family slipped legally through the tight net that enclosed Tibet and arrived undetected first in Nepal and from there to Delhi and later Dehra Dun.

On 27 January 1994, Shamar Rinpoche proclaimed in New Delhi that the Karmapa's reincarnation had been discovered. His terse statement said, "I, Shamar Rinpoche, announce that the authentic reincarnation of the XVIth Karmapa Ranjung Rigpe Dorje has been found. The XVIIth Karmapa is presently in India. Details regarding the traditional procedures for his installation will be made known in the near future." The family name of the XVIIth Karmapa was Trinley Thaye Dorji. Shamar Rinpoche had done the first half of the work, which he had to do traditionally. The other half was the installation of the XVIIth Karmapa.

In a formal letter addressed to the Dalai Lama, representatives from various Kagyu monasteries in India and Nepal stated that they disagreed with Shamar's decision, which they described as illegal. They emphasised that there could only be one Karmapa and reminded the Dalai Lama of his approval of Ugyen Trinley as the Karmapa.

At the end of February 1994, Shamar Rinpoche announced that Trinle Thaye Dorje, the new Karmapa, would be ordained on 17 March in the Karmapa International Buddhist Institute (KIBI), New Delhi.

On the evening of 16 March, the day before the planned ceremony, Shamar Rinpoche was aware that the following day Situ's men would try, at all costs, to stage a demonstration in front of KIBI. Under such circumstances, his original idea to bring Trinley Thaye Dorji to KIBI in the early hours of 17 March was laced with risks. The only reasonable solution, then, was to fetch the child under the cover of the night before the protestors began to gather at the entrance to KIBI. It was proposed that the next morning an empty car should be sent anyway, as if dispatched to bring the young Karmapa to KIBI. With little time to waste, Shamar Rinpoche put the plan into action, and within a few hours the young Karmapa was safely delivered to KIBI. Not even the KIBI residents suspected that their main teacher was enjoying the comfort of the institute that bore his name.

The next day, in the early hours, a large crowd gathered at the gates of KIBI. The hundreds of visitors who came to attend the historic function were frisked by the institute volunteers before being allowed in. Some monks, obviously owing allegiance to

Situ Rinpoche, took a defiant position on the pot-holed street that ran parallel to the institute. They came armed with numerous banners that not only denounced Shamar and Topga Rinpoches but also promised to confront the duo's 'puppet Karmapa'. Surprisingly, a few slogans raised were pointers to the development that the rally enjoyed the Dalai Lama's support.

While the group outside continued to swell, a black Mercedes inched out of KIBI's driveway and sped off to an unknown destination. The vehicle caught the protesters' attention. They shifted their focus from the building to the street and from the street to the vanishing car. The leaders of the mob concluded that the limousine would soon return with the 'fake'Karmapa. The trick proved as deft as it was timely. While the Situ's men flexed their muscles and blocked the street in an effort to prevent Trinley Thaye Dorje's ingress to KIBI, Shamar Rinpoche signalled that the ordainment ceremony could commence.

Preceded by Shamar Rinpoche and sheltered by the traditional umbrella, Trinley Thaye Dorje, the XVIIth Karmapa, entered KIBI's main shrine and slowly walked towards the Buddha statue that dominated the lofty room. The sound of horns and the jingle of cymbals filled the air. The hall was packed to bursting point. The Karmapa's monks, together with several hundred European and a few Chinese visitors from South East Asia, were seated on the floor facing the altar. As the boy moved through the hall, everyone rose to catch a glimpse of the new Kagyu leader.

With *èlan*, the young Karmapa prostrated himself in front of the Buddha statue and climbed, for the first time in public, on his throne. Nendo Tulku, the *vajra master* of ceremony at Rumtek, offered him a symbolic replica of the black hat and put a brocade robe around his shoulders. The blare of horns and the beat of drums heightened; the Karmapa, fully concentrated, placed the black hat on his head. The official *puja* began.

Some hours later, as the ordainment ceremony was drawing to an end, the tinkling of bells was suddenly drowned by the sound of windowpanes breaking. Wild screams reached those in the hall. The guests exchanged curious and increasingly bewildered looks. The protestors, having closed the street and waited in vain to intercept the "false" Karmapa, had finally noticed that Karmapa's welcome ceremony had got underway hours ago and was now all but over. Furious at failing to stop the event, a group of monks rushed towards the entrance of KIBI. The security men unlocked the gate and took to their heels. Armed with stones and clubs, the assailants stormed forward.

As the first windows in the shrine room shattered, some guests taking part in the rites dashed out of the building. A hail of bricks and bottles descended on them. About 20 monks, well past the gate, were charging ahead, trying to gatecrash into the hall. They were deterred by a barrage of brickbats coming from KIBI side and had to pull back to the street, beyond the KIBI's premises. The disciples of the Karmapa from the West attempted in vain to lock the gate.

The hall resembled a bastion under siege, most windows gone, frenzied yells resounding in the courtyard. It was a free for all. The sound of brickbatting and pitched battles mingled with the menacing slogans of the assailants outside and the chanting of *mantras* inside the shrine hall. The Karmapa appeared completely relaxed; accompanied by Shamar Rinpoche, he stayed behind a curtain next to the altar. After the mob had been driven away, the Karmapa was quickly escorted to his quarters on KIBI's third floor from where he could safely watch the developing situation.

The pitched battle lasted about 15 minutes. Nine persons were arrested. Several, including a Pole, were injured. One of the injured sustained head injuries. Flying pieces of glass inflicted cuts on many.

The spectacle of men in robes, anchored in two opposing camps, fighting each other right in front of a Buddhist institute, gave little credit to Buddhism and the Tibetan cause. It took the police some time to curb the unruly crowd. The main building had escaped serious damage but almost all the windows of KIBI had been smashed, the walkway leading to the hall destroyed, the rails and posts making up the fence ripped apart, and the sentinel box housing the guards ravaged. The courtyard, strewn with stones, broken glass and other objects that had been used as missiles during the attack, resembled a deserted battlefield.

The Dalai Lama, the Tibetan leader-in-exile, was addressing a human rights congress at exactly the same time as the attackers were charging KIBI. Some foreign delegates sent a memorandum the same day to the Dalai Lama questioning on what basis he planned to discuss the Chinese human rights policy in Tibet when his own people in India had no respect for the freedom of religion in the world at large.

Two persons from the Chinese embassy were spotted outside KIBI. One of them was equipped with a still camera and another with a video, clicking away the demonstration. It irked South Block.

Lt. Col. (Retd.) T.N. Atuk, whose brother is in the Indian Foreign Service, had come with two busloads of musclemen. He told newsmen that his plans were frustrated as the ceremony was advanced from 20 to 17 March in 1994. The brother of Situ Rinpoche, Gyaltshan, too was spotted among the violent protestors.

In August 1994, the Government of India banned the entry of Situ Rinpoche from India. He was virtually declared *persona non grata*. As expected, his case was taken up by Tashi Wangdi, *kalon* in-charge of health in the bureau of the Dalai Lama. He wrote a letter to Arvind Verma, then Special Secretary in the Ministry of Home, Government of India, in this regard. The joint action committee, too, sent a memorandum to the then Union Home Minister S.B.Chavan urging revocation of the order. S.M. Limboo, a minister in Sikkim, also wrote to the home minister in this regard. Virbhadra Singh, the then Chief Minister of Himachal Pradesh, pitched in with a request to Indrajit Gupta, the Union Home Minister, on 17 December, 1996. At the prompting of Pinto Narboo, a former Jammu & Kashmir state minister, Dr Farooq Abdullah, Chief Minister of Jammu & Kashmir, wrote to Indrajit Gupta. Phunchog Rai, Himachal Pradesh Minister of State for Tribal Development, also wrote to Indrajit Gupta.

A memorandum was sent to the Prime Minister by Karma Topden, an M.P. from Sikkim, Lama Lobzang, member of the National Commission for Scheduled Castes and Scheduled Tribes, P.K. Thungan, former union minister, and Lochen

Rinpoche, Head Lama of Lahul and Spiti. They also wrote a letter to then Union Home Secretary K. Padmanabhaiah. Karma Topden and Lama Lobzang wrote a joint letter to Indrajit Gupta. A joint letter was sent to I.K. Gujral, Prime Minister of India, by P. Namgyal, member of the Lok Sabha, Sushil Barongpa, member of the Rajya Sabha, and Karma Topden, member of the Rajya Sabha. The most steadfast supporter of Situ Rinpoche, Ram Jethmalani, wrote to Rajesh Pilot and Indrajit Gupta, the successive union home ministers and even went to describe the conduct of the Deve Gowda government for not lifting the ban on the entry of Situ Rinpoche as 'irrational' and 'anti-national'.

In September 1994, Ugyen Trinley was summoned to Beijing. According to reports in the Chinese mass media, during a meeting with a Politburo official, "the living Buddha Karmapa declared that he would study well and always follow the Communist Party of China." *People's Daily*, the Communist Party's mouthpiece, quoted the ten-year-old as saying: "Long live the People's Republic of China".

In the meantime, in an well-orchestrated campaign, the Dalai Lama and supporters of the Situ Rinpoche repeatedly urged the Government of India to allow the Karmapa in Chinese captivity to visit Rumtek. In July 1992, the Dalai Lama wrote to the then Prime Minister P.V. Narasimha Rao to facilitate his entry into India. His request was followed by a letter from the secretary, department of religion and culture of the Dalai Lama government to the foreign secretary of the Government of India. Copies of the letter were also sent to Situ Rinpoche and the union home secretary in January 1993. Again, a similar letter was sent to K. Srinivasan, the new Foreign Secretary, in December 1993. A series of letters was sent by the successive Sikkim Chief Ministers Bhandari and Chamling, urging the government to allow the boy to visit India.

The third prong of campaign by the supporters of Situ Rinpoche and the Dalai Lama government was against Shamar Rinpoche. A memorandum in the name of the followers of the Kagyu order at Rumtek was sent to the union home minister describing the activities of Shamar Rinpoche as sacrilegious. The joint action committee also repeated the allegation in a memorandum to Deve Gowda on January 31, 1997. Earlier, in November 1994, the Dharamsala government wrote to C. Phuntysog, Joint Secretary, Union Home Ministry, and K.A. Vardhan, Chief Secretary, Sikkim, 'about the plan to take the candidate of Shamar Rinpoche to Rumtek at the time of the state assembly elections. Apprehending serious law and order problem, the Government of India was requested to alert the state government in this regard and not to allow such a visit.

On 8 August, 1995, Topga Yulgyal and the Kagyu monks marched peacefully towards Rumtek to regain their place of worship. Situ Rinpoche alleged that Topga Yulgyal brought a convoy of about eight trucks, crammed with about 200 men to take over the Rumtek monastery by force. The intruders preceded their attack by cutting off all the telephone lines in the monastery. They were met with force and denied entry to their cloister.

Situ Rinpoche has a different tale to tell. According to him, when the men brought by Topga entered about 500 yards into the compound of the monastery, the residents realised what was going on. The Rumtek residents lined both sides of the road and stood in front of the attackers, singing prayers. Then the Sikkim police intervened and did not allow them to proceed to the monastery. In order to protest against the continuing occupation of Rumtek, the monks started an indefinite hungerstrike at the gates to the temple. Two months later, with no prospects of winning the place back, the strike was called off.

On the night of 11 September, three monks suddenly appeared at a secluded place while Tsewang Chorden, representative of the laity in Rumtek, in his sixties, was returning home. He had served the XVIth Karmapa and his family. Three monks shouted, "It is him, it is him" and attacked him. He fainted. When he regained consciousness, he found himself lying in the ditch next to the road with multiple injuries. He was taken to the hospital where he remained for a fortnight. The old man recognised one of the assailants known as Patru.

Rumtek today remains in the hands of outsiders while the monks, living the lives of refugees, are still prevented from returning to their homes.

In December 1996, Trinlay Thaye Dorje presided over the *monlam chenmo*, great aspiration prayers, in Bodh Gaya, the place of the Buddha's enlightenment. For the first time in history, a Karmapa had his hair cut in Bodh Gaya — a ceremony that formally initiated his activity in the world. Over 6000 monks and nuns as well as a large number of lamas from the Himalayan region attended the event.

In September 1997, Topga Rinpoche died of liver cancer. Later, at his cremation in Thimphu (Bhutan), Trinlay Thaye Dorje was officially welcomed by the Bhutanese royal family as the XVIIth Karmapa.

A 79-member delegation comprising activists of the joint action committee led by Situ and Gyaltshab Rinpoches met the Dalai Lama and the *kashag* (cabinet) of the Tibetan government-in-exile at Dharamsala on 29 and 30 January in 1997. The delegation expressed its reservation to an audience promised to Shamar Rinpoche by the Dalai Lama. The Dalai Lama conceded the request and did not grant an audience to Shamar Rinpoche. A letter in this regard was sent to Shamar Rinpoche by the office of the Dalai Lama on 3 February. However, Shamar Rinpoche says he still holds the Dalai Lama in high esteem but in the same breadth adds that the process of the reincarnation of the Karmapa does not need the seal of approval *bukhta rinpoche* of the Dalai Lama.

8

The Trial of Gods

Narain Singh, a resident of Munger (Bihar) and a disciple of the XVIth Karmapa, in a letter to the President of India on 28 July 1998 alleged that Situ Rinpoche was a threat to national security He also resorted to a *dharna* (sit-in) at Jantar Mantar, New Delhi from 27 to 31 July, 1998.

He alleged that Situ's men were involved in criminal activities such as trafficking in animal products of endangered species — skins, bones, etc. On two occasions in 1992-93 in Delhi, Situ's men were arrested by customs officials.

According to Narain Singh, Thrangu Rinpoche, a supporte of Situ Rinpoche, who was constructing a massive complex a Khajuhi, Sarnath, known as Vajra Vidya Mandir, has a Nepal passport. Similarly, Bokar Rinpoche and his nephew Lodro Donyo at Mirik in Darjeeling were flitting around the world unde Nepali passports and frequently visiting China. Situ's supporters have reportedly organised smuggling rings in India, Nepal and China. He has formed two parallel Khampa business groups one in Kathmandu and the other in Lhasa (Tibet). His interna secretary Ngoche Kargyay is in charge of the Kathmandu group Bhu Chung Chung, a member of the Bureau of Public Security in China, heads the Lhasa venture. According to the Delhi police Bhu Chung Chung and his associate, Ugyen, came to Delhi with *pashmina* (antelope fur) worth $ 2.5 million in the open market. Ugyen was arrested but Bhu Chung Chung escaped.

Altogether 62 permanent residents of Rumtek sent a joint memorandum to the prime minister demanding a ban on the entry of Gyaltshab Rinpoche into India for his alleged anti-Indian activities. Gyaltshab Rinpoche heads the Palcheenling monastery at Ralang.

Once the Sikkim government was rapped on the knuckles by the Government of India for accommodating Tibetan refugees. The state government was directed to take action against such persons who visited Tibet or Nepal and re-entered India. Instead of being pushed back, they were allowed re-entry. V.S. Ailawadi, Joint Secretary, Home Ministry, Government of India, wrote to K. Vardhan, Sikkim Chief Secretary, on 8 February, 1994 in this regard.

The letter said:

> It could be seen that no such action appears to have been taken by the state government in the case of the Tibetan refugee(s). I would therefore request you to please look into the matter and let us know the circumstances in which the Tibetan refugees who had left India without proper permission were allowed to re-enter the state. Also please take action against Lama Lodro Tharchin, a close associate of Situ, who visited Kathmandu to re-enter India and others, under the Foreigners Act, and send state government's recommendations/views/comments regarding their pushback after completion of legal proceedings..."

Lama Lodro Tharchin, 72 years old, is the tutor of Situ Rinpoche. He travels with him and shares the same hotel room.

In January 1994, Mrs. Rosalia Findeisin, a 40-year-old German pursuing Buddhist studies at Rumtek, was told to quit India. She had been to India in the past. After a short spell of absence from India, she had reappeared in Gangtok in December 1993, soon after the visit of Taiwanese minister Chen Lu Aan. She first came to Sikkim in 1985, armed with a multiple-entry visa, after a long stint in Beijing. Her declared mission was to study Buddhism and Buddhist architecture. She was associated with Situ Rinpoche. New Delhi was alerted by reports about her operations only after 1991. Suspicions about her questionable activities mounted by July 1993, when the ministry of external affairs ordered that no Indian mission abroad should give her a visa without its approval. Rosalia was away at that time, leading the ministry to believe that it had got rid of one problem.

Intriguingly, Rosalia turned up again. How she was issued a visa in Hamburg and an entry permit by the Sikkim House in New Delhi was a matter of inquiry. What baffled the mandarins in the Indian foreign ministry even more was her timing of the visit.

Chen Lu Aan had visited India between 28 November and 4 December, 1993. Subsequently, his entry to India was banned in January 1994 by the external affairs ministry, following his objectionable activities. The Taiwan minister's conclave was organised by Karma Topden. It is reported that Situ Rinpoche, too, attended the meeting. Chen Lu Aan belongs to the KMT party of Taiwan which stands for united China and is said to be pro-mainland China, though Taiwan pursues an independent role and is an eyesore for Communist China.

Dourmo was appointed the 'disciplinary master' to groom Ugyen Trinley, the claimant to the throne of the Karmapa but under the captivity of China. He, along with Bakezu, wanted to come to India via Nepal. Karma Topden and Gyaltshab Rinpoche both pleaded with home ministry officials to allow them to visit India. Frequent rendezvous of some Sikkim leaders with Chinese Public Security Bureau officials in Kathmandu have also baffled the Indian intelligence men.

And then a French connection thickened the Sikkim plot. Even the then governor of Sikkim became a part of the puzzle. Beijing-based but India-born French national Rajender Nath, who calls himself Regie Nath, was a friend of the Governor Admiral (Retd.) T.H. Tahiliani. A former Indian Air Force engineer, Nath had quit prematurely in the late seventies to take up a job in France. Between 28 October and 1 November, 1993, he visited Sikkim without an inner line permit. A junior Sikkim police officer escorted him from Bagdogra airport, but the West Bengal police did not allow him to enter Sikkim without an inner line permit. Then a senior Sikkim police officer intervened. Records were later created in Gangtok to legitimise the visit. Nath spent several days in Rumtek. His visit was followed by those of Taiwan's Chen Lu Aan and Rosalia Findeisin.

In fact, the Chinese have been penetrating the monasteries in India since the 80s — in Sikkim, the Tawang area in Arunachal and in Ladakh. Chinese citizens disguised as monks or as refugees have been coming through Nepal. The Chinese also use Tibetans who come under disguise. Once permitted to enter, such persons mingle with the crowd and develop links with the monasteries. Penetrations occur particularly during the *kalchakra* festival. The Chinese gameplan is to learn more about the activities of Tibetans in India. Also, they seek to influence their minds, particularly the second generation Tibetans, about the actual state of affairs in Tibet.

Situ Rinpoche has claimed that on 19 April, 1994, he and Gyaltshab jointly met the additional foreign secretary of the Government of India and gave the latter in writing that they were proceeding to Tibet via Beijing, as early as possible, to pursue the visit of the XVIIth Karmapa to India. Within a few months, Situ Rinpoche was declared *persona non grata* by the Government of India. In contrast to such activities, Shamar Rinpoche was met by Chinese officials seven times between 25 July and September 1993 but he stood his ground. The charge d'affaires of the Chinese Embassy admitted that the Karmapa was number one while Shamar Rinpoche was number two in the hierarchy. Shamar Rinpoche was also told that the Chinese government accepted the fact. He was urged to accept the Karmapa, recognised by China. But he did not yield.

In the meantime, a notice under Section 80(1) of the CPC dated 2 April,1997 was served on the chief secretary and secretary for ecclesiastical affairs of the Sikkim government on 14 April, 1997. The cause of action for this statutory notice first arose on 2 August, 1993 and again on 8 August and 29 November, 1995. Earlier a similar notice on 16 October, 1996 had been served. Thereafter a court case was filed before the district court, Gangtok, by the Karmapa Charitable Trust, T.S. Gyaltshen, Shamar Rinpoche and Gyan Jyoti Kansakar through L. Tshering Bhutia, duly constituted attorney against the state of Sikkim, the secretary for ecclesiastical affairs, Gyaltshab Rinpoche and (pro-forma defendant) Jigdral Tashi Densapa.

Earlier, Topga Yulgyal had written a letter to the district magistrate, East District, Sikkim on 18 May, 1995 and requested for the return of the key to the main entrance of the monastery. It had been in the hands of the legal caretakers till 2 August, 1993. He acknowledged that a letter came from the office of the district magistrate, addressed to the *dhuche* (committee) of the Rumtek Dharma Chakra Centre, calling for a meeting. He admitted that he was unable to attend the proposed meeting. He demanded that since he had returned to Rumtek and assumed his normal functions, he be given back the key.

He also sent a letter to the secretary, land revenue department of Sikkim on 11 May, 1995 drawing attention to the illegal use and occupation of the head office of the trust by unauthorised persons after the unsavoury incidents of 2 August, 1993. He also alleged the illegal use of the stationery of the trust by unauthorised persons. He added that Tenzin Namgyal alias Dungche Tenzin and Gyurme Tsultrim alias Tenpa Rapgay were posing as general secretary and secretary, respectively, of the trust. Such action was patently illegal under the deed of the trust and the laws of the land, he said.

In his capacity as general secretary, he sought the cooperation of the state government in order to restore law and order, peace and tranquillity in the holy place of worship. The copy of the letter was also sent to the minister for ecclesiastical affairs, director-general of police, superintendent of police, and secretary of the ecclesiastical affairs. Shamar Rinpoche, too, had written a letter to the chief secretary on 3 March, 1993 in this regard.

The state government, the Party no. 2, objected on technical grounds. Defendant no. 3, Gyaltshab Rinpoche said that no office of the trust was maintained during and after the lifetime of the late Karmapa. At another place, he said the trust lay dormant for a period of 23 years from 1961 to 1984. The traditional administration was in the hands of the Tsurphu *labrang*, in accordance with the undisputed 800-year-old tradition. He added that the Dalai Lama had consulted the Tibetan state oracle, confirming the recognition of the reincarnation, before putting his seal of approval.

He asserted that the Karmapa was enthroned during a ceremony according to the Kagyu tradition at the Tsurphu monastery following the search conducted by Situ and Gyaltshab Rinpoches. Topga Yulgyal and Shamar Rinpoche, both being nephews of the late Karmapa, had conspired to gain unlawful possession of the properties as a matter of right. He said that the Gyaltshabs traditionally lived at the Tsurphu monastery in Tibet and were regarded as regents during the absence of a Karmapa. The word *gyaltshab* in Tibetan means 'regent' in English.

Denzong Nang-ten Sung-kyob Tsogpa, a Gangtok-based Organisation, too sent a letter on 1 August,1996 to Shamar Rinpoche, T.S. Gyaltshen, J.T. Densapa, Topga Yulgyal and Gyan Jyoti Kansakar, all trustees of the Karmapa Charitable Trust, stating, "We have come across a written complaint dated 12 July, 1994 addressed to the chief secretary to the government of Sikkim by the Pal Karmae Sangha Dhuche, constituted by the late Karmapa. We assume that you have also received a copy of the said letter."

The letter expressed concern about the safety of the most precious/invaluable articles of religious worship and significance.

> It appears that neither the state government nor the trustees of the Karmapa Charitable Trust have hitherto taken a positive step to check and verify the safety of the precious religious articles including the Vajra Mukut (Black Hat) of the Karmapa. It is believed that the Pal Karmae Sangha Dhuche has also not received any communication from the concerned authorities of the government and trustees of the trust on such a vital complaint concerning the articles of religious worship.

The letter also drew attention to rumours in Gangtok regarding the articles being missing from Rumtek. It was signed by Lachen Gomchen Rinpoche, Chairman, and Palden Lachugpa, Vice-Chairman.

The right wing Bharatiya Janata Party-led alliance government lifted the ban on the entry of Situ Rinpoche in 1998. Ram Jethmalani, a minister in the Government of India, pleaded his case. Dugo Bhutia, a former MLA of Sikkim, filed a special leave petition in the Supreme Court of India challenging the revocation of the ban order. Earlier, a writ petition in this regard in Delhi High Court had been dismissed by 26 August, 1998 with the observations that as the matter concerned the policy of the Government of India in relation to the neighbouring country, it was not appropriate for the high court to entertain the public interest litigation.

The Supreme Court too dismissed the petition and observed that in all questions like this where the Government of India decided not to allow a person to enter this country, it was not appropriate for any court to decide otherwise or to interfere in such a decision.

Legal luminaries Kapil Sibal and Prashant Kumar appeared on behalf of the petitioner while the respondents were represented by Soli Sorabjee, Attorney-General, K.N. Rawal, Additional Solicitor-General, Gopal Subramaniam and Rajeev Dhawan, senior advocates.

N. D. George, Director in the Home Ministry, in a counter affidavit on behalf of the Government of India, admitted that the situation in Sikkim had become fragile and capable of being exploited by anti-national elements as also by the external agencies with possibilities of attempts to divide communities and groups. The situation was extremely delicate and sensitive, involving imminent danger of breach of peace and public order as there were frequent clashes between the two rival groups.

In 1994, Situ Rinpoche went abroad without intimation to the Government of India. Even in the past he had frequently visited foreign countries including Nepal and China without intimation and without seeking permission of the government. Under the existing rules, Tibetan refugees in India are required to obtain a 'No Objection to Return to India Certificate' before proceeding to any foreign country. At the same time, complaints were received about Situ's involvement in a deal of land measuring 534 *bighas* in Gurgaon in Haryana without permission from the Reserve Bank of India and in violation of the provisions of FERA. The Central Bureau of Investigation (CBI) began investigation into the case. Situ Rinpoche was also reported to be in possession of a Bhutanese diplomatic passport.

After considering his frequent visits to Nepal and Tibet (China) without prior intimation or permission of the Government of India, and his role in the discovery of reincarnation of the Karmapa with suspected active assistance of Chinese authorities coupled with the possession of a Bhutanese diplomatic passport, making him liable to lose his Tibetan refugee status, the Government of India decided to put Situ Rinpoche in the 'suspect list'. The warning circular 28/94 dated 2 August, 1994 placing him in the 'prior-reference category' stated that he should not be allowed visa (entry, transit or tourist) without prior reference to the Government of India.

The Government of India admitted receiving a number of representations and communications for review of the restrictions. The matter was periodically reviewed in inter-departmental meetings at various levels. The matter was finally considered at the level of the home secretary where it was noted that the intelligence agencies had opposed revocation of the warning circular, as it would result in serious law and order situation in Sikkim in case Situ Rinpoche went there.

However, he is still debarred from entering Jammu & Kashmir, north-eastern states and Sikkim. A lookout circular has been issued in place of warning circular. The order gave the reasons as (1) CBI inquiry regarding purchase of land, (2) anti-India activities.

N. D. George said the reasons were given inadvertently as the orders were issued by a different division of the home ministry. The correct reason was "apprehension of law and order problem". The two orders were released on 5 August and 31 August, 1998, respectively. They prohibited Situ Rinpoche from leaving India without prior clearance from the CBI. It was also mentioned in the last circular that he should not be allowed to enter Darjeeling district of West Bengal besides the other states mentioned.

Situ Rinpoche returned to India on 25 August, 1998. He was received at the Indira Gandhi airport in New Delhi by a crowd of his supporters. A reception was held in his honour by the Himalayan Buddhists Cultural Association at the India Habitat Centre next day. The Dalai Lama welcomed him back on 3 September. After eight days, the Dalai Lama gave him a certificate, putting aside all doubts about his anti-Indian activities.

Situ Rinpoche denied his involvement in the land deal. He said that no land had been purchased either by him or any one on his behalf; that no document had been executed either by him or any one on his behalf and, therefore, the question of violation of any law did not arise. However, he admitted that there was a proposal. There is still a proposal to purchase land for constructing a retreat for monks, he said. This retreat would be part of the Palpung Foundation just as the Sherab Ling Institute of Buddhist Studies forms the part of the same foundation. The foundation is of Indian origin and has nothing to do with the Chinese government at all, he claimed. However, he admitted that he had received a questionnaire from Interpol in this regard.

Soon after his return to India, Situ Rinpoche met Pawan Kumar Chamling, Chief Minister of Sikkim, in New Delhi. He reportedly told the chief minister that he came to India when he was barely six-year-old and since then he had always regarded India as his own country. He added that branding him as anti-India or pro-Chinese was only a design by certain vested interests to tarnish his image among his followers. The Dalai Lama too vouched in September 1998 that Situ Rinpoche was not an instrument of Chinese political intrigue.

Situ Rinpoche requested the chief minister of Sikkim to use his good offices in bringing the XVIIth Karmapa (reincarnate) to India and thus resolve the vexed issue. He apprised the chief minister that the Dalai Lama had also urged the then Prime Minister P.V. Narasimha Rao for the same. The chief minister told him that the role of the state government was confined to maintaining law and order, which it was doing in a fair and impartial manner. As for bringing the XVIIth Karmapa to India, the chief minister advised that nobody should seek to extract capital out of religion and all political parties in Sikkim should unitedly request the union government to bring the XVIIth Karmapa to India.

Chamling later requested the prime minister to acknowledge Situ's candidate as the XVIIth Karmapa of the Kagyu order. In a letter to the prime minister, Chamling pointed out that the reincarnate of the XVIth Karmapa was recognised by the Dalai Lama way back in 1992. He said that immediate steps in this regard would clear doubts in the minds of devotees and followers of the sect within and outside the country, besides putting an end once and for all to the decade-old controversy laden with international ramifications. He also requested the government of India to assist in bringing the XVIIth Karmapa to the Rumtek monastery in Sikkim from Tibet. However, he reiterated that notwithstanding the succession of the Gyalwa Karmapa, the state government had maintained a clear and transparent policy confined to maintaining law and order at the Rumtek monastery in a fair and impartial manner.

The chief minister has also demanded lifting of the ban on the entry of Situ Rinpoche into Sikkim. He said, "by no stretch of imagination can Situ Rinpoche be branded as an 'agent' of the Chinese government." In his three-page letter, the chief minister explained the background of the controversy over the reincarnation of the XVIth Karmapa.

K. Sreedhar Rao, the then Chief Secretary of Sikkim, sent a detailed assessment report on the Rumtek affairs to the union cabinet secretary in May 1997.

The 14-page report, marked secret on every page, forms the annexure of a one-para covering letter, sent by the then chief secretary from his camp office in Delhi to the then cabinet secretary. The letter stated:

> I had sent a brief report to you on the Rumtek situation on 18 December 1996. Taking into account certain recent developments I have carried out a more detailed assessment outlining possible options before us. I am sending herewith

> this assessment for your kind perusal. I am endorsing copies of this (report) both to the DIB (Director of the Intelligence Bureau) and the Chairman JIC (Joint Intelligence Committee) with whom I have discussed this matter.

The report continued:

> Given the fact that Sikkim occupies a strategic position, it would be most undesirable to have a situation where a Tibetan reincarnation, who is basically a Chinese national recognised by the Chinese, occupies a position in a monastery in Sikkim. The reincarnation of the Karmapa, if at all brought into Sikkim, will not come alone and may be accompanied by a very substantial entourage. Such an event can lead to consequences quite unpredictable, and may affect the security interests of the country very substantially. Clearly, we cannot allow a situation where a Tibetan reincarnate is brought into Sikkim, however vociferous such a demand may become.

Regarding the role of the Dalai Lama in the controversy, the chief secretary said:

> In a hurried manner and that also without evidence and proper verification, the Dalai Lama recognised the candidate of Situ Rinpoche. It is possible that a small coterie around the Dalai Lama had been influenced by the Chinese. The belief is reinforced by the fact that this small group has influenced His Holiness (Dalai Lama) to continue to support the Situ group even though the Dalai Lama himself has been briefed about the controversy and the lack of unanimity among the regents with respect to reincarnation.
>
> The second explanation could be that the Dalai Lama was at that point of time carrying on delicate negotiations with the Chinese with respect to Tibet and he was influenced to think that such a recognition may go in his favour during his further discussions with the Chinese.
>
> A third explanation put forth by the religiously inclined is

that the Dalai Lama heads the Gelug order which is not favourably inclined towards the Kagyu order, particularly because of the growing influence of the latter. (After the establishment of the Dharma Chakra Centre in Rumtek in the early 1960s, the Kagyu order has opened no less than 600 centres all over the world.)

The fourth explanation is that the recognition given by the Dalai Lama is not religious recognition but basically a temporal act placing the Karmapa in a hierarchy next to the Dalai Lama and Panchen Lama. It is an act which need not be given any religious significance.

While this matter needs to be studied in more detail, what is important to note is that following the recognition of the Karmapa in Tibet and its approval by the Dalai Lama, China put its seal of approval on the reincarnation. This is, perhaps, the first time that the People's Republic of China has given such an approval and is possibly calculated to demonstrate to the world the decisive say that China has in the affairs of Tibet, both spiritual and temporal.

Since then Situ Rinpoche has been influencing local opinion in Sikkim to continuously pressurise the authorities for bringing the Karmapa reincarnate to Rumtek and formally install him in the monastery.

Situ Rinpoche had wittingly or unwittingly played into the hands of the Chinese. Reports indicate that Situ Rinpoche, a Tibetan national, had been visiting Tibet on and off and in 1984-85 he travelled extensively and drafted a programme for so-called development in the country (Tibet). He records that 'at the end of 1984 and beginning of 1985 I visited for four months my country (meaning China) after 26 years abroad and travelled the areas of Sitron Tsongol, Gangsheo Yunnan and Shingkiang. The development pogramme includes education, health care, culture, handicrafts, increase in income and living standards etc.' What is noteworthy is that throughout his report he talks about friendly connections between the Chinese and the people of other countries, study of the Chinese language and study of Chinese medicine. He talks about Chinese in the friendliest terms, referring to the Chinese as Chinese brothers. He talks about Chinese brothers living abroad as well. He talks about the autonomous region of Tibet and indicates that his plan has the honest intention to benefit the people of China, and, in particular, the autonomous regions of Tibet, Sitron, Yunnan, Gangshuo, etc. He profusely thanks the two leaders of China, namely, Hu Yao Ban and Deng Niao Peng, as well as other leaders for their excellent political stance. His report is addressed to the director of the Chinese Communist government. All this indicates that Situ Rinpoche has built up a good relationship with the Chinese possibly from 1984.

It would be appropriate to consider the Chinese interest in the entire matter at this stage. From the time of Chinese occupation, and indeed, after the departure of the Dalai Lama from Tibet, the Chinese have been strengthening their control over Tibet in a variety of ways. Apart from the well established efforts to reduce the religious influence of the Dalai Lama and changing the demographic composition of Tibet by large scale influx of Han Chinese into Tibet, it would appear that the Chinese having got their own Panchen Lama, have, by formally recognising the XVIIth Gyalwa Karmapa, extended their control over the religious reincarnations of the Tibetans. It is also very much possible that the Chinese are preparing to get themselves into a position of strength in the post-Dalai Lama Tibet. It is not inconceivable that having established their right to recognise the reincarnates, the Chinese would not hesitate to identify the successor of the present Dalai Lama when the time comes. This would complete their hold on the religious consciousness of the Tibetans both within and outside Tibet. The Chinese may not attach too great an importance to the declaration by the Dalai Lama that there will be no more reincarnation of His Holiness. It is important from our point of view to take note of this. It is also important to note that along the entire Himalayan belt, right from Ladakh to Arunachal Pradesh, the influence of Tibetan Lamaistic Buddhism is extensive, with a string of monasteries. It is

> reported that the Chinese have been making efforts to penetrate into these monasteries and, as of now, no less than eleven monasteries are headed by lamas who can be considered proteges of China. It would be most undesirable to allow the Chinese to extend their influence in this manner and it is in this context that the present situation in Rumtek needs to be carefully viewed.

He drew attention to the fact that the Chinese were out to expand their influence on the religious consciousness of not only Tibetans but also of the population in the entire Himalayan region. He said that the monastery itself had to be cleansed of all unruly elements and of offensive material which could be used to prevent anyone entering the monastery or otherwise creating an ugly law and order situation,

He added:

> Taking into account the fact that the Chinese government is actively interested in the Rumtek affairs and the emerging situation there, it would be necessary to anticipate events and consider a possible course of action. The Sikkim government right now would be hesitant to act because of the belief that a large proportion of the Bhutia/Lepcha population is inclined to accept the Tibetan reincarnation, primarily because of the blessing given by the Dalai Lama and would not like to do anything which can be construed as offending the sentiments of Bhutias/Lepchas. He concluded with the remarks that while keeping India's security interests in mind we should recognise the fact that the legitimate trustees have been disallowed from functioning from the monastery by an act of the state government and that within the next few years both the regents and the trustees would lose their status as religious and temporal authorities of Rumtek once the Karmapa reincarnate attains the age of 21. Interestingly enough, the Sikkim government has denied the existence of the copy of the said letter in its files and records. When asked by the state government, Rao has kept mum.

In November 1997, Ugyen Trinley, the candidate of Situ Rinpoche as the Karmapa, recognised a four-year-old boy from Chushul near Lhasa as the reincarnation of Jamgon Kongtrul Rinpoche. Situ Rinpoche and his secretary Ngoche Kargyay smuggled the purported reincarnation to Kalimpong in Darjeeling district of India and installed him at the retreat centre of the monastery of Jamgon Kongtrul Rinpoche at Lava near Kalimpong. On the other hand, Trinlay Thaye Dorje, the candidate of Shamar Rinpoche as the Karmapa, recognised the son of Beru Khyentse Rinpoche in 1996 as the reincarnation of Jamgon Kongtrul Rinpoche. This boy is studying in the monastery of his father. Situ Rinpoche too searched the reincarnation of Kalu Rinpoche. The reincarnation is the son of Gyaltshen, who was the secretary of the previous Kalu Rinpoche. The Dalai Lama too recognised this reincarnation. In April 1993, when the Dalai Lama consecrated Kalu Rinpoche's stupa at Salugara on the outskirts of Siliguri, he performed the hair-cutting ceremony for Kalu Rinpoche's reincarnation and also attended another ceremony in the monastery of Kalu Rinpoche at Sonada. The daughter of Beru Kyentse Rinpoche is the reincarnation of Gelongma Pag-Mo, a nun (mother of Indian movie star Kabir Bedi). The succession war again hotted up in January 2000.

9

Postscript

Dharamsala (India), 31 March, 2000: Situ Rinpoche again staged a coup of sorts. Lama Ugyen Trinley Dorje, a 14-year-old boy, who was recognised by Situ Rinpoche as the XVIIth Karmapa, arrived at McLeodganj in Himachal Pradesh on 5 January, 2000 around 10.30 a.m. Within two hours, he was granted an audience with the Dalai Lama, who was in the winter retreat. The lama boy was accompanied by his mentor Situ Rinpoche, whose monastery, Sherab Ling in Baijnath district of Himachal Pradesh, was about 60 km from McLeodganj. The presence of Situ Rinpoche at McLeodganj smacked of his successful manoeuvring. A few days later Situ Rinpoche realised his mistake and denied that he accompanied the lama boy. He claimed that he reached McLeodganj around 2.30 p.m. after getting the news of the arrival of the lama boy.

A call was made from McLeodganj to the office of the *Daily Telegraph*, London, which broke the story of how the lama had "feared for his life" in Tibet. The Dalai Lama's government-in-exile seemed ready to cooperate and information was voluntarily provided. The lama, referred to as the Karmapa, could be photographed fairly easily, though he was not available for interviews. The task of publicising achieved the desired result. The British media, giving a lead to Indian papers, grabbed the news. But for the intervention by Shamar Rinpoche on

8 January, claiming that the arrival of the lama boy was a Chinese ploy, meant to grab the Vajra Mukut and other valuable relics from the Rumtek monastery, the newspapers and magazines continued to refer to the lama boy as the Karmapa. Shamar Rinpoche told newspersons at New Delhi on 8 January that "Ugyen Trinley is an innocent boy who should not be used for political purposes. I do not believe he escaped or came without permission from China. The flight was designed to divert attention from Thaye Dorje, who was recognised according to our sacred traditions."

Significantly, *Kuensel*, Bhutan's only newspaper, reported guardedly. It preferred to bury the story in the inside pages and all it seemed to deserve was an eight-para story with a double-column heading. The story, quoting officials, said:

> In what is described as the most significant defection from Chinese-ruled Tibet in decades, a 15-year-old lama recognised by a section of Tibetan Buddhists as the 17th Karmapa, arrived in India.
>
> Robbie Barnett, a Tibet scholar at Columbia University in New York, said the lama left the 800-year-old Tsurphu monastery on 28 December with a handful of attendants and walked over to India, arriving on Wednesday (5 January) in Dharamsala.
>
> International reports point out that Lama Ugyen Thinley has not officially sought political asylum in India. Meanwhile other Buddhists recognise another lama residing in India, Lama Thaye Dorje, as the real Karmapa.
>
> The Karmapas virtually ruled Tibet until they were supplanted by the Dalai Lama and the Gelugpa order 350 years ago.

The Tibetan government-in-exile made arrangements for the stay of the lama boy at Chonor lodge of the Norbulingka Institute. A week later, he was moved to the Gyuto monastery of the Gelug bordering Siddhabari, about 15 km from McLeodganj. From 9 January, the lama boy went incommunicado and was perennially 'tired and resting'. He again met the Dalai Lama on 8 and 14 January, though the latter was supposed to observe silence during the period of retreat.

His arrival was greeted almost like the coming of a messiah and potential successor to the aging Dalai Lama, who would be 65 this coming July.

There were exotic stories doing the rounds in McLeodganj of how the lama escaped from the Chinese captivity. The crux of the stories was the same. The lama boy opened his bedroom window on the sixth floor at 11 p.m. on a cold wintry 28 December, 1999 at the Tsurphu monastery in Tibet. The escape plan was drawn up meticulously. The lama consulted the oracles before escaping. He said he was going into retreat. His personal staff went about their duties as usual. Food was cooked, served and other everyday routines were undertaken normally. A look-alike even impersonated for the lama who had actually left the monastery. The lama had left a letter declaring that he was going to India to retrieve some religious artefacts. He said the Chinese authorities had rejected an earlier request for his travel to India. He was thus left with no recourse but to go without permission.

When a Chinese official went to meet him on New Year's Day, the lama had disappeared. Five days later he surfaced at Dharamsala. It is surprising that the Chinese authorities did not raise an alarm and tried to increase surveillance on the border. It is difficult to believe that the lama's entourage, during its 11-day trek of about 900 km across frozen terrain from Tibet, managed to dodge the heavy Chinese security presence in Tibet.

He was accompanied by Ngodup Palzon, his sister, 10 years older, and five male attendants. The lama and his followers changed into civilian clothes. He wore a denim jacket and trousers and his sister a loose robe. The party ate only *tsampa*. From the Tsurphu monastery, the group set out in two jeeps. Before every checkpost, the lama and his entourage would get off and head for the mountains. After the jeeps crossed the checkpoints, the lama and his companions would join the vehicles. This they did nearly 20 times till they reached west Nepal through Nyichung in Mustang region. He thought it better to flee in winter for two reasons. First, the Chinese guards are not as alert and the checks not that stringent. Second, most of the mountain lakes are frozen and can be crossed on foot. Escape from the guards in Tibet is possible only in the cold months, by daredevils who have the will and the stamina to face the hazards before the weather 'opens up'.

Another equally fanciful account says that the lama and his party first reached Shigatse in transport vans disguised as helpers and then went to Khumbu La, on to Katari in Nepal. After reaching Kathmandu, the party did not even get in touch with the office of the Dalai Lama's representative in Nepal. Normally escapees from Tibet drop in at this office from where arrangements are made for their coming to India. His mentors had arranged Nepalese and Indian currency and guides to ensure that the party did not lose its way in blizzards in the high mountain terrain, and shelter points were all worked out in advance.

Another account puts it altogether differently. The lama left Tsurphu in a Toyota Land-cruiser and another car, travelling for 36 hours. When the mountain terrain became unmotorable, he began a trek. His team walked for 12 hours, entering Nepal. The border was fairly easy to cross. It was only a few hours' journey by train from Gorakhpur to Lucknow from where the seven-member group reached Dharamsala via Delhi in two taxis. The Dalai Lama's office was informed by telephone on arrival.

The travel account treads the fine line between the happenstance and coincidence. It rather smells of a deliberate action. As if to divorce the lama from Chinese links, there are stories doing the rounds in McLeodganj of how he called Tsurphu on reaching Nepal, how the phone was answered by a Chinese voice, how the 'Karmapa' heard the sounds and shrieks of searching and interrogation in the background. Intriguingly, the lama boy surfaced at Dharamsala and met the Dalai Lama instead of going to the traditional seat of the Karmapa at the Rumtek monastery in Sikkim, which could be easier for him and his entourage to travel than going to Dharamsala.

The response from China was surly. Initially, the Chinese issued a statement that the young 'Karmapa' had come to India to collect some of his belongings — the black hat and an ancient bell among them. In fact, it is the China factor that had the ministry of external affairs of India in a bit of a tizzy. If it really was a defection, it was a public relations disaster for Beijing whose Tibet policy in recent years had moved from suppression of religious authority to its manipulation. Initially, Beijing sought to wipe out the monks' privileges, denounce their faith and swamp Tibet with ethnic Chinese migrants. It came to realise that the average Tibetan cherished the Buddhist faith and its institutions with an uncommon fervour. The ministry of external affairs has realised over the years that Tibet-China relations were an enormous game of chess, one in which India at times seemed no more than that hapless chessboard. Therefore, the ministry of external affairs has been circumspect in reaction, waiting for other players to show their hand.

Four days after the arrival of the lama boy at McLeodganj, Zho Bangzao, Chinese foreign ministry spokesman, hinted that granting political asylum to the 'Karmapa' would violate the 'panchsheel' (five principles of peaceful co-existence) on which Sino-Indian relations were based. A few days later, Zhou Gang, Chinese Ambassador to India, advised India not to use the presence of the 'XVIIth Karmapa' in India for "anti-political and anti-social activities against China".

The Government of India denied having received any request from the lama boy or the Dalai Lama for granting asylum to the visitor. However, it admitted having received a 'personal' memorandum from Mrs. Dolma Gyari, a member of the Tibetan parliament-in-exile, seeking grant of political asylum to the lama boy.

Tshering Lama and Lama Narain Singh wrote a joint letter to the President of India, expressing their concern over the activities of Situ Rinpoche and his group in connivance with the Chinese authorities to usurp the heritage of the Karmapa.

At the same time, Ms. Julia Teft, US Coordinator for Tibet, arrived in India. She is also the Assistant Secretary of State for Population, Refugees and Migration. The US was at pains to explain that her visit to Dharamsala had nothing to do with the arrival of the 'Karmapa'. The US officials emphasised that her trip to India had been in the pipeline for five months and she was to visit Tibetan refugee camps as she visited those of Afghan refugees.

They pointed out that her visit had been mandated on the understanding that it would take place when the Dalai Lama was on his annual retreat. Was it merely an embarrassing coincidence that she came just when the 'Karmapa' arrived in India.

India sought to deflect Chinese pressure over the 'Karmapa' presence in India, asking Beijing to provide 'specific details' about the journey of the 14-year-old 'Living Buddha' from Tibet. Beijing had sought information on Lama Ugyen Trinley Dorje. The spokesman of the Indian ministry of foreign affairs said, "The Chinese side has been asked to share with us specific details about the 'Karmapa's' departure from Tibet, the route taken and other relevant matters."

In a seemingly desperate bid to hide its role in the departure of the lama boy, Chinese police detained at least two monks of the Tsurphu monastery on 15 January. Reports say that all monks in the monastery have been confined in the premises by armed police — a sign that some are being questioned — while at least two have been taken away to the headquarters of the autonomous council of Tibet at Lhasa. Perhaps the move was meant to create confusion about China's stance.

Intrigue, deception and an air of mystery have made a China-Tibet puzzle difficult to decode. Preliminary Indian official investigations do not show that the boy lama and his entourage slipped through the heavy Chinese security cover. On the contrary, the investigations suggest that they had a fairly smooth passage out of their Chinese-controlled homeland, indicating that Beijing may at least have acquiesced in the departure.

Ugyen Trinley Dorji cannot indefinitely sustain his 'Karmapa claim without the *vajra mukut*. It is vital for him and those who propped him up to secure that spiritually indispensable item. Moreover, his presence in India could aid the Chinese designs to divide the Tibetan exile community by fostering open discord between the rival contending sides and bringing a bad name to the holy institution of the Karmapa.

Since the ban on the entry of Situ Rinpoche in India was lifted in mid-1998 by the right-wing Bharatiya Janata Party-led government, the activities of the pro-China group in the succession war again hotted up. In a vilification campaign against Shamar Rinpoche, a news item appeared in an Indian newspaper alleging his links with China. Shamar Rinpoche vehemently denied it.

In the last week of November 1999, Beru Kyentse Rinpoche organised an ordination ceremony at Bodh Gaya for his son who was recognised by Thaye Dorji (recognised by Shamar Rinpoche as the reincarnation of the Karmapa) as the reincarnation of Jamgon Kongtrul Rinpoche, one of the senior Kagyu order *tulkus*. Tashi Wangdi, the Minister for Religious and Cultural Affairs in the Tibetan government-in-exile, wrote to the Indian Home Minister apprehending trouble over the investiture of the 'fake' lama. At the same time, Beru Kyentse received a letter from Dharamsala in which it was written that they (the Dalai Lama government) have told Situ Rinpoche and his party not to create trouble during the ceremony at Bodh Gaya. The scheduled ceremony could not take place since Beru Kyentse Rinpoche was indisposed.

The Sikkim government made a turn-around. Despite change of guard at the helm of affairs, it remained steadfastly with Situ Rinpoche. It helped the Situ group to grab the Rumtek monastery. From time to time, the successive chief ministers pleaded the case of Situ Rinpoche to allow entry to Ugyen Trinley Dorje in India. Even in Novemner 1999, Pawan Kumar Chamling, Chief Minister of Sikkim, wrote a letter to the Prime Minister of India iterating his request in favour of Ugyen Trinley Dorji. However, the Sikkim government and politicians alike preferred to maintain a studied silence when Ugyen Trinley Dorji landed in India. But with a foot in his mouth, Sikkim Chief Secretary Sonam Wagdi volunteered information on phone to an Indian newspaper that Sikkim locals were 'rejoicing' and were hopeful that the historic Rumtek monastery which had not had a head for almost 17 years would finally have one. He added that once the Dalai Lama accepted Ugyen Trinley Dorji as the Kagyu leader, the people of Sikkim had come to repose their faith in the 14-year-old lama.

A few days later he invited an Indian wire agency man at Gangtok to give information that the visiting lama was already an Indian since he was the reincarnation of the late XVIth Karmapa. He was blissfully unaware that the status of the late Karmapa was that of a Tibetan refugee. It is an utterly preposterous idea. Following the logic that the XVIth Karmapa — or any Karmapa — is of Indian origin simply because Buddhism has its roots in India, one would be tempted to accept that all Buddhist masters from around the world are of Indian origin. This argument will also include all Buddhists across the world as having an Indian origin. Contrary to the popular notion that was highlighted with motives other than religious, a majority of the Buddhist population in Sikkim has faith in the Nyingma order, the oldest among the four orders of Tibetan Buddhism.

In the meantime, Shamar Rinpoche had iterated his old proposal. Way back in 1995, he proposed to Drugchu Lachaungpa, a former Sikkim minister and member of the joint action committee, and Palden Lachaungpa, secretary of the Sikkim's ecclesiastical department:

> Tai Situ is a Buddhist teacher, and so am I. We should both behave accordingly. Therefore, we should both respect each other's nominee, which would prevent any schism in the lineage. Since the Chinese government had authorised Ugyen Trinley to take over the Tsurphu monastery in Tibet, which was the Karmapa's traditional seat before the exile of the XVIth Karmapa, it was only logical to allow my nominee, the Indian Karmapa, to take the Rumtek monastery in India.

However, Situ Rinpoche says that there is only one Karmapa, that is his nominee, whose recognition has been validated by the Dalai Lama.

Dharamsala will not give its mind to journalists. However, a letter from the Dalai Lama to Rabi Ray, former Speaker of the Lok Sabha (Lower House of Indian Parliament) clearly stated that the Dalai Lama wanted the visitor from Tibet to stay in India. The Dalai Lama forewarned India that she would make a terrible mistake if she did not let the 'Karmapa' stay. Earlier, Rabi Ray had pleaded the case of the lama boy for political asylum. After a two-month-long studied silence, the Dalai Lama told BBC: "The Indian Government has informally and unofficially indicated to me that the Karmapa Lama, who recently fled from Tibet to India, would most probably be allowed to remain in India." A number of right-wing politicians and academicians have also joined the chorus to support Situ Rinpoche.

10

Epilogue

The Karmapa is the first Tibetan Buddhist master who has continually reincarnated in an unbroken line since the year 1110 AD.

The first Karmapa, Dusum Khyenpa, left three short oral instructions indicating the next incarnation as Karma Pakshi with three disciples. In addition, Karma Pakshi himself declared that he was the incarnation of Dusum Khyenpa. Also, his teacher Pomdragpa had a vision of Dusum Khyenpa declaring that he was, in fact, reborn as Karma Pakshi. Karma Pakshi said he would return to an area in northern Tibet called Lato. He did not leave any written instructions indicating his reincarnation. It was the IIIrd Karmapa Ranjung Dorje himself who stated that he was the incarnation of Karma Pakshi.

Thus, it is evident that they do not always leave written instructions indicating the details of their next birth. Even when a written message was left behind, it was the reincarnations themselves who always proved their own authenticity. The Karmapas also showed extraordinary abilities and convinced people by their unusual behaviour and statements.

Up to the VIIIth Karmapa, Mikyo Dorje, there seemed to be no difficulties in identifying the reincarnations. At the time of Mikyo Dorje, a scholar called Amdo lama indicated that his son was the incarnation of the VIIth Karmapa Chodrag

Gyamtso. He claimed there had been unusual signs at the birth. Amdo lama made offerings to Tashi Namgyal, the then Gyaltshab Tulku and the monks and administrators of Tsurphu supported his claim. At the same time, in eastern Tibet near Karmagon, another boy proclaimed himself to be the Karmapa. This five-year-old child announced that he was the incarnation of the VIIth Karmapa. He added that the other candidate at Tsurphu was the incarnation of a lama from the Surmong monastery. Both the claimants were brought together and an investigation was made. They were confronted with possessions of the previous Karmapa, to check which one would recognise them. It then became evident that the boy from Karmagon was the genuine incarnation.

The recognition and finding of the XVIth Karmapa, Rangjung Rigpe Dorje, also brought some difficulties. The XVth Karmapa had given a letter predicting his incarnation to his close disciple, Jamgal Tsultrim, who at first did not disclose this information. After the death of the XVth Karmapa, a very powerful Gelug minister got his son recognised as the reincarnation of the Karmapa. This was even confirmed by the XIIIth Dalai Lama. Perforce, the people from Tsurphu had to accept the child. Later, however, the boy fell from the monastery's roof and died. Some years later, the genuine letter was presented which led to the recognition of the true XVIth Karmapa. Lea Terhune, Secretary of Situ Rinpoche, writes in *Relative World, Ultimate Mind*, edited by her:

> The XIth Situpa (predecessor of the present one) recognised the XVIth Karmapa's incarnation without benefit of seeing the XVth Karmapa's predictive letter, which had been spirited away after the latter's death by an absconding monk who was afraid of the Situpa. When the letter was finally recovered, it confirmed that the *tulku* recognised by the Situpa was correct, supporting every detail.

The Dalai Lama nullified his confirmation in favour of the candidate of Situpa at that time because there was no senior

Kagyu lama willing to seek support from, or extending support to, the Dalai Lama.

In the earlier disputes concerning the Karmapa's reincarnations, the true one has always proved himself beyond any doubt. According to Tibetan belief and lore, there exist extraordinary qualities which only an unsurpassable *bodhisattva* like the Karmapa can manifest.

Appendix A

Precious Treasures of the Kagyu Order

Preserved at the Rumtek monastery:

(1) Inside a golden relic-box, a self-made marble statue of Mikyo Dorje, the eighth Karmapa. The face is painted and the rest of the image covered with gold and precious wrappings. It is said that "anyone beholding this image quickly becomes liberated". After completing the statue, the Karmapa was left with a small piece of marble. Unwilling to discard it, he squeezed it in his palm, leaving a clear impression of his palm. The piece is kept preserved above the main statue, along with a small personal image of Vajravarahi, the protector-goddess of the Karmapas.

(2) Inside another golden relic-box is a statue of Phagmo Khachodma, once the personal icon of the Siddha Naropa who presented it to his disciple Marpa. The image is of copper and heavily ornamented. This image is one of the most precious treasures of the Karmapa reincarnates.

(3) A statue of Pema Jungnes Chinlab Pal Barma, a form of Guru Padmasambhava, which was miraculously discovered from a mine by the XVth Karmapa.

(4) A statue of Nor Lha Jambhala, made of *dzi chim* metal. It was presented to the IIIrd Karmapa by the protector of the Tsari lake in southern Tibet.

(5) A statue of Chakrasamvara and Vajravarahi made of mixed white, red and yellow *dzi chim* metals discovered from the relic-box of the ruler of Derge in Kham.

(6) A statue of Mahakala, named Gonpo Gya Nakma, consecrated by the IInd Karmapa.

(7) A five-pronged sceptre (*vajra*), made of *dzi chim* metal, which belonged to Dorje Lingpa, a *terton* (great discoverer of treasures) who discovered it.

(8) A statue of Tong Drol Chenmo, a form of Guru Padmasambhava, in a relic-box of silver. It was discovered by Chogyur Lingpa, a *terton*, from the Champa Trak rock in Tsari Tso Kar.

(9) A statue of Guru Dewa Chenpo Chema Atrong, a form of Guru Padmasambhava. A very important relic from the Tsurphu monastery of the Karmapas and preserved within a golden relic-box, it is decorated with the dancing figures of *dakinis*.

(10) A statue of Tamang Khanon Dule Namgyal, a form of Guru Padmasambhava, made by Tami Gonson of *ekadhatu* metal and discovered by Terchen Ratna Lingpa, a *terton*, is preserved within a golden relic-box with auspicious symbols engraved on it.

(11) A statue of Tsogyal Sangdrup, a form of Guru Padmasambhava, discovered by the Terchen Ratna Lingpa and presented to the XVth Karmapa, it is preserved within a silver relic-box inscribed with auspicious symbols.

(12) A statue of Dolma Ngodrup Pel Barma, of the Goddess Tara, made from *li kadur*, a kind of bell metal. The image is heavily gilded, with many precious red coral stones decorating the upper part. It is preserved within a beautiful relic-box. This statue is said to help successive Karmapas to make their important predictions.

(13) A statue of Yeshe Norbu, a form of Padmasambhava, discovered by Taksham Nuden Dorje, a *terton*. Inserted into the head of the image is a precious jewel.

(14) A statue of Lord Buddha made in eastern India of *li kadur* metal, it was presented to the XVIth Karmapa by Situ Tulku, after his ordination ceremony.

(15) A statue of Vajravarahi made of red *dzi chim* metal. She is the guardian deity of the line of Karmapas.

(16) A statue of Lord Buddha, in earth-witness *mudra*, made in eastern India of *li kadur* metal. It was once the property of Oser Gocha, the King of Nepal, whose daughter was the first Buddhist queen of Tibet. This precious image was presented to the Xth Shamar tulku by King Mantrasimha of Nepal. It is considered to be as important as the Lord Buddha statue called Jowo Yeshe Norbu, which is in the great Jokhang temple of Lhasa.

(17) A Yab-Yum statue of Guru Padmasambhava, discovered by Terchen Urgyen Chogyur Dechen Lingpa whilst he was preparing precious medicines in the cave known as Khandro Bum Dzong Gi Dechen Phug in lower Kham. This small statue was recovered from within a lump of the medicinal mixtures. It is preserved within a golden relic-box.

(18) Relics of Lord Buddha discovered by Taksham Nuden Dorje, a *terton*. They are preserved within a golden relic-box.

(19) A statue of Jetsun Dolma, the goddess Tara, known as Zi Ji Barwa, the guardian deity of the Buddhist King Indrabhuti of India. It is completely inlaid with precious jewels.

(20) White funerary relics (*rinshel*) inside a statue of the Ist Karmapa. It is made of *li kadur* metal from eastern India and was consecrated by the Karmapa himself. This extremely precious image has thrice preached the 'six yogas' of *siddha naropa*. It is heavily gilded and painted.

(21) A statue of the Ist Karmapa, made of mixed red, yellow and white *dzi chim* metal. It preserves the funerary relics of the Ist Karmapa and is believed to be a good likeness of him. Though paint has many times been applied to the top of the head, it always peels off or disappears

completely. This phenomenon has occurred every time, and tests have proved its authenticity.

(22) A statue of Vajradhara, the Adi-Buddha and root-guru of the Kargu order. It was made by Chos Ying Dorje, the Xth Karmapa, from a rhinocerous horn. It is partly gilded and painted.

(23) Four statues of Siddha Tilopa, Siddha Naropa, teacher Marpa and Jetsun Milarepa carved by the Xth Karmapa from rhinocerous horns. They are partly gilded and painted.

(24) A statue of Vajrapani, called Chag Dor, holding a kite-bird, presented to the Xth Karmapa by Sherab Jungnes, a great doctor. It was his protector deity.

(25) A Yah-Yum statue of Purpakila, named Dorje Shonu Dule Namgyal, presented to the XVth Karmapa by Sherab Jungnes, a great doctor. It was his protector deity.

(26) A round golden relic-box (*gau*), usually carried by the Gyalwa Karmapa, containing relics found in the head of Dharmadhoti, son of Marpa. When Dharmadhoti was cremated, a small statue of Vajravarahi was found within a cluster of relics.

(27) A golden relic-box containing the original green silk used to wrap up the *namgyal purpa* (ritual knife) worn by Teshe Tsogyal, the disciple of Guru Padmasambhava. It was found beneath the Thang La rock, one of the eight great pilgrimage centres of Tibet.

(28) A relic of the IInd Karmapa, his cheekbone in the form of the Tibetan letter 'Dhi', along with several other relics, all preserved within a fine golden relic-box.

(29) A stone statue of Avalokiteshwara discovered from a large round stone by Dzigar Dorje Trakpa.

(30) A rib-bone of the VIIIth Karmapa preserved in the form of the Tibetan letter 'Ah' in a fine relic-box.

(31) A bone of Lhacham Pema Sel, the consort of Guru Padmasambhava, in a golden relic-box showing the self-formed (*rangjung*) statue of Jetsun Dolma, the goddess Tara.

(32) A small golden box in a larger golden box containing a statue that, King Srongtsan Gampo, the Siddha King of Tibet, used to wear in his hair. It is called De Chung Wang Gi Gyalpo, meaning 'Fulfiller of Desires'. It is a golden form of Jambhala, the wealth deity, and was retrieved from the precious lake of Tsari Tso Kar by Ranjung Dorje, the IIIrd Karmapa.

(33) A *namchak purpa* (ritual knife) believed to have fallen from the sky and discovered by Terchen Chogyur Lingpa. It is kept within a relic-box.

(34) A *namchak purpa* believed to have fallen from the sky, of mixed *dzi chim* metal of a red and white colour, discovered by Terchen Chogyur Lingpa.

(35) A white statue showing the ten miracles of Lord Buddha. It was made by Siddha Nagarjuna, who discovered the material *lu zim* from the great Naga lake in India. It was presented to Rolpe Dorje, the IVth Karmapa, while en-route to China.

(36) A grey-green statue showing the ten miracles of Lord Buddha. It was made by Siddha Nagarjuna out of *lu zim*, a metal-like material recovered from the Nagalake. It was presented to Rolpe Dorje, the IVth Karmapa, while en route to China.

(37) A statue of Lord Buddha made of *li* metal from eastern India. This was the personal guardian of Palden Atisha, from whom it passed on to Je Tsongkhapa, founder of the Gelug order. When Debzhin Shegpa, the Vth Karmapa, was returning to Tibet from China, Je Tsongkhapa, his disciple, presented him the statue.

(38) A statue of Lord Buddha, made of *li* metal from eastern India, presented to Shamar Tulku by the present Dalai Lama. This statue is called Marwe Senge.

(39) A statue of Vajrapani made of Chinese bell-metal.

(40) A painting (*thanka*) of Palden Atisha, drawn and painted by himself, with an inscription on the reverse, in his own hand.

(41) A series of forty-six scroll-paintings (*thankas*) of the Kagyu order lineage of teachers.

(42) A statue of Lord Buddha in standing posture, known as Thup Pa Trong Cher Ma, which was the prized possession of King Ashoka of India. It was presented to Marpa by Siddha Maitripa.

(43) A statue of Lord Buddha, known as Thup Pa Cham Shug Ma, the personal guardian deity of the Indian Siddha Jowo Ser Lingpa, the teacher of Atisha.

(44) A statue of Lord Buddha made of yellow *li* metal, the guardian deity of Sakya Kunga Nyingpo.

(45) A statue of the white Tara made of red *dzi chim* metal by the Xth Karmapa.

(46) A statue of Avalokiteshwara, known as Sa Yi Nyingpo, made of *dzi chim* metal by the Xth Karmapa.

(47) A statue of Vajravarahi made of *dzi chim* metal. It was the main guardian deity of Lama Ngogpa, one of the important disciples of Marpa. It is a statue that has spoken on occasions (*Sung Chon)*.

(48) A statue of Jetsun Dolma, the goddess Tara, known as Ngodrup Pal Barma, of yellow *li* metal, the guardian of the great Kenchen Shiwa.

(49) A statue of the IInd Karmapa, made by him and named Pakshi Nga Tra Ma ('My likeness'). It is composed of mixed white, black and multicoloured *dzi chim* metal. It was consecrated by himself.

(50) Books:

(a) *The Tenjyur*: in 104 volumes
(b) *The Tenjyur*: in 206 volumes
(c) *The Rinchen Terdzod*: in 61 volumes
(d) The *Dam Ngag Zod*: in 10 volumes
(e) The *Ngag Zod*: in three volumes
(f) The *She Cha Zod*: in three volumes
(g) The *Padma Karpo Sung Bum*: in 14 volumes
(h) The *Drukpa Kuntu*: in 10 volumes
(i) The *Kha Chab Dorje Ka Bum*: in 10 volumes
(j) The *Khongtrul Ka Bum*: in 10 volumes
(k) The *Mila Gur Bum*: in one volume
(l) The *Seng Treng Namthar*: in two volumes

(m) *Shamar Kha Chod Wangpo Ka Bum*: in four volumes of ten each
(n) *Yeshe Kor Sum*: in one volume
(o) *Dvagspo Ka Bum*: in two volumes
(p) *Chag Chen*: in three volumes

(51) Three hundred and fifty pairs of dancing costumes made of rare Chinese silk-brocade, about 200 years old, preserved on the first floor of the monastery.

(52) Thirty-two lengths of embroidered curtain-like decorative material used for draping on each pillar of the main shrine hall and other rooms in the monastery.

(53) Two pieces of over a century-old massive *thanka*, depicting the images of Lord Buddha and the Karmapas, used on special occasions to cover the front view of the main monastery building.

(54) About 350 intricately designed masks of various sizes depicting the deities worn by the lama dancers on special dance ceremonies.

(55) One thousand gold-plated Buddha statues preserved in the main shrine hall of the monastery.

(56) One huge embroidered curtain used as a decorative piece for the main shrine hall.

(57) Two elephant tusks with silver rims at the base, preserved in the enthronement room of the Karmapa.

Immovable Properties

1. The Pal Karmapae Densa Shedrup Chokhorling, Dharma Chakra Centre, i.e. the main monastery building at Rumtek, East Sikkim district, built within 74.86 acres of land allotted by the then Chogyal of Sikkim on 20 January, 1961 and recognised vide Land Revenue Secretary's letter dated 26 June 1979.

2. Buildings

(a) Karma Shri Nalanda Institute for Higher Buddhist Studies (old and new buildings).

(b) The Linga, i.e. the personal residence of the Gyalwa Karmapa located within the Dharma Chakra Centre premises, Rumtek.
(c) Jamyang Khang School (for Tibetan Studies).
(d) Hotel Kunga Delek.
(e) Tashi Delek Guest House.
(f) Drub Khang-Meditation Centre located above the main monastery.
(g) Zoo House.
(h) Kitchen House of the late Karmapa, near the zoo house.
(i) Chorten.
(j) Old Dispensary.
(k) The Carpet Weaving Centre.
(l) Rumtek Primary School.

3. Shareholding in the Star Cinema Building, M.G. Marg, New Market, Gangtok, Sikkim.
4. The paddy field, gifted together with its boundary, under Plot No. 792, covering an area of 2.82 acres, situated at Middle Camp (Martam), and recorded in the records of the Registrar of East Sikkim District at Gangtok.
5. The entire building on Plot Nos. 214, 197, 213 and 265 and part of plot No. 221 covering areas of 69, 2.54, 1.54 and .42 acres, respectively, in Rumtek, recorded in the records of the Registrar of East Sikkim District at Gangtok.
6. The 90-year lease-hold cardamom field of reserve forest at Rumtek Majhitar, granted vide orders of the State Government, measuring 50 acres.
7. Four paddy fields — area 6.57 acres, two dry fields — area 3.99 acres and three groves of bamboo — area 5.58 acres, situated at Rumtek (Limburtar) recorded in the records of the Registrar, East Sikkim District, Gangtok.
8. The paddy field and three dry fields on Plot Nos. 343, 350, 351 and 352 covering areas of 1.6, 1.88, 1.46 and 36 acres, respectively, at Rumtek and recorded in the records of the Registrar, East Sikkim District, Gangtok.

Appendix B

Tibetan Calendar

Gregorian Year	Name	Gregorian Year	Name
1944	Wood Monkey	1966	Fire Horse
1945	Wood Bird	1967	Fire Sheep
1946	Fire Dog	1968	Earth Monkey
1947	Fire Boar	1969	Earth Bird
1948	Earth Mouse	1970	Iron Dog
1949	Earth Bull	1971	Iron Boar
1950	Iron Tiger	1972	Water Mouse
1951	Iron Hare	1973	Water Bull
1952	Water Dragon	1974	Water Tiger
1953	Water Snake	1975	Wood Hare
1954	Wood Horse	1976	Fire Dragon
1955	Wood Sheep	1978	Earth Horse
1956	Fire Monkey	1977	Fire Serpent
1957	Fire Bird	1978	Earth Horse
1958	Earth Dog	1979	Earth Sheep
1959	Earth Boar	1980	Iron Monkey
1960	Iron Mouse	1981	Iron Bird
1961	Iron Bull	1982	Water Dog
1962	Water Tiger	1983	Water Pig
1963	Water Horse	1984	Wood Mouse
1964	Wood Dragon	1985	Wood Bull
1965	Wood Snake	1986	Fire Tiger

1987	Fire Rabbit	1994	Wood Dog
1988	Earth Dragon	1995	Wood Pig
1989	Earth Snake	1996	Fire Mouse
1990	Iron Horse	1997	Fire Bull
1991	Iron Sheep	1998	Earth Tiger
1992	Water Monkey	1999	Earth Rabbit
1993	Water Bird	2000	Iron Dragon

The Tibetan calender is divided into major cycles of sixty years duration. These sixty-year cycles are themselves divided into five minor 12-year cycles, each year of which is identified by the name of an animal, bird or reptile. The twelve years are also paired consecutively with a distinguishing element. There are five such elements, with alternating male and female attributes. Thus each sixty-year cycle runs:

1. Female Fire Rabbit
2. Male Earth Dragon
3. Female Earth Snake
4. Male Iron Horse
5. Female Iron Sheep
6. Male Water Monkey
7. Female Water Bird
8. Male Wood Dog
9. Female Wood Pig
10. Male Fire Mouse
11. Female Fire Ox
12. Male Earth Rabbit
13. Female Earth Rabbit
14. Male Uron Dragon
15. Female Iron Snake

A year is based on the Lunar calendar, certain days of which are generally considered to be particularly auspicious, as those falling on the 8th, 10th, 15th and 25th of the month. When a day is deemed especially unfavourable, owing to a specific combination of the phase of the moon and the point at which it occurs within the 60-year cycle, such a day may be omitted from the calendar altogether and a more beneficial day of the month doubled in its place. (Tibetan time-systems can be further understood through the great *kalachakra* tantra.)

Appendix C

The Kagyu Family — Genesis

The Buddhist philosophy has two streams — the Mahayana school and the Hinayana school — with different approaches. Mahayana asks the seeker to work for the betterment of the world. The seeker is advised to dissolve his ego into the common good. Hinayana, on the other hand, asks the seeker to withdraw from the world and seek individual salvation through meditation. Hindu philosophy too advocates much the same thing. The Buddhism introduced in Tibet by Guru Padmasambhava was Mahayana with elements of Tantricism therein. All the Buddhist orders of Tibet are classified under two schools: the Ancient School and the Gelug or the Reformed School. The difference between the two lies in the inclusion of *tantras* in the first only while the *sutras* are the same in both.

The Western usage is to divide Tibetan Buddhism into red and yellow. By 'red' is meant the three earlier orders: Nyingma, Kagyu and Sakya while the 'yellow' denotes the later Gelug. The Nyingma dates back to the advent of Guru Padmasambhava, i.e. the second half of the eighth century. The Kagyu traces its heritage to a great *siddha* from eastern India named Tilopa, the Sakya to a scholar and patron of learning from central Tibet named Khongyal (1034-73) and the Gelug to a great monk-scholar from Kokonor named Tsongkhapa.

There is a sharp difference of opinion regarding esoteric practices and monastic discipline between the so-called Red orders on the one hand and the Yellow on the other. For laity in general, temples and monasteries of all sects are equally holy both for congregation and pilgrimage. Reincarnations connected with *red* have been found in *yellow* households while some highest *yellow* reincarnations have come from *red* families.

In Tibet, there are two kinds of temples, *lhakhang* and *gonkhang*. The former house images of the Buddha, *bodhisattvas* (saints) and scholar saints while the latter have *tantric* deities and guardian spirits. The two stand out in sharp contrast. Distinct and separate atmospheres prevail in both. People offer *chang* and *chema* (*tsampa* and butter) to the tantric *gonkhangs* twice a month. The hideous-looking gods and goddesses, with their multiple heads and hands are petrifying for children. Their faces are curved in violent anger. Their multiple hands are armed with spears, axes and daggers, and they wear necklaces of human skulls. These grotesque images are supposed to provide appropriate objects for meditation. Some are guardian spirits — spirits of the dead who by the law of their karma are forbidden further rebirth and compelled to remain perpetually in this state. They are believed to be able to help Tibetans achieve secular and materialistic ends in this world. Most of these *gonkhangs* are built on the hills, side by side with the *lhakhangs*.

Hanging on the walls of each *gonkhang* are stacks of swords and muskets used in the wars of conquest that had made Tibet the greatest military power in Central Asia during the seventh and eighth centuries before Buddhism killed the martial spirits of Tibetans. Perhaps no religion in the world ever changed a people's way of life so dramatically as did Buddhism in Tibet. The Tibetans, at one time the most dreaded and fiercest warriors in Central Asia, literally 'put down their weapons at the lotus feet of lamas' and followed the 'white path of non-violence' shown by the Buddha.

Whole families would go to the *lhakhangs* to replenish the butter-lamps on the tenth, thirteenth or fifteenth of every month; these dates are considered the auspicious days, and charities and offerings made then are considered sacred. The calm and tranquillity in *lhakhangs* is altogether different from the terrifying *gonkhangs*. The statues, images of Buddha, *bodhisattvas* and saintly scholars look benevolent and beautiful. The interior decorations, all of a religious nature, hold the pilgrims spellbound. Usually three protestations and prayers are offered. Wall paintings and frescoes depict the lives of saints or of the Buddha, or illustrate their teachings. The *lhakhangs* contain four chapels, in which golden chortens hold relics of the departed lamas, and accommodate a good number of monks with separate quarters. This is a *sutra* institution, and its monks do not follow *tantric* practices. However, in the established monasteries in Tibet, both the *sutra* and the *tantric* aspects of Buddhism are considered necessary for the attainment of *nirvana* (enlightenment). Monks, to the north of the Sakya river, generally practise *tantric* Buddhism while those in the south follow the *sutra*. Such a division of religious practice and specialisation indicates the extent to which Buddhism has become institutionalised in Tibet.

Halfway up the snow-clad mountains, among the rocks and shale, a number of caves are carved out for hermits — monks who have renounced the monastic life of ease and plenty — and laity who have permanently left their families, herds of yaks and fields of barley behind.

Unlike the various Christian, Hindu or Muslim denominations, the lay Tibetan Buddhists are not rigid about their sectarian faith and practice. They usually worship all reincarnate lamas, regardless of their orders. It is also not theologically necessary for the laity, whose average ambition may be simply to lead a decent Buddhist life, to follow a particular order. Only the lamas, by their theoretical renunciation of the world, are supposed to choose the most suitable means — and so a particular order — and then concentrate on attaining *nirvana*.

The formation of four major orders (Nyingma, Sakya, Kagyu and Gelug) and their numerous sub-orders was a creative Tibetan response to Buddhism. The orders went their separate ways, each following vigorously and continually transmitting its own tradition and practice. This was partly due to lack of communication. But the basic difference among the orders centred on their different interpretation of 'emptiness', which is the basis of Buddhism, and with the rise of each order, there have been momentous theological debates whether the phenomenal objects really exist or not. These debates contributed greatly to the development of Tibetan religious literature. The various orders grew from the interpretations of four or five extraordinary Buddhist scholars. Naturally enough, great numbers of monks in a particular region began to accept readymade interpretations of the Buddha's teachings because it was easier to do so. Samyukta-nikaya records the Buddha's premonition about the *bhikhus* (monks) of the future. He said, "Monks will no longer wish to hear and learn the *suttantas* proclaimed by the Tathagata, deep, deep in meaning, reaching beyond the world, dealing with the void, but will only lend their ear to the profane *suttantas* proclaimed by poets, poetical, adorned with beautiful words and syllables." Perhaps, the Buddha was aware that what he had preached was a new, pristine doctrine and it would be distorted in later times.

Gradually as Tibet became increasingly religious, the various orders came to play significant roles like political parties in democratic countries. The high lamas of Sakya, Kagyu and Gelug sects ruled Tibet at different periods of history, and the ruling order exercised the greatest power. However, it would be wrong to conclude that all monasteries or orders exercised political power.

The historical Buddha, Sakyamuni, accommodated the different capacities of beings in his teachings. All these teachings can be subsumed under the *Sutrayana* and the *Tantrayana*. Although the Buddha only gave oral teachings, his early disciples recorded his instructions in writing and thus passed them on in their original form. Buddhist masters also authored many treatises explaining the meaning of the Buddha's teachings. Throughout the centuries different lines of communication, with their own characteristics, came about.

In the eighth century the Tibetan king, Srongtsan, invited two Buddhist masters, Padmasambhava and Shantarakshita, to Tibet. At the same time the king initiated translation of important Buddhist texts into Tibetan. This early activity of teaching and translation brought about the Nyingma order, known as the 'old tradition'. The teachings in the Nyingma order are based on the texts of this early period of translation.

During the 11th century, there was a second phase which involved the revision of earlier terminology as well as new translations. The traditions that base their transmission on that period are referred to as the *sarma* (the new) traditions. Of these the Kagyu, Sakya and Gelug are the most well known.

The Kagyu Lineage

The Kagyu Lineage originated with the great *yogi* Tilopa who lived in northern India sometime around the 10th century AD. Tilopa received the four special transmissions and mastered them.

Although there is some discrepancy in historical sources regarding the identities of the masters associated with each of the four transmissions, there is consensus that the first of the four came from Nagarjuna and consists of two *tantras*, the *sangwa dupa tantra* and the *denshi tantra*. It also incorporates the practices called 'illusory body' and 'transference'. The second special transmission came from Naropa and includes the *tantra* called *mahamudra* and the practice called 'conscious dreaming'. The third special transmission came from Lawapa. It includes the *demchok tantra* (the practice of *'clear light'*). The fourth was transmitted from Khandro Kalpa Zangmo and includes the *tantra* known as *hevajra*, and the practice called *tummo*.

These teachings were passed on from Tilopa to Naropa, and were systematised as the six *yogas* of Naropa that are considered a central theme in the Kagyu order. Naropa transmitted his knowledge to Marpa, the great translator, who came to India from Tibet in order to receive instructions. He spread the teachings of *dharma* in Tibet.

His disciple Milarepa became one of Tibet's great *yogis*. Through perseverance in the practice of *mahamudra* and the six *yogas* of Naropa, he achieved profound realisation of the ultimate nature of reality.

Milarepa's transmission was carried on by Gampopa. He studied the Kadampa tradition, which is the gradual path that includes what is called the Lam Rim teachings. He attained realisation of ultimate reality under Milarepa's guidance and established monastic institutions, taught extensively and attracted many students.

Four of his disciples founded the four major Kagyu orders. Babrom Dharma Wangchuk founded the Babrom Kagyu; Pagdru Dorje Gyalpo founded the Pagdru Kagyu, Shang Tsalpa Tsondru Drag founded the Tsalpa Kagyu, and Karmapa Dusum Khyenpa founded the Karma Kagyu.

It was the Ist Karmapa, Dusum Khyenpa, who received the complete *mahamudra* transmission from Gampopa.

The eight minor Kagyu orders also originated disciples. These eight orders are the Taglung Kagyu, Trophu Kagyu, Drukpa Kagyu, Martsang Kagyu, Yerpa Kagyu, Yazang Kagyu, Shugseb Kagyu and Drikung Kagyu.

None of the different Kagyu orders is referred to as major or minor in terms of the instructions they contain. In that respect they are equal. The four major orders are known as major in that they originate with Gampopa himself, whereas the eight minor orders originate with a later generation of masters. At present, among the four major Kagyu orders, only Karma Kagyu remains prevalent. That is why it is generally referred to as the Kagyu order. Among the eight minor Kagyu orders, only Taglung, Drukpa and Drikung Kagyu still exist as independent orders.

One can distinguish several transmissions within each order. However, all major Buddhist traditions in Tibet have a lineage of *pratimoksha* vows and a lineage of *bodhisattva* vows.

The Karmapa himself always chooses the teacher who will pass on the lineage to him in his future reincarnation. In this respect, he is considered a great *bodhisattva* with the capacity to perceive the realisation and qualities of others. And, it is through this ability that he selects his own guru. There is no fixed rule which defines the teacher in advance. In some cases the lineage-holders are eminent reincarnates, while in others they are exceptional practitioners without high status in the religious hierarchy.

Sometime, interim caretakers look after the Karmapa's monasteries during the period when the reincarnate is searched or until the reincarnate attains adulthood. These caretakers are not lineage-holders. The XIV Karmapa, Theg Chog Dorje installed the head of the Drugpa Kagyu, the IXth Drugchen Mipham Chokyi Gyamtso (also known as Mingyur Wangi Gyalpo), as the interim director of administration. The XVIth Karmapa installed a legal body, the Karmapa Charitable Trust, and appointed the trustees in accordance with the Indian law. As per the deed of the trust, it is the responsibility of this trust to run the affairs of the seat of the XVI Karmapa and the affiliated monasteries and centres till the coming of age of the XVII Karmapa.

Tilopa (988-1069 AD)

Tilopa was born into a Brahmin family in east India. At an early age, he met the great master Nagarjuna who, by means of his magical powers, induced the state oracle to choose Tilopa as the ruler of one of the then Indian kingdoms.

Barely a few years later, Tilopa began to be weary of a life of luxury. Renouncing the kingdom he became a monk. He was ordained by his uncle at the *tantric* temple of Sonapuri in Bengal. One day, while he was engaged in his priestly duties, an ugly hag appeared before him and asked if he would like to attain true enlightenment. Tilopa recognised her as a *dakini*, a keeper of esoteric secrets, and begged for her instructions. The *dakini* initiated him into the *chakrasamvara tantra*, which he was able to comprehend and absorb fully. Tilopa practised these teachings for 12 years at Sonapuri. He took a *yogini* (a female practitioner of *yoga*) as his consort. This action led to his expulsion from the monastic community.

Travelling far and wide throughout India, he met many accomplished teachers and received their instructions. For livelihood, he would pound sesame seeds (*til*) to produce oil, hence his name Tilopa. His main guru was the Buddha Vajradhara from whom he received direct transmission of the teachings, in particular the *mahamudra*. He lived in desolate places and grew famous as a great master. Once Tilopa appeared seated on a lion and manifested the power of controlling both the sun and the moon, putting to shame a non-Buddhist *yogi* called Mati who used to boast that he possessed the greatest occult power. On another occasion, Tilopa flew high in the air with his consort and could be seen hovering over a crowded marketplace.

Among his outstanding disciples, Naropa became the lineage holder. His teaching was the expression of the highest realization of Yoga.

"Do not imagine, think or deliberate,
Meditate, act, but be at rest.
With an object do not be concerned" (Tilopa).

Naropa (1016-1100)

Naropa was born in a royal family in Bengal. He was given the name Samantabhadra and was brought up to become a king. Being more inclined towards a spiritual path and intellectual studies, at the age of eight he sought permission to go to Kashmir for higher education. Three years later, he went to Kashmir and began his studies in art, science, grammar, rhetoric and logic with the most eminent teachers of that time.

He remained there for three years and completed his studies. He returned home to find that his parents had arranged for his marriage to a Brahmin girl named Vimaladipi. He lived with her for eight years during which period she became his disciple. Later, at Naropa's insistence, this marriage was dissolved. Thereafter, he again went to Kashmir for further studies. Ordained as a novice there, he spent another three years in studies and earned himself great renown for his remarkable scholarship and learning.

At the age of 28, Naropa returned from Kashmir and lived at Pullahari. He joined the nearby Nalanda University which was presided over by four great Buddhist masters. When one of them died, he was elected to the vacant place. Thus, taking the name of Abhyaakirti, he became an abbot of Nalanda where he taught for eight years.

One day a *dakini* appeared before him, manifesting 37 ugly features. As an embodiment of the Vajra Dakini, she revealed to him the importance of meditation practice suggesting that he should seek instructions from her brother Tilopa. Naropa deserted his exalted position at the university, gave up his books and set out in search of his destined teacher.

Travelling further east, clad in only a robe, with just one companion and with only a begging bowl, he encountered numerous strange manifestations in the search for his teacher. In despair, and on the verge of committing suicide, he at last suddenly met Tilopa, "a dark man with protruding blood-shot eyes, dressed in cotton trousers, his hair knotted in a tuft."

Tilopa revealed the lineage teachings to Naropa and put him through 12 hard tests, each of which ultimately resulted in the transmission of an important esoteric teaching. Having absorbed the full transmission of his teacher, Naropa travelled to a remote region and engaged himself in meditation.

After some years, Tilopa instructed other disciples to fetch Naropa, declaring that there was some more work for him to do. Naropa came back to Pullahari, where he envisioned the arrival in India of the Tibetan pilgrim Marpa, who was soon brought to him. Marpa was accepted as a disciple, initiated into the higher *tantras* and taught the *mahamudra* to perfection. On two other occasions, Marpa travelled from Tibet to meet Naropa, thus enabling the oral transmission to be preserved for future.

Naropa spent his last years in isolation, appearing occasionally to his closest disciples in times of need. He died at the age of 84. One of his disciples, Siddha Dombhi Heruka, was the teacher of Lama Drogmi (992-1072), the founder of the Sakya order. A distinguished scholar, Dipankara Atisha, who was instrumental in spreading the message of the Buddha in Tibet, was also his disciple. Marpa, the Tibetan translator, carried the teachings to Tibet, giving rise to the Kagyu order.

Marpa (1012-1097)

Marpa was born in south Tibet. His father had prophesied that his son had the potential for great spiritual attainments. At an early age, Marpa embraced Buddhism, changing his name to

Dharmamati. He studied Sanskrit with the Sakya lama Drogmi. Then he set out for India. The journey took him through Nepal where he met two disciples of the Siddha Naropa who impressed him greatly with their practical knowledge. After a long and difficult journey, Marpa was led directly to Naropa, who accepted him as a spiritual son and began to transmit the teachings to him.

For sixteen years, Marpa received initiations and teachings from Naropa. Then he returned to Tibet where he spent many years translating the manuscripts of the *tantric* teachings brought with him from India. He established a community farm and monastery at Lhobrag, and married Dagmema who bore him several sons. He was a teacher to only a select group of disciples, among whom he dispersed the essence of his understanding.

Marpa made a second journey to India in order to bring back more teachings to Tibet. Upon his return, he took Milarepa as a disciple, but not before the latter passed a number of trials and tests. Pleased, Marpa bestowed the secret teachings on Milarepa. In answer to a query from Milarepa concerning the most secret Drong Jug teachings (for entering the bodies of others, used for the animation of corpses or the *transformation yoga*), Marpa found himself wanting. He once again returned to India to receive those teachings though he was of advanced age.

In India, Marpa met Dipankara Atisha, who informed him that Naropa was just about to leave the world. However, Marpa was able to have a miraculous meeting with his teacher, who appeared in a vision and transmitted the required teaching to him. Marpa returned to Tibet.

He always utilised dreams and omens for understanding the course of destiny. He was a hard taskmaster, famous for his ungovernable temper and frequent rages, yet equally noted for sudden moments of great generosity and good humour. Among his four main disciples including Jetsun Milarepa, he distributed the esoteric teachings, along with the various holy relics brought with him from India. At the age of 86, he passed away, having firmly established the Kagyu order in Tibet.

Milarepa (1052-1135 AD)

Milarepa was born in the Gungthang province of western Tibet, close to the Nepal border. His father died when he was only seven, and the family property was usurped by greedy relatives who treated him and his mother shabbily. The embittered widow, impatient for revenge, sent him off to learn black magic as soon as he came of age.

The young man quickly learned the powers of destruction. He brought havoc to his village and caused the death of many people. However, his teacher resented the misdeeds and sent him off to find someone who could help him counteract all the bad karmas accumulated through his magical incantations. He became a pupil of a Nyingma lama who soon directed him to Marpa, then living in Lhobrag.

Marpa had had a vision of his coming and allowed him to remain at Lhobrag but refused to admit him to the inner circle of initiates and would not give him any teaching. For six years, Milarepa was treated like a servant and subjected to backbreaking labour. After several futile attempts, he finally built a nine-storied tower according to the specifications of Marpa.

Finally, the difficult trials were over, the bad karmas used up, and Milarepa was quickly given the full teachings and initiations. Marpa prepared him for a life of solitary meditation and imparted the secret teachings of Naropa, in particular the *mystic heat yoga*. Clad only in cotton, Milarepa lived for many years in total isolation in high mountain caves. He engaged himself in the perfection of the teachings transmitted to him.

The years passed and the cotton-clad *yogi* became fully enlightened. People got to hear about him and sought him out to listen intently to the mystic song through which he expounded his teachings. After completing nine full years in isolation he began accepting disciples. Living a very simple life, he spread his teachings through his mystic songs, many of which survive to this day. Tibet resounded with his fame.

Among his well-known disciples was Gampopa who became the next lineage-holder after Milarepa passed away at the age of 84.

Gampopa (1079-1135)

Born in Nyal in eastern Tibet, Gampopa was brought up by his father who was an excellent physician and imparted him a thorough knowledge of the profession. At the age of fifteen, Gampopa was well-versed in many of the *tantras* and also a competent doctor. At the age of 22, he married and had two children, a son and a daughter. An epidemic in the region claimed the children suddenly. The young man was distraught, especially when his wife also fell victim to the disease. In her death throes, she asked Gampopa to devote his life to Buddhism.

Four years later Gampopa, 26, received ordination as a monk, taking on the name Sonam Rinchen and following the doctrines of the Kadampas (founded by lama Domtonpa). He studied under many illustrious teachers and quickly developed a good understanding of Buddhism. When he was 32, he overheard some beggars talking about the *yogi* Milarepa and realised that this *yogi* must be his destined teacher.

He set out in search of Milarepa and after many hardships, managed to find him. For 13 months, he received teachings directly, the doctrines of Naropa, the *mystic heat yoga* in particular and also the complete teachings of the *mahamudra*. He spent many years in deep meditation in retreat and founded a monastery, which came to be called Dvagslha Gampo. He soon attracted many disciples.

Gampopa blended the doctrines of the Kadampas with his own realizations of the *mahamudra*, producing the basis for the many aspects of the Kagyu order. He was a fine writer, renowned for his clarity and deep analytical insight. He always stressed the importance of simplicity in matters of doctrine. Soon, he became known as Dvagspo Lharje, the doctor of Dvagspo, though most of his later years were devoted to the healing of spiritual rather than physical sickness.

There are Tibetan traditions declaring him to be the incarnation of Chandraprabhakumara (the son of a wealthy householder in Rajgir in Bihar who had asked the Buddha to preach the *samadhirajasutra*), whereas some declared him to be that of King Srongtsaṇ, the first Buddhist ruler of Tibet.

The four main disciples of Gampopa formed the four 'major' or 'larger' branches of the Kagyu. At the age of 75, having firmly established the Kagyu teachings, he died. At this time there were many remarkable and auspicious omens. One of his disciples, Dusum Khyenpa, founded the line of successive reincarnate Karmapas. He was the first incarnate (*tulku*) of Tibet:

According to predictions in the Buddhist scriptures, 21 Karmapas will appear.

Dusum Khyenpa: The First Karmapa (1110-1193 AD)

Dusum Khyenpa was born in village Ratay in east Tibet. As his father was a Buddhist practitioner, Dusum Khyenpa received teachings from him as well as from many other teachers. At the age of 20, he was fully ordained as a monk. He had already acquired the *mantra* of *ekajata*, learnt the rites of the great protector Mahakala, obtained *siddhi* (miraculous powers), studied the rites of Chakrasamvara, learnt the doctrines of the future Buddha Maitreya and the Prajnamula teachings, six treatises of Siddha Nagarjuna, doctrines of the Kadampas, and initiated into five important esoteric practices. Now he set himself to the task of thoroughly studying the Vinaya precepts.

Dusum Khyenpa travelled to the Penyul Gyal monastery where he met the great teacher Pal Galopa and others, who gave him the teachings of the great *kalachakra* cycle, together with those of Mahakalakakamukha, the crow-headed form of Mahakala. Meeting Gampopa at the age of 30, he obtained precepts from the teacher, who taught him the Lam Rim of the Kadampas and said, "I meditated on it! So should you!" Sometime later Dusum Khyenpa was initiated into the mysteries of Hevajra. During the empowerment rites, Gampopa manifested before him in the form of Hevajra himself.

Dusum Khyenpa received the full transmission of the esoteric teachings. His inner heat was developed and he felt a strong feeling of wellbeing. Wearing only a single cotton-cloth he went into retreat for nine months, fasting and meditating under the guidance of his teacher. His great faculty for concentrated trance was born in him at this time and out of the hundreds of disciples,

Gampopa realised that it was Dusum Khyenpa who had the greatest ability at meditation. Gampopa prophesied that Dusum Khyenpa would gain complete control of the inner heat, which he did. Many wonderful signs manifested, so he returned to Gampopa who told him to continue with his meditation for some more months. Six months passed, and like the sun bursting through the clouds, he attained true enlightenment. Gampopa recognised the great attainment of his disciple and laying a hand on Dusum Khyenpa's head, he said, "My son, you have severed your bond with the world of phenomenal existence," adding that it would henceforth be Dusum Khyenpa's duty to impart his realisations to others.

According to a *sutra* (an ancient scripture) the Buddha had once prophesied that approximately 1600 years after his own passing there would be born a man of great spiritual attainment and infinite compassion. This man would spread Buddhism for many successive reincarnations and would be known as the Karmapa (man of karma). Gampopa and the two great masters of that time, Lama Sakya Sri from Kashmir and Lama Shang recognised that Dusum Khyenpa was indeed the Karmapa foretold in the prophesy.

Acting on the instructions of Gampopa, he travelled all over Tibet on pilgrimage and began preaching and teaching. He attained the power of being able to pass right through solid rocks and mountains. For four months he remained on the 'flat white boulder' at Phabong Karleb, which had been a seat of Guru Padmasambhava. He was fed there by the *dakinis*.

The Karmapa heard of the departure of the soul of his teacher. He returned immediately to the Dvagslha Gampo monastery. He had a vision of Gampopa in the sky and then engaged in extensive rites for the propagation of the Kagyu order. It was here he promised his disciples that he would live until his 84th year. In his fifty-sixth year, he established the large Kampo Nesnang monastery at a place which is noted for the huge rock upon which the Tibetan letter 'ka' appears whenever a new Karmapa reincarnates into this world. (The letter appears in a line, next to the previous one.) He arranged for the building of a large new monastery at Tsurphu, which became the principal seat of the Karmapa reincarnates. Beside it, he established Gampo Kangra monastery and Karmagon monastery.

The seat of a Buddhist master is the place where he creates the facilities for the study and meditation of *dharma*. A seat is not just the place where the master lives. How should a Buddhist master supervise the activities at his seat? Supervising the seat has to do with the study and the meditation of *dharma*. A Buddhist master's activity concerns nine aspects. The master has to be learned in the Buddhist teaching; he has to be someone who adheres to the Buddhist code of ethics and should be a 'good person', that is, someone of good character. He should also study, reflect and meditate regularly. And his work for others is to teach *dharma*, to refine understanding of the teachings through the art of debate and to write compositions in which he clarifies the meaning of the teachings. This is how the masters of old times cared for their seats. It is not just the master who must engage in these activities, his associates must also practise them. They also need to live in *dharma*, not profit from it.

The Ist Karmapa made a prediction containing all the details of the place where his next incarnation would be found and left it in the care of Drogon Rechen, one of his foremost disciples. He declared that there would be many Karmapas in the future, adding that there were already his other incarnations in existence. (Several incarnations can exist simultaneously: e.g. of body, of speech, of mind, of knowledge, etc.) During the later years of his life the letter 'ka' appeared on the large rock at Kampo Nesnang. In 1193, he passed away. One of his disciples, Drogon Tsangpa Gyare (1161-1211) founded the Tsangpa sub-order and Gyalwa Lingrepa founded the Drukpa branch.

Karma Pakshi: The IInd Karmapa (1204-1283)

Karma Pakshi was born in Drilung Wonthod in a noble family tracing its link with the great Tibetan king, Srongtsan. There were many auspicious signs at his birth and he was soon noticed to be quite an exceptional child. By the age of six, he was fully proficient in the art of writing, even though he had no teacher.

At ten, he had completed the study of the religious texts available to him and only needed to glance at a text or hear it once in order to know it fully. It was this awesome power of natural knowledge which finally convinced his parents that the child had a high spiritual birth.

His first teacher was Lama Gyalsay Bom Trakpa, a disciple of Drogon Rechen, whom the first Karmapa had entrusted with the prediction details of his future incarnation. The lama said to him," Today the *viras* (heroes) and *dakinis* appeared in the sky like a mass of clouds. You will be blessed by *dakinis*!" The same night the tutelary deities informed the teacher that the boy was the new Karmapa and there were many auspicious indications to confirm it.

At the age of 11, he received the primary ordination. Disturbances broke out in the region and the young Karmapa left for Tashi Pom Trag in eastern Tibet and engaged himself in meditation. He also travelled to the Tsurphu monastery, badly damaged during local wars. He rebuilt it.

Once Khubilai Khan sent 30,000 soldiers to arrest him. When they confronted the Karmapa, they were immediately paralysed by his two-finger *mudra* (the *tantric* paralysing gesture). Feeling compassion for them, he restored their movements and allowed them to seize him. They wrapped him in a cloth and tried to tie him up, but his body was like a rainbow, with no substance and they found the task impossible. Then they forced him to drink poison. Instead of any injurious effect, blinding rays of light began to stream from his body. The soldiers were terror-stricken. They took him to a high mountain and pushed him off, but he glided down, landed on a lake and travelled across the surface like a duck. Unsuccessfully they tried to burn him, throwing him with two of his disciples into a blazing fire. Streams of water came out of their bodies and soon put out the flames. Khubilai Khan heard of the events and ordered that the Karmapa should be locked up without any provisions. For seven days, people observed heavenly beings coming to provide him with food and drink. At last the emperor relented and became his disciple.

A few years before, the Karmapa had had a vision telling him to arrange for the building of a large statue of the Buddha, 26 arm-spans in height. He recalled the vision. The task took three years. But the image curiously appeared to be leaning over to the left. After a few years, the Karmapa sat in meditation posture before the huge new statue, lining his body up with the tilt of the image. Slowly he straightened himself up into a vertical position and simultaneously the statue did likewise.

The Karmapa told the Siddha Ugyen that the latter would be the teacher of his reincarnation. A couple named Chosphel and Changden, from Tengri Langkor in southern Tibet, came to Tsurphu on pilgrimage and had an audience with the Karmapa. He told them that his reincarnation would be born as their son and that he had already transmitted part of himself into the womb of the woman.

Five months passed, and then, in 1283 he passed away at the age of 80, having performed the rite of consciousness-transference. There were many curious and auspicious omens at the time of his last rites.

Ranjung Dorje: The IIIrd Karmapa (1284-1339)

Ranjung Dorje was born in the evening, just as the moon was rising, on the roof of a house in Tengri Langkor in south Tibet. After his birth he sat cross-legged and said, "the moon has risen!" His mother took this to be a bad omen and threw ashes into his mouth, but his father recalled the words of the IInd Karmapa and restrained her from acting further. Consequently, the boy did not speak again until he was three years old.

When he was three, while playing with some other children, he suddenly asked them to make for him a throne out of squares cut from turf. He sat upon it, produced a black hat, which he put on his head and then declared that he was the Karmapa. Once, on a visit with his parents to Tengri, after perceiving the image of the Buddha there, he experienced the sensation of a rainbow merging into him. He learnt some Buddhist precepts from his father. He knew the alphabet without having it taught to him. In his dreams he had many pure visions.

At the age of five, he told his father that he would like to see Siddha Ugyen. He, along with his father, travelled to the place where Siddha Ugyen was staying. The day before they reached there, Siddha had a dream in which the IInd Karmapa appeared and told him that he would be coming to see him on the following day. Early in the morning, he shared the dream with his disciples. A throne was set up and a large procession organised.

The child arrived and went straight up to the high throne and sat upon it. "Who are you that you sit upon the throne of my teacher?" asked Siddha. "I am the famous lama Karmapa!" replied the boy. Siddha then asked him to relate how they had met before, to which the boy replied, "One great Siddha came to me. He was you and told me about all the pilgrimages and travels made throughout that breath-taking land of India." The child then climbed down from his throne, prostrated before the Siddha and said that in the previous life he had been the teacher, but that in this life he would become the Siddha Ugyen's disciple. The prediction details left by the IInd Karmapa were consulted and it was established beyond any doubt that the child was the reincarnation of the Karmapa.

He composed a treatise on astrology, which later became established as a new system, the Tsurphu system. The other system is the Central Tibetan one. At the invitation of successive emperors of China, he visited that country several times. Once as the guest of the Emperor of China, he let it be known that the time was approaching when he would leave his body and would be reborn in the region of Kongpo. To his personal secretary, Kunchok Rinchen, he gave precise details of where and how to find his reincarnation, adding that he would declare himself at the appropriate time. He passed away at the age of 56.

There was great lamentation. However, in the wee hours of the next morning, the sentries of the palace looked up in the sky and there in the full moon they could clearly see the Karmapa. Shamar Trakpa Senge, first Shamar Tulku (1283-1349) was one of his five prominent disciples.

Rolpe Dorje: The IVth Karmapa (1340-1383)

Rolpe Dorje was born at sunrise. His mother was a natural wisdom-*dakini*. While still in the womb he could be heard reciting the *mani mantra* and his body frequently assumed strange postures, which caused her to shake. As soon as he was born he sat cross-legged and uttered, " Om Mani Padme Hum, Hri! I am the Karmapa." Then he recited the letters of the alphabet. His father was very sceptical but his mother told him not to doubt as she had had many highly auspicious dreams.

When three years old, the child was taken to Nyangpo and there he told his mother 'I am the reincarnation of Karma Pakshi. I shall have many disciples in this world, you just wait and see!" He assumed the meditation posture of Amitabha, the Buddha of Boundless Light, and then told his mother not to mention their conversations to anyone else, adding that he would eventually go to Tsurphu.

A search party, looking for the Karmapa's reincarnation in the Kongpo province, heard of the remarkable child. Convinced that the reincarnation had been found, the searchers took the child to the Dvagslha monastery of Gampopa. Reaching there, he immediately pointed to the statues of the past Karmapas, saying 'That is me!' to each of them. At the age of 18 he received the final ordination. He observed all the Vinaya precepts. He even forbade anyone to bring even the smallest piece of meat into his presence. Always surrounded by books, it was said of him that he could read them even in his dreams. He knew more than 60 different scripts and always amazed his teachers with his vast knowledge.

Once a family brought a young boy of three-and-a-half years to him for the primary ordination. Instead of that, he bestowed the fuller ordination and at the same time (year 1361) prophesied that the child would eventually become a great spiritual leader. He was Lobzang Trakpa, who later became the great teacher Je Tsongkhapa, the founder of the Gelug sect.

Once, on way to Karmagon while crossing the Shamnam Dzung river, he met the reincarnation of Shamar Trakpa Senge, recognised him and named him Kha Chod Wangpo. The reincarnate was only seven years old at that time. Later, the Karmapa journeyed towards a solitary mountain in the far north, preaching extensively on the way. He set up camp on the barren mountainside and said, "Should the remains of a good monk be cremated on the summit of this mountain, then Chinese troops will not invade Tibet!" He performed a ceremony, packed up all his personal books and ritual items, explaining that they should be carefully preserved for his reincarnation who would be reborn in Nyang Dam. He circumambulated the holy objects 55 times and passed away at the age of 44 years.

His remains were cremated on the mountain, amidst numerous auspicious signs such as rainbows, glowing lights, tremors and showers of flowers. Disciples saw him in the sky, sitting inside a rainbow circle, riding on a lion and sitting on the sun, the moon and the stars. His foremost disciples included Shamar Kha Chod Wangpo, IInd Shamar Tulku (1350-1405) and Je Tsongkhapa, who established the Gelug sect.

Dheshim Debzhin Shegpa: Vth Karmapa (1384-1415)

Debzhim Debzhin Shegpa was also born at sunrise in the region of Nyang Dam in southern Tibet. His father, Guru Rinchen, was a *tantric*, and his mother a *yogini* called Lhamo Kyi. Even before his birth, he could be heard reciting the *Mani Mantra* and the alphabet inside his mother's womb. At the time of his birth, his mother and numerous persons dreamed of the coming of the Karmapa, of railings made from rainbows, showers of flowers and sweet fragrances. As soon as he was born auspicious rainbows appeared everywhere. The child wiped his face and said, "I take refuge in the Buddha, the *dharma* and the order of monks. I am the Karmapa! Om Mani Padme Hum, Hri!"

The lamas at Tsurphu heard of the birth of the prodigy. Brought to the monastery, he was immediately recognised by the Shamar Kha Chod Wangpo, who had been his disciple in the previous incarnation. At the age of 20, he took the final ordination at the Namdruk Riwo monastery in Kongpo.

At the invitation of the Emperor of China, he visited China. The emperor was so impressed by him that he referred to the

Karmapa as the Tathagata. The emperor told the Karmapa that there were too many different orders of Buddhism and that it would be much better if there was only one, the Kagyu, offering to bring this about by force. The Karmapa explained to him that neither this was his desire, nor could it be beneficial to humanity since mankind requires varying methods of teaching and that in reality all orders are but one great family of Buddhism. The emperor took teachings and initiations from the Karmapa, eventually becoming a great *bodhisattva* himself.

Once, during a ceremony, the emperor saw the mystic *vajra mukut* made from the hairs of 100,000 *dakinis*, hovering over the Karmapa's head. Realising that it was visible only on account of his own advanced spiritual attainments, he decided to make a hat that would be visible to all. On completion, he presented it to the Karmapa. This same 'black hat' has been worn by the successive reincarnations of the Karmapa since that time. It is also said that this hat has the power of conferring deliverance-on-sight to all living beings who behold it.

The Karmapa met the young reincarnation of Shamar Tulku, Chospal Yeshe, and supervised his ordination and bestowed many initiations on him. When the Karmapa became afflicted by a serious disease and it seemed that he was ready to leave the world, his disciples held a propitiation ceremony to prolong the Karmapa's life, but he said, "Following an omen, I have projected myself to a place in the vicinity of Karmagon. You should address your prayers in that direction and I shall protect you." To his main attendant he said, "Do not scatter the books and images, for an owner will soon be coming." Then he handed over all his ritual implements, precious relics and personal books, prophesying that he would be reborn at She Kyong. He assured his disciples that he would meet them again in reincarnation.

In the Potala palace, at the age of 32, he passed away. At the time of his cremation, many rainbows, haloes and showers of flowers were observed. Shamar Chospal Yeshe, IIIrd Shamar Tulku, Situ Choskyi Gyaltshen, Ist Situ Tulku and Trung Mase Tokden, Ist Trungpa Tulku were among his foremost disciples.

Tongwa Donden: The VIth Karmapa (1416-1453)

In accordance with the prophecy, Tongwa Donden was born at Ngamtod in She Kyong, near Karmagon. While he was in his mother's womb, his parents had highly auspicious dreams. As soon as he was born, he sat upright, looked at his mother and laughed. When the umbilical cord was cut the smell of beautiful incense pervaded the whole region.

On the 12th day of the third month, his parents took him on a begging round and on this occasion he met Ngompa Cha Gyalwa, a disciple of the previous Karmapa. The infant became very excited at the sight of him and began to recite the alphabet (*ali-kali*: the vowels and consonants). Ngompa then took him to a solitary place and asked him who he was. The small baby grasped his finger and said, "I am unborn, free from all names, place-less and the glory of all living beings! I shall lead many to liberation!" Later he told the lama that he was the new Karmapa, but forbade him from disclosing this yet.

At the age of seven months, he made a throne, stood on it and recited the name of the Buddha and the *mani mantra*. He also bestowed blessings on the people around him. When one year old, he was taken towards Lha Chim and on being asked why he had come there he pointed to the monastery and said: "For this!" Upon reaching the main building he pointed out the stupa of Karmapa Dusum Khyenpa, grasped hold of a black hat and said, "It's mine!" For three days there was a great shower of flowers from the sky and afterwards he was proclaimed to be the new Karmapa. The IIIrd Shamar Tulku, a disciple of his previous reincarnation, came and recognised him officially and performed the enthronement ceremony. Later, the IIIrd Shamar Tulku took him to his own monastery where the child recognised all the previous possessions of the past Karmapa reincarnations and made a number of prophecies.

In 1452, while staying at Tse Lha Gang, it appeared that his passing was imminent. Therefore, Lama Sangye Senge began to offer prayers for the prolongation of his life. The Karmapa said, "This year nothing will happen to me. For nine more months I shall take responsibility for my life." Then he travelled to the Tsurphu monastery and went into retreat. At the age of 37, he imparted all the Vajradhara teachings to Gyaltshab Goshir Paljor and entrusted to his care a sealed letter giving all the details of his reincarnation. Many unusual signs were witnessed such as earth tremors, sudden darkness and showers of flowers and all knew that the Karmapa would be leaving the world soon. One day he said, "I also belong to the lineage of the Kagyus!"

The Karmapa collected his books, images, garments and black hat and gave them into the care of his chief attendant. He made some secret prophecies and then passed away at the age of 37. Gyaltshab Goshir Paljor Dondrup, Ist Gyaltshab Tulku and Situ Tashi Namgyal, IInd Situ Tulku were among his foremost disciples.

Chos Trag Gyamtso: VIIth Karmapa (1454-1506)

The VIIth Karmapa was born at Kyi Lha in northern Tibet. At the time of his birth he wiped his face and said, "Ama-la" (mother). At the age of five months he said, "Ah Hung! (There is nothing in the world but void.) People may think there is something, but they are really quite wrong. For me there is neither birth nor death!"

At the age of nine months, he met first Gyaltshab Tulku, who immediately recognised him and arranged for his enthronement. All the details of the prediction letter were found tallying with the facts of his birth. Many people came to pay their respect and the young child astounded them all by reciting the alphabet correctly.

During his life, he preached the message of peace relentlessly and pacified warring groups. The internecine fights ceased following his interventions. Once he travelled to Lhasa, where he had a vision of the future Buddha Maitreya, who advised him that a monastery should be built around the large statue of the Buddha there. The local ruler, Nuipa, who supported the Gelug order, would not permit it. The monastery was then built outside Lhasa. The monks from the neighbouring Gelug monasteries descended on it under the cover of night and razed it.

A Karmapa lama, Ghostrag Gyamtso, narrowly escaped being killed. He took refuge in Lhasa.

The supreme ruler of Tibet at that time was IVth Shamar Tulku, Choskyi Trakpa, who had been elected by the then ministers. Hearing of the great insult to the Gyalwa Karmapa and the Kagyu order he decided to punish the local ruler. The Karmapa would not hear of this and told him the matter was already well into the past. He left Lhasa.

During his next visit to Lhasa, he met IInd Gyaltshab Tulku, Tashi Namgyal and presented him with an 'orange hat' in recognition of his high attainments. Later in Tse Lha Gang, he gave his last teachings, informing his closest disciples of his imminent passing. All the prediction details of his reincarnation were left in the care of IIIrd Situ tulku, Tashi Paljor. At the age of 53, he passed away.

Shamar Choskyi Trakpa, IVth Shamar Tulku, Situ Tashi Paljor, IIIrd Situ Tulku, Gyaltshab Tashi Namgyal, IInd Gyaltshab Tulku, Sangye Nyenpa Druptop, Ist Sangye Nyenpa Tulku, Karma Tinlaypa, Ist Karma Tinlay Tulku were among his foremost disciples.

Mikyo Dorje: VIIIth Karmapa (1507-1554)

Mikyo Dorje was born one early morning in the province of Dam Chu in eastern Tibet. There were many auspicious signs and a strong smell of incense pervaded the region. A rainbow pillar formed over the house of his birth and many flowers fell down from the sky. The newly born baby wiped his mouth and declared, "I am the Karmapa! I am the Karmapa!"

IIIrd Situ Tulku heard of the birth of a very unusual child in the province indicated in the prediction letter. He sent a messenger to determine if it could be the new Karmapa. Soon he visited the place himself and enquired: What are the names of the mother and father? Are there any palm-trees near the house? Which direction does the doorway face? Is there a stream nearby, and if so, in which direction does it flow?" All the answers tallied with the details given in the letter of prediction, so it was established that the child must indeed be the new Karmapa.

When he was only a month and a half old he declared, "Eh-Ma-Ho!" (Don't doubt me, for I am the Karmapa!") When he was three months old, Situ Tulku took him to the Karmagon monastery. There, the child got a royal reception.

At the age of four months, the Karmapa met Gomchen Ser Phuwa, who had been his disciple during his last reincarnation. Gomchen Ser Phuwa presented him with a ritual ball and a double-drum. Immediately the small boy became very happy and played them both with great delight. When asked by the Gomchen which teachings he had transmitted to him in his past life the boy replied, "I gave you the *mahamudra* and the six *yogas* of Naropa."

When he was five, he was invited to the house of a nobleman from Ri Wo Che, in Eastern Kham. One day, while sitting there he was asked by Lama Sonam Rinchen to say who he really was. The boy laughed and said, "Sometimes I am Padmasambhava, sometimes Saraha and at other times I am the Karmapa!"

At about the same time, the mother of a child born in the Amdo region declared that her son appeared to be the new Karmapa. The news of this new boy spread rapidly. Gyaltshab Tulku, Tashi Namgyal, and Lama Yang Ripa travelled to Ri Wo Che in order to settle the matter, and vowed not to show any distinction between the two little boys until it was determined beyond doubt which of them was the true reincarnation. However, when they were presented before Mikyo Dorje they found themselves automatically doing full prostration to him and thus realised that he must undoubtedly be the real Karmapa.

In Leh, Ladakh, a huge python entered the palace assembly-hall and refused to be driven out. Several meetings were held to find a way to get rid of it, but no solution could be found. Finally one of the lamas suggested that the Karmapa be contacted for advice. Laden with gifts of dried plums, apricots and grain, a delegation was sent to Kongpo. The Karmapa sent a letter back, with a message, saying, "Oh python, it is my personal order that you return to your own place in the lake, without any more bother", and gave the instructions that the letter should be read out loudly from the window of the hall.

This advice was followed and upon hearing the contents of the letter the python started shaking so violently that even the palace walls seemed to tremble. Slowly it unwounded itself and leaving the assembly-hall went straight to a nearby lake and disappeared into the water. This story is still recalled in Ladakh.

At the age of 22, the Karmapa received the full ordination. While travelling to the pilgrimage place of Tsari, where there is a natural image of Chakrasamvara, the Karmapa was met by a group of pilgrims who rushed to prostrate before him. Among them was a small boy whom he recognised to be the reincarnation of the Shamar Tulku, so he took him along. At the age of five, the Vth Shamar Tulku, Kunchok Yenlak was enthroned by the Karmapa.

Once, while staying at the Tsurphu monastery, the Karmapa had a vision of Sakya Pandit who appeared to him surrounded by many Bodhisattvas, from whom he received important teachings. At this time, he made a small marble statue of himself and with a piece of leftover marble he made an impression of his palm by squeezing it. When the statue was consecrated, in the presence of many lamas, the Karmapa addressed it, asking if it was a good likeness of him. The statue replied, "Yes, of course!" much to the amazement of all those present.

The Karmapa recognised the reincarnation of the IVth Situ Tulku, Choskyi Gocha, enthroned him and took him as a disciple. Later he also recognised the IVth Gyaltshab Tulku, Trakpa Dodrup. He entrusted Shamar Tulku with all his personal books, relics and ritual items, as well as the letter containing the prediction of his next birth. Then he prepared to leave the world. At midnight, while staying at the Dvagspo Shedrup Ling Monastic College of the Shamar Tulku, he passed away in his forty-eighth year. His foremost disciples included Shamar Kunchok Yenlak, Vth Shamar Tulku, Situ Choskyi Gocha, IVth Situ Tulku, Gyaltshab Trakpa Dodrup, IVth Gyaltshab Tulku and Pawo Tsuklak Trengwa, IInd Pawo Tulku.

Wangchuk Dorje: IXth Karmapa (1556-1603)

Wangchuk Dorje was born in the region of Treshod in eastern Tibet. Before his birth, his mother dreamed that she was blowing on a white conch-shell and that many people were rushing towards her. While still inside his mother's womb, the baby could be heard reciting *mantras*. When he was born, he sat cross-legged, wiped his face and said, "I am the Karmapa!" He remained sitting in that position for three days and his father was so overawed that he started prostrating before him. At this the child stood up, said "Om-Āh-Hum!" and started to laugh. His mother untied her apron strings and tried to wrap up the child in it, but he threw it off saying "Oh No! No!" Then he was wrapped up in a sheepskin, which he accepted.

Neighbours told his father that the child must surely be the Karmapa, but he doubted them. However, on returning to the house he found the baby sitting in the lotus-posture of the Buddha, gazing up at the sky, with a bright light moving around his head. By the time he was eighteen days old, he could walk very easily and was totally independent. The fame of the child spread far, reaching the ears of the IVth Shamar Tulku, Kunchok Yenlak, who asked Lama Gyaltshen to investigate.

It was found that the letter of prediction correctly indicated the place of his birth, for it read, "My reincarnation will be born in a place called Treshod Horkok, close by a rock bearing a naturally-formed statue of Avalokiteshwara, near to a river coming out from the Himalaya mountain." As soon as Lama Gyaltshen reached the place, the baby boy looked very pleased and started to call out "Shamarpa! Shamarpa!" and told those near him that Shamar Tulku would soon meet him.

When six months old, he was taken to the Tsurphu monastery, and on the way there he started saying "Situpa! Situpa!" Everyone was very surprised when a messenger from the Situ Tulku arrived the very next morning. Some days later the IVth Situ Tulku himself appeared, recognised the child as the reincarnation of the Karmapa, and bestowed on him the empowerment of Amitabha.

A few days before reaching the monastery the Karmapa joked with his attendants, saying that it was time that Shamar Tulku come in person to see him. Upon reaching Lung Se, the party met IVth Shamar Tulku, who immediately took a great liking for the little boy. Together, they proceeded to Tsurphu. At the age of 24, he received the final ordination from Shamar Tulku.

While staying at Tsari, the Karmapa engaged himself in deep meditation for nine months. He had visions of Chakrasamvara, Kalachakra and deities and protectors of the Kagyu order appear before him. He travelled to the Phagmo monastery of Denso Hill, where he met the reincarnation of Shamar Tulku, Garwang Choskyi Wangchuk. The Karmapa formally recognised him and performed his enthronement ceremony at the Dvagspo Shedrup Ling Monastic College.

One of his representatives, a lama, visited Sikkim and founded three monasteries at Ralang, Potang and Rumtek. The Karmapa was requested to consecrate the new monasteries, to which he replied that he would do so from Tibet, as he was unable to make the journey there himself. He sent instructions indicating the auspicious month, day and time of the ceremony, saying that everything should proceed accordingly. At the time of consecration of the Ralang monastery, three large eagles came from the direction of Tibet, flew three times around the new monastery and dropped consecrated grains of yellow rice right on top of the new roof. There are persons in Sikkim who still preserve these yellow grains.

The Karmapa recognised the reincarnation of the Vth Situ Tulku, Choskyi Gyaltshen. During a visit to the Kagyu order monastery of Sungrab Ling he began to refer to his own imminent passing and his health began to decline. He sent all the prophetic details of his future birth to Shamar Tulku. At the age of 47 he passed away. His foremost disciples included Shamar Choskyi Wangchuk, VIth Shamar Tulku; Situ Choskyi Gyaltshen, Vth Situ Tulku; Gyaltshab Trakpa Chos Yang, Vth Gyaltshab Tulku; Pawo Tsuklak Gyamtso, IIIrd Pawo Tulku.

Chos Ying Dorje: Xth Karmapa (1604-1674)

Chos Ying Dorje was born at Golok Khansi Tang, in the extreme north-east of Tibet. During her pregnancy his mother dreamed that Guru Padmasambhava came towards her and entered into her. There were many other auspicious omens. When the baby was born, he took one step in each of the four directions, sat cross-legged in the centre and said, "Om Mani Padme Hum, Hri! I pity the sufferings of humanity, for I am the Karmapa!"

VIth Shamar Tulku, who was staying at the Tsari Tso Kar monastery, sent his personal secretary, accompanied by several lamas, to bring the Karmapa reincarnation. They were very surprised when the small boy asked if Shamar Tulku was well, even before they announced who had sent them. They found that all the details of his birth tallied with the letter of prediction.

The Karmapa received his final ordination from Shamar Tulku. At the Tsurphu monastery, he made five beautiful statues out of rhinoceros horn, depicting the Kagyu order of Vajradhara, Tilopa, Naropa, Marpa and Milarepa.

The Karmapa foresaw that the time of political oppression was approaching. He went to Lhasa, visited monasteries before continuing on to the Yang Dop monastery, where he engaged himself in contemplation of the future.

The King of Tsang at that time, Desi Karma Tenkyong Wangpo, who was one of the Karmapa's disciples, became strongly anti-Gelug and practised religious discriminations during his reign. The Vth Dalai Lama, Ngawang Lobzang Gyamtso, sent three representatives to Mongolia, asking for military help from the chieftains there. The chief of the Qoshot Mongols, Gushri Khan, responded favourably to the invitation and supported the Gelugs.

Deeply disturbed by the bigotry and anti-Gelug acts of the King of Tsang, the Karmapa also foresaw the approaching storm from Mongolia. He sent a letter to the Dalai Lama explaining that he was not in favour of military action in the name of religion and that neither he nor the Kagyu order in any way sanctioned the activities of the King of Tsang. The Dalai Lama replied that he understood this to be the case and to rest assured that nothing untoward would happen. The Karmapa realised, however, that events would take a different course.

He also went to see the King of Tsang and told him to stop his sacrilegious actions as they were contrary to the Buddhist *dharma*. He forewarned that if the King of Tsang were to initiate attack he would surely get killed.

In the meantime, Gushri Khan marched into Kham and engaged the non-Buddhist (Bon) Behri chieftain in fighting. The Behri chieftain had entered into an alliance with the King of Tsang, with the intention of eliminating the Gelugs. Defeated by the Mongols, he was captured and put to death by Gushri Khan. A year later, Gushri Khan brought all the Kham under his control and moved his armies towards Tsang.

The Dalai Lama, who perhaps had not been kept fully informed of the developments, was very upset at the sacrilegious turn of events and desired that the Mongol chieftain should be persuaded to return to his own lands. But the Dalai Lama could not do anything since he was the slave of the political intrigues of his ministers.

The Karmapa began to distribute all his accumulation among the poor. Knowing that he too must eventually get involved in the dangerous situation, he appointed Gyaltshab Tulku as his temporary representative at the Tsurphu monastery. He then moved to Yam Dur, where he set up a camp. After some days, Shigatse, capital of Tsang, fell and the King of Tsang was captured and executed. At Yam Dur, the Karmapa received a letter from the Dalai Lama, asking whether he was preparing to wage war against the Gelugs and demanding that he send his word of honour that he would refrain from taking any hostile action. The Karmapa replied, "How dare we ever harm the Gelugs in the future, even as we have never harmed them in the past", and added that he would comply with any request from the Dalai Lama to prove his sincerity on this point.

But the Gelug administration quibbled over the words of his letter and their exact meaning. Dismissing the reply as gobbledygook, the Gelug ministers pointed out that the Karmapa had not, in exact terms, promised to harm the followers of the Dalai Lama. Consequently, forces were sent to attack the

Karmapa's camp. The Gelugs put to sword many of his followers and destroyed their tents and belongings. The Karmapa somehow escaped the slaughter. After the Gelug forces withdrew, he sent the survivors away to disperse throughout the country. Then with his servant Kuntu Zangpo, he flew in space to Kurtod district of northern Bhutan. Those who witnessed him leaving saw him in varying forms; some saw him taking the shape of a vulture, others that of a deer, while some simply saw him flying in his human form.

During this period, the Kagyu order was pushed back to the point at which there were just three of its monasteries left in central Tibet — Tsurphu, Yangpachen and Nenang. All other Kagyu monasteries had been forcibly converted to the Gelug order.

Thirteen years younger than the Karmapa, the Vth Dalai Lama, Ngawang Lobzang Gyamtso, was born in 1617 into a Nyingma family. With the help of the Mongol ruler, Gushri Khan, he established himself as the Supreme Ruler of all Tibet. And rebuilt the great Potala palace in Lhasa. He died in 1682.

The Karmapa was caught up in political events totally at variance with his religious way of life. A remarkable character, typical of the best of Tibetan lamas, he avoided fighting and lived for many years, sometimes disguised as a simple monk and always accepting hardship of every kind.

The King of Jyang, the host of the Karmapa, in a sudden battle, succeeded in defeating the Mongol army in the border region of Amdo. The King and his Council of Ministers wanted to send forces to attack the Mongol armies in Tibet itself and install the Karmapa as the Supreme Ruler. But the Karmapa forbade any such action, saying that warlike activities were contrary to the tenets of Buddhism.

The Karmapa resolved to settle things peacefully and set out for Lhasa. There he went straight to the Potala and met the Dalai Lama. The latter, feeling great compassion towards the Karmapa, gave instructions that he should be free to return to the Tsurphu monastery. Some months later, the Karmapa indicated that he expected to leave the world soon and gave predictions of his reincarnation to Shamar and Gyaltshab Tulkus.

He had lived tumultuous years fraught with suffering, patience and the indomitable will to overcome all obstacles through the practice of *dharma*. This truly remarkable man breathed his last at the age of 71.

His foremost disciples included Shamar Yeshe Nyingpo, VIIth Shamar Tulku, Situ Mipham Chogyal Rabten, VIth Situ Tulku, Gyaltshab Norbu Zangpo, VIth Gyaltshab Tulku and Pawo Tsuklak Trinlay Gyamtso, Vth Pawo Tulku.

Yeshe Dorje: XIth Karmapa (1676-1702)

Yeshe Dorje was born in Meshuk in eastern Kham. As soon as he was born, he wiped his face, sat cross-legged and said, "I am the Karmapa!" At this time a rainbow formed over the house and many flowers fell down from the sky. During his childhood he saw Chakrasamvara and other protectors and deities in the sky above him. He pointed them out to those who were present, but they saw nothing and mocked him. In reply to their scorn, he rose up in the air, hovered for a while and then returned to the ground. The news of this miraculous feat spread far and reached Shamar and Gyaltshab Tulkus, who both sent off their representatives to investigate further.

The searchers found all the details of the birth tallying with the letter of prediction left by the previous Karmapa. The new Karmapa was thus brought to the great Yangpachen monastery where the VIIth Shamar Tulku recognised him immediately. The young Karmapa was taken to the Tsurphu monastery and enthroned there. He performed the 'black hat' ceremony shortly afterwards. During his time, the Tsurphu monastery was rebuilt as it was badly damaged by the Mongol soldiers. As part of his duties, he sent the letter of prediction concerning his reincarnation to the young Shamar Tulku. Soon after, he passed away at the early age of 27. His foremost disciples included Palchen Choskyi, VIIIth Shamar Tulku and Tenzin Chogyal, Vth Trungpa Tulku.

Changchub Dorje: XIIth Karmapa (1703-1732)

The XIIth Karmapa was born at Litsa Tok in Derge province of eastern Tibet. Two months after his birth, he suddenly declared himself to be the Karmapa. Shamar Tulku heard of the birth of the remarkable child in the place mentioned in the letter of prediction and sent a search party. Reaching the village, the party was astonished to witness a white rainbow which ended right on the roof of the house where the child had been born, Everything tallied with the details given in the letter of prediction. The child correctly chose all the items which had belonged to the previous Karmapa and threw away all the others in disgust.

The new Karmapa set out for Tsurphu where he was enthroned by Shamar Tulku. He visited Nepal, India and several regions of Tibet. In Tibet both of them performed many rites, giving special instructions to their disciples, saying that they should try their utmost to propagate *dharma* in difficult times. In this period of severe religious discrimination, the Karmapa and Shamar Tulku saw fit to leave their bodies and reincarnate. Early in the morning of the new moon, after sending the letter of prediction to the Situ Tulku, the Karmapa passed away at the young age of 29. Two days later, Shamar Tulku followed him. The foremost disciples of the Karmapa included Choskyi Jungnes, VIIIth Situ Tulku (1700-1774); Kunchok Oser, VIIth Gyaltshab Tulku (1699-1765); Tsuklak Gawa, VIIth Pawo Tulku and Kargyud Tinlay Shingta, VIth Drukchen Rinpoche.

Du Dul Dorje: XIIIth Karmapa (1733-1797)

Du Dul Dorje was born in Chawa Drong of Nyen Chowa province. As a small child he started recounting stories of his past visits to India, Nepal and China. One day a 16-year-old boy dressed in white, holding a basket of flowers appeared before him. Scattering the flowers at his feet, the boy danced around him and said, "I am Mahakala! I come from the Light of Knowledge, sometimes in a wrathful form! As teacher and protector, there is no difference between you and me!" Before disappearing the figure scattered the last handful of flowers and laughed. As many people witnessed this curious event, the fame of the young boy spread far and wide. A search party led by the VIIth Gyaltshab Tulku met the boy and found that everything tallied with the letter of prediction left by the previous Karmapa. Thus, the reincarnate was recognised and taken to the Tsurphu monastery, where he was ceremoniously enthroned.

Once water started pouring out from a breach underneath the great statue of the Buddha in the Jokhang temple of Lhasa. The people feared that if the image was submerged, it would probably be taken off to the land of the *nagas* (serpent kings). A book written by Guru Padmasambhava carried the prophecy that only the Karmapa could stare off the danger. The Dalai Lama requested the Karmapa to come to Lhasa, and save the precious statue. Circumstances beyond his control prevented the Karmapa from personally visiting Lhasa. So, he sent a letter with instructions to place it on the water. When the letter, addressed to the king of *nagas*, was presented, the water immediately started receding until it dried up. Later the Karmapa himself travelled to Lhasa on a hornless yak. Going directly to the Jokhang temple, he prayed before the great statue of the Buddha. He offered a white silk scarf to the image. The arms of the statue moved into the 'receiving' position, remaining permanently outstretched from that time on. A grateful Dalai Lama honoured the Karmapa with an audience, bestowing many gifts besides.

The Karmapa gave the letter of prediction to his disciple, Situ Tulku and passed away at the age of 65. His foremost disciples included Padma Nyingche Wangpo, IXth Situ Tulku; Chosdrup Mipham Gyamtso, Xth Shamar Tulku; Tsuklak Choskyi Gyalpo, VIIIth Pawo Tulku; Kunzig Choskyi Nangwa, VIIth Drukchen Rinpoche and Ladakh Hemi Gyalsay, a Prince, from the Hemis monastery in Ladakh.

Theg Chog Dorje: XIVth Karmapa (1798-1868)

Theg Chog Dorje was born in Danang village of Zalmo Gang in Domed region of Kham in eastern Tibet. Many rainbows were to be seen over the village and like most of his predecessors, at the time of his birth, the baby wiped his own face and said, "*Om Mani Padme Hum, Hri! Ah Ahh I Ii Uu UU...*" (The vowels of the alphabet). The fame of the child spread far. Search parties were sent. They took the boy to the Karmagon monastery, where he was welcomed by the IXth Situ Tulku. Finding all the details in the letter of prediction to be exactly correct, Situ Tulku officially recognised him as the new incarnation of the Karmapa and bestowed the primary ordination.

Once the Karmapa made a pilgrimage to Kang Rimpoche, Mount Kailash in western Tibet, and during his stay there some people claimed they could see him sitting meditating in a tent in the middle of lake Mansarovar. He circumambulated the holy mountain, visited all the shrines, and had a wonderful vision of Chakrasamvara. While returning, he passed by a crag, notorious as the abode of a demon. Large boulders suddenly began rolling down towards the party of pilgrims, and it looked as if everyone would be crushed to death. The Karmapa glanced up and at that moment the large rocks stopped right where they were. Even the rubble and dust completely disappeared. He left the letter of prediction with his two brothers, Dodrup and Choswang Tulkus, and passed away at the age of 71.

In the biography of Chogyar Kingpa, a Nyingma master and *terton* (an individual who reveals the hidden teachings of *Padmasambhava*), it is recorded that in between the XIVth and XVth enthroned Karmapa reincarnations, one reincarnation who did not live to become a throne-holder was born. He lived for only two years. He was born in a family related to the XIVth Karmapa. When one counts this reincarnation, Khachab Dorje becomes the XVIth Karmapa and Rangjung Rigpai Dorje becomes the XVII Karmapa.

That clarifies the Vth Karmapa, Dheshin Shegpa's prediction that between the end of the XVIth Karmapa's life and at the beginning of the XVIIth Karmapa's life the Buddhist doctrine would deteriorate in Tibet, that the people of China would rise against their emperor, his family line would come to an end, the people of China would invade and occupy Tibet and that the two countries will suffer and become poor. This prophecy has been interpreted differently.

The first fourteen Karmapas were solely individuals whose activities were based on the nine aspects. However, during the period of the XVth Karmapa, things changed due to the political climate as well as the way religious institutions had been operating. In the past, religious institutions had been able to support themselves without interference of politicians and the like. But, during the nineteenth century attitudes changed. Interference in monastery affairs became the norm. In most cases this happened because an individual or a group of individuals desired to profit. Thus, lawsuits concerned with monastery property and other disputes became common. The root of these profit-oriented practices lay in the fact that, unlike in the past, people around lamas departed from the nine practices.

Khachab Dorje: The XVth Karmapa (1871-1922)

Khachab Dorje was born in Shelkar village of Tsang province in western Tibet. As soon as he was born he looked up at the sky and declared himself to be the new Karmapa. He had a white mole in the centre of his forehead. Within a year of his birth, he already had an astonishingly profound understanding of many subjects and was able to pass his knowledge on to others. He continued to be his own teacher until the age of six.

The *terton* Chogyur Dechan Lingpa, Drukchen and Jamgon Kongtrul Rinpoches felt convinced that he must be the reincarnation of the Karmapa and upon consulting the letter of prediction, it was found that all the details tallied. As a final test, the boy was asked to select items of clothing placed before him, and he immediately chose those which had belonged to the previous Karmapa. Therefore, he was taken to the Tsurphu monastery where he was ceremoniously enthroned.

At the age of fourteen, he received an invitation to consecrate a newly restored monastery in Li Thang. Drawing a map of the place, he dropped a holy grain on it. Showers of grain fell on the roof of the monastery simultaneously. Once, visiting Bonpo Gon in Li Thang, he performed a miracle by pushing his finger right into a hard rock. When he withdrew it, a stream of milky water flowed out of the hole. On the first day of the Tibetan calendar in 1912, he insisted that the New Year trumpets be blown towards the east instead of south, as was customary. This was interpreted as indicating the direction in which his incarnation would be born.

Leaving a letter indicating details of his next rebirth in the care of Jampal Tsulten, his confidant attendant, he passed away at the age of 52. His foremost disciples included Padma Wangchuk Gyalpo, XIth Situ Tulku (1886-1952); Khyentse Oser, IInd Jamgon Kongtrul Tulku; Tsuklak Nawa Wangchuk, Xth Pawo Tulku; Jambyang, XIth Shamar Tulku; Trakpa Gyamtso, XIth Gyaltshab Tulku; Choskyi Nyinje; Xth Trungpa Tulku.

Rangjung Rigpe Dorje: the XVIth Karmapa (1924-1981)

The XVIth Karmapa was born at Denkhok on the banks of the Dri chu (river), near the 'Athup' palace in Derge (eastern Tibet). Before his birth, it was prophesied by two eminent monks that a great Bodhisattva would soon come to Athup. The monks advised the family to set up camp outside the palace so that the birth would not take place in a lay environment.

While still in his mother's womb, one could hear the baby reciting the *mani mantra*. One day, shortly before the birth, his mother noticed that her stomach had become completely flattened as if she was not pregnant at all. She proceeded to the camp set up on a hill behind the palace, and at sunrise the next morning she felt a great heaviness and her stomach began to swell very rapidly. Soon afterwards the baby was born.

There was a drizzle and rainbows appeared all around, some ending at the camp and others at the palace. When the child was born he took seven steps, saying, "Mother, Mother!" As she wrapped him in a blanket she noticed that all the water in the offering basins had turned into milk. Realising the importance of the birth, the family let it be known that a girl had been born in order to protect the child from ill-luck.

In the meantime, Situ and Jamgon Kongtrul Tulkus had opened the letter of prediction left by the XVth Karmapa and found the following detailed instructions:

> East of Tsurphu, close by a river, in a place that long ago had belonged to Pawo Denma Yulgyal Tokgod (a famous archer) and to the minister of King Kesar, on the Pat Hill, decorated with the letters 'A' and 'thup', is a house made of earth, belonging to a royal and religious family. The birth will take place there on the fifteenth day of the sixth month of the rat year (according to Tibetan calendar).

Both Situ and Jamgon Kongtrul Tulkus had clear visions of the Athup Palace and sent off a party to determine if the new incarnation was to be found there. The foray party heard of the birth of the remarkable child in conditions exactly as had been predicted in the letter. The search was over. Thus the XVIth Karmapa was recognised. For some years he remained in the palace in the care of his parents.

He was a child of extraordinary natural insight; if horses or cattle were missing from the area he could always give an exact description of the place where they could be found. His room in the palace was on the third floor. Once, some visitors brought him tea in earthenware. The Karmapa flung it into the courtyard below and then sent a servant to pick it up. Miraculously neither was the pot broken nor had a drop of the tea spilled. Laughing, the Karmapa squeezed the neck of the pot and sealed it completely. For a long time it was preserved in the Athup Palace.

His primary ordination was performed when he was seven-year old. He left for the Tsurphu monastery, the traditional seat of the Karmapas. The way lay through a valley near the palace of the greatest protectors of Tibet, Nyenchen Tang Lha, which was situated on the crest of a mountain. The Karmapa sent sacred grain and a white yak as offerings to this protector and the yak was seen to run straight up to the top without any guidance.

He travelled to Lhasa to meet the XIIIth Dalai Lama who performed his 'hair-cutting' ceremony. The Karmapa was wearing his *ne shu* (his small hat), but the Dalai Lama saw another hat on top of it and pointed it out to his chief minister. When the Karmapa performed the traditional prostration he took off his small hat, but afterwards the Dalai Lama asked why he had not taken off the other hat also as it was customary to be bareheaded on such an occasion. Those present protested that he had indeed been bareheaded. Then people realised that the Dalai Lama must have seen the ethereal *bodhisattva* hat, visible only to those of the highest spiritual attainment, and had thought that everyone else could see it also.

Once, at the age of twelve, the Karmapa travelled to Kham. En route, at a place called Lorong, he told Dechang Yeshe Palwar to open the window of his palanquin, saying that he could see many well-dressed people riding towards him on very beautiful horses. His entourage realised that these riders must be the protectors of that place coming to honour the Karmapa, since none else could see them.

The Karmapa and his party reached Tardzi Chutsen, the hot water springs, and stopped to rest and bathe in the curative waters. It was the middle of winter yet many snakes suddenly started crawling out from between the rocks. The Karmapa rushed into them and was soon covered in them. He started to dance, saying, "I am the king of the snakes!" Everyone was terrified and begged him to stop, but he only laughed and did not seem to be worried at all. The snakes unwound themselves and went back into the hot springs.

At Chite, the Karmapa discovered a new stream, naming it 'Five Nectars'. While passing once more through the neighbourhood of the protector Nyenchen Tang Lha, a white yak came straight up to the Karmapa, bowed before him and disappeared. Everyone was astonished but the Karmapa just said, "It is only natural!"

The Karmapa and his party reached Shakshu Kar, where Drukchen Paljor Rinpoche came to receive the Karmapa. They began chaffing each other about their respective miraculous powers. Suddenly the Karmapa took a sword from his attendant's scabbard and tied a knot in the blade with his bare hands. Paljor Rinpoche was dumbfounded and did not dare compete. The party reached Tsokpur, where a frozen river had to be crossed. There, the Karmapa left his footprint on the ice. Later, when the river melted people found that this footprint was still visible in the water and again on the ice the following year.

The party reached the Riwa Barma monastery, where a ceremony to pay reverence to Guru Padmasambhava was performed. At the end of the rite, the offering cakes were thrown in different directions in order to dispel evil forces. When they were thrown to the east flames could be seen coming out of them. It was at this time that there was a sudden and unaccountable pause in Chinese aggression on the eastern borders.

At the Tungnak Lhachen Gon monastery, the Karmapa was asked to perform a consecration ceremony. After the holy grains were thrown, it was found that they had all turned into dazzling white holy relics. A very famous hunter of the region came to the Karmapa, prostrated himself and confessed that he had killed many innocent animals unnecessarily. Afterwards, he presented his hunting dog to the Karmapa. At the same time, another visitor brought three baby deer and presented them to the Karmapa. Soon the hunting dog and the three deer became very good friends, completely at ease in each other's company. Other people brought cats, guinea pigs, mice and rats and soon all these animals were sleeping side by side.

The Karmapa reached the Dil Yak monastery, where the party stayed in tents, several of which were joined together. On one occasion he was seen high up off the ground, riding a deer along the ropes from one tent to another. The party reached Radza Dzong in the mountains, where there was a drinking water crisis. Lama Samten Gyamtso explained to the Karmapa that the nearest spring was three miles away and asked for a blessing to help the situation. The Karmapa called for a wooden tub to be brought and placed near the monastery. Saying that he wished to bathe, he asked the people to bring water and fill it up. After the bath, he told the attendants to empty the water onto the ground. Immediately, it began to rain and a spring broke forth from the spot where the tub had been standing. The water shortage of that area was permanently resolved.

Passing by Chos Gon in Kham, where the local protector had a palace on the top of a very high mountain, the Karmapa offered the protector a beautiful red horse which ran straight up the mountain to the summit. The party reached the

Karmagon monastery and as the Karmapa entered the great assembly hall, all the tops of the relic-stupas were seen to raise themselves, as if in salute.

The Karmapa travelled to the Tukshi monastery, quite close by, and there staged the dance of Mahakala. Two neighbouring provinces were fighting and many people had been killed, so the Karmapa visited the area and made peace between the warring parties. Though the dictator of China, General Chang Kai-Shek, invited the Karmapa to visit his country, he declined.

While travelling to Tsurphu, he visited the Penchen monastery on the way. In that place there was a statue of the protector Zhing Kyong, riding on a horse. As soon as the Karmapa approached the place the horse started to neigh, much to the surprise of everyone. Thence, he proceeded to Dam Chung, where the main deity offered him a large unpierced nine-eyed *zi* stone, a type of precious banded-agate. At the age of 26, he received the final ordination.

Later, he visited Bhutan, Nepal, India, Sikkim — which is a part of India now — and China extensively. During his long trips, he made three complete circumambulations of the holy mountain of Kailash (Kang Rimpoche), taking three days for each one, and also went all around the holy lake of Mansarovar (*Tso Mapham*).

In 1950, an epidemic of smallpox struck Tsurphu, so the Karmapa performed the *vajra kila* (the tantric knife-deity) rites. Soon it subsided and all those who were affected recovered very quickly. Once he visited the Kar Chung monastery and before entering it, he spat on the ground. An elderly lady devoutly gathered up the spittle and carefully preserved it. Later it was found to have turned into precious shining relics, which kept on multiplying. Many of these were given to sick people, curing them fully. Many of these relics are still preserved by his followers.

In 1953, he journeyed to Lhasa where he had audience with the XIVth Dalai Lama, Tenzin Gyamtso (born in 1935). The following year, accompanied by the Dalai Lama, Chong Rinpoche and other high lamas, he visited China. He again visited Lhasa briefly, where he had an important discussion with the Dalai Lama. Accepting his invitation, the Dalai Lama visited Tsurphu. Meanwhile, fighting broke out in eastern Tibet, between the Khampas and the Chinese. The Chinese authorities requested the Karmapa to visit the area. He did so and advised both sides to cease further hostilities. He also made them promise to keep a five-year truce but the Chinese did not abide by that. He travelled to Lhasa to explain the situation to the Dalai Lama before going back to his monastery at Tsurphu.

In the fifties of the twentieth century, before the exodus of Tibetans to India, following the Chinese aggression, the Tsurphu monastery, the seat of the Karmapa, was astonished to receive the news that the *labrang* (administration) of the nearby monastery of XIth Gyaltshab Rinpoche had sued the Tsurphu *labrang* in a court of law at Lhasa for fraud and theft. More surprising than the most was the fact that the plaintiff was none but Gyaltshab Rinpoche's *labrang*. The dispute lingered for about 12 years. Ultimately, the verdict went in favour of the Karmapa administration at Tsurphu.

Further east, in Palpung (Kham) lay the monastery of Situ Rinpoche. Despite having had good relations with the Tsurphu administration, there had been moments of strain and Situ's administration had developed distrust of the Karmapa's administration. Time to time, the then General Secretary of Tsurphu, Ngedon Gyatso, clashed with Situ's administration on several issues, ranging from breach of protocol to lack of respect, some years before the court row in Lhasa.

Though on account of his seniority, the XIth Situ Rinpoche was requested by the Tsurphu administration to instruct the young XVIth Karmapa, there were several instances when the sentiments of the followers of the Karmapa were hurt by the action of XIth Situ Rinpoche. During a visit to the Palpung monastery in Kham (east Tibet), XIth Situ Rinpoche had the Gyalwa Karmapa seated on a throne similar to his own, clearly denoting an equal rank. Formal photographs were clicked. However, it was not long before the Tsurphu administration extracted retribution.

A few years later, the opportunity cropped up when XIth Situ Tulku, during a visit to Tsurphu, got the cold shoulder from the Tsurphu administration. Thereafter, on several occasions, he was deliberately ignored by the Tsurphu administration. However, the XVIth Karmapa remained aloof from such petty one-upmanship games. But he too was surprised to learn while leaving his motherland that some *labrangs* and their *tulkus*, were unhappy on account of their positions being secondary to his.

During his visit to India in 1956, the elderly lamas of the ravaged Rumtek monastery asked him to visit the monastery. The Karmapa told them that the time was not yet ripe, but promised that he would come later. He returned to Tsurphu, by which time further hostilities had broken out in the Domed region of Kham.

Fighting broke out all over Tibet and the Karmapa was begged by his disciples to flee the country while he had the chance. He told them not to worry and said, "It is not necessary for me to leave yet. But if the time comes you can be assured that there will be no difficulty for me." Sometime later, the Karmapa sent Situ and IXth Sangye Nyenpa Tulkus to Bhutan. He gave instructions for the restoration of the Nyide Gon monastery in Lhobrag in the south, telling the monks to go about life in their normal way. At this time a new monastery was being built for the Karmapa at Kur Tod, in northern Bhutan, under the patronage of the aunt of the King of Bhutan. This monastery was finished and prepared for use.

The Chinese hostilities became intolerable and the possibilities for a peaceful existence were very unlikely. Realising that the cause of *dharma* would best be served by escaping from the ever-tightening grip of the Chinese, the Gyalwa Karmapa decided to move to more peaceful areas. Accordingly, accompanied by an entourage of 160 lamas, monks and laymen, the Karmapa left the Tsurphu monastery, the ancient seat of the Karmapas since the twelfth century, and proceeded to Bhutan. Accompanying him were Shamar, Gyaltshab and Ponlop Rinpoches as well as many other incarnate lamas. Jamgon Kongtrul Rinpoche was already in Kalimpong (Darjeeling) and Situ Rinpoche in Bhutan.

The party was able to ferry out with them the most precious of the sacred statues, ritual items, relics, icons, paintings, books and costumes preserved at the Tsurphu monastery for centuries. The hazardous and difficult journey, taking 21 days, passed through Lhobrag in southern Tibet, the birthplace of Marpa. Rites were performed at various sacred places on the way for the welfare of all and for the preservation of Buddhism in the difficult times ahead.

The party safely arrived in Bhutan. At this time, discussions ensued with the Government of India in respect of future plans for the resettlement of the Karmapa and his many followers. It was decided that all should transit through Bhutan and settle temporarily in Dharamsala (Himachal Pradesh). Tashi Namgyal, the Chogyal (King) of Sikkim, too invited the Karmapa to settle in Sikkim.

Uppermost in the Karmapa's mind was one thought. It was that, though in exile, he must not rest but take full responsibility for rekindling the torch of *dharma*, with the material and spiritual cooperation of the many Buddhists throughout the world. He felt that *dharma* had become like a lamp which needed an immediate and sustained supply of vital oil in order to give off a clear, strong flame.

The Karmapa felt that Sikkim would undoubtedly be the best place to set about creating the conditions for the fulfilment of his mission. He considered Sikkim especially suitable on account of the natural Buddhist inclinations of the people and particularly as the country had been sanctified by a visit of Guru Padmasambhava in the distant past. Therefore, he readily accepted the Chogyal's invitation to set up base in that country. He arrived at Gangtok.

The *labrangs* of Situ and Gyaltshab too decided to establish themselves in Gangtok. The Gyathon Tulku, a Kagyu lama who belonged to the Palpung monastery of Situ Rinpoche, was already firmly ensconced in Sikkim at that time. He also had been invited to settle in Sikkim in 1954 when he accompanied the XVIth Karmapa during his visit to that region. In 1962, Thondup Namgyal succeeded his father as the Chogyal of Sikkim. By that time, Gyathon Tulku had begun to wield considerable influence over the Sikkimese royal family, to the extent of becoming the confidant of the queen mother of Sikkim. Incidentally, the queen mother was not favourably inclined towards the Karmapa.

Gyathon Tulku with Situ's *labrang* hatched a conspiracy in league with the queen mother to expel the Karmapa from Sikkim. The same Gyathon Tulku had earlier succeeded in getting Dujom Rinpoche, an eminent Nyingma lama, expelled from Sikkim. He wanted Situ Rinpoche as the Guru of the Chogyals and the presence of the Karmapa in Sikkim would be an obstacle in his designs. However, the plot failed miserably due to the Chogyal's tough stand on this issue. Ably guided by his minister, Tashi Dadul Densapa, and an influential secretary, Tratin Sherab Gyaltshen, the Chogyal ensured the Karmapa's arrival and settlement.

In 1967, before his death, Gyathon Tulku declared himself publicly as the last in the lineage of the Gyathons. Many years later, however, the present Situ Rinpoche declared that the reincarnation of the Gyathon was born in the politically influential Martam's Topden family. But the Rumtek administration refused to recognise the reincarnation of the Gyathon Tulku. Since then, the Topden family had reason to nurse a grudge against the Karmapa and his administration.

Sikkim again witnessed an unsavoury dispute. The Gyaltshab administration laid a claim on the property of the father of the Gyaltshab Lama. He had given all his assets into the care of the queen mother. The Gyaltshab administration approached the Karmapa. Pretending to have buried the hatchet, it asked for forgiveness and succour. The Karmapa then helped the Gyaltshab administration to recover the belongings from the queen mother. He also provided lodging and education to the young Gyaltshab Tulku at the Rumtek Dharma Chakra Centre.

At the same time, Situ's *labrang* tried in vain to build its power and influence in Gangtok. In its heyday, it had enjoyed a big say in the eastern region of Tibet. Therefore, the Situ's *labrang* was not willing to merge its identity with, or be influenced by, that of the Karmapa.

Rising above rancour, the Karmapa permitted the young reincarnate of Situ Rinpoche to receive his education in Rumtek monastery. However, Situ's *labrang* put a rider. It made it clear that Situ Rinpoche would have a separate board and kitchen from that of the Karmapa. A jittery Rumtek administration feared the prospect of having to deal with the haunting past that Situ Rinpoche had brought with him. However, the Karmapa was least worried. He had already recognised and appointed Shamar Rinpoche as the second in the hierarchy of the Kagyu order.

Then came an offer from the Chogyal — magnanimous and opportune: An offer to the Karmapa giving him the choice of several sites in his kingdom, for the location of the new monastery. It greatly strengthened his position. The Karmapa selected the site at Rumtek, where a Kagyu monastery had been built during the time of his IXth reincarnation as Wangchuk Dorje. This place possessed all the auspicious attributes needed for the site of a seat of the Karmapa: seven streams flowing towards it, seven hills facing it, a mountain behind, snow ranges in front and a river below, spiraling downhill like a conch-shell.

The Karmapa and his party left post-haste for Rumtek. Those days Rumtek consisted of a monastery in shambles, encircled by a cluster of huts and surrounded by forest. Inadequate accommodation and non-existent kitchen — that was Rumtek then. Conditions were extremely difficult. The need of the hour was to render the place habitable. Land was cleared, tents were pitched and everyone persevered to fulfil the dream of establishing a new centre for the Karmapa.

The Karmapa visited New Delhi to meet the Indian Prime Minister Jawaharlal Nehru who promised all help. The Chogyal of Sikkim gifted 74 acres of land at Rumtek to the Karmapa, in perpetuity. Besides that, the Sikkim government generously donated towards the preliminary construction cost. It also provided free timber. A motorable road was constructed, electric cables brought in and water lines were laid. The Government of India gave a large grant for the construction of an assembly hall, residential quarters for the monks, a dispensary, and a house for the medical officer. Contributions were also received from public though no appeal was made. The Karmapa contributed a large amount from his own resources.

Work started in 1962 and it took four years to complete the new centre, designed in the most beautiful traditional Tibetan style. It was named *Pal-Karmapa-Densa-Shed-Drup-Chos-Khor-Ling*, meaning 'The seat of His Holiness the Gyalwa Karmapa: A centre for teaching and practice of *dharma*'. The treasured religious relics, icons and books brought from Tibet were installed in the new monastery. In 1966, the Karmapa entered the new centre.

In 1974, the Karmapa led a party of Kagyu lamas to the West visiting Europe, USA and Canada. He performed the 'black hat' rite on a number of occasions. At the age of 58, he passed away.

The Shamar Lineage: The 'Red Hat' Karma-Kagyu Lama

Reincarnations:

Ist	Trakpa Senge	(1238-1349)
IInd	Kha Chod Wangpo	(1350-1405)
IIIrd	Chospel Yeshe	(1406-1452)
IVth	Choskyi Trakpa	(1453-1524)

(He had been elected supreme ruler of Tibet by the then ministers)

Vth	Kunchok Yenlak	(1525-1583)
VIth	Garwang Choskyi Wangchuk	(1584-1630)
VIIth	Yeshe Nyingpo	(1631-1694)

(During this period, just three Kagyu monasteries — Tsurphu, Yangpachen and Nenang — were left. All other Kagyu monasteries had forcibly been converted to the Gelug order.)

VIIIth	Palchen Choskyi Dodrup	(1695-1732)

(The VIIIth Shamar Rinpoche was born in Nepal, though he spent most of his time in Tibet. He is held in particular reverence in Nepal.)

IXth	Kunchok Jungnes	(1733-1741)
Xth	Chodrup Mipham Gyamtso	(1742-1792)

The Xth Shamar Rinpoche was poisoned. During those times of political uncertainty in Tibet, a Qing dynasty emperor had decreed in the eighteenth century that the Kunzig Shamar Rinpoche would no longer be recognised. It all developed when the Gelug Kundenling of Lhasa was the regent at the time as there was no Dalai Lama. When the Xth Shamar Rinpoche was on a pilgrimage to Nepal, the Gelug administration seized the opportunity to accuse Shamar Rinpoche of treason. To make matters worse for the Shamar Rinpoche, war between Nepal and Tibet broke out over a currency dispute. The accusation-cum-request made by the Gelug *kundenling* officials led the Qing ruler to impose a ban on the reincarnations of Shamar Rinpoche.

The Chinese rulers by then were already certifying and often dictating the reincarnations for the higher incarnate posts, including the Dalai and Panchen Lamas, but never for the reincarnation of the Karmapa. The Chinese emperor had innovated a way to recognise some reincarnates, particularly Gelugs, with his 'chin golden vase'. He had devised a lottery-like draw from where one chit among the many would be picked up by the emperor or his representative, containing the name of the 'right' reincarnation. Of course, such interference by the rulers in religious matters and its acceptance by the Gelugs, sullied the milieu of *dharma* in Tibet.

XIth	Jambyang Rinpoche	(1880-1947)
XIIth	Tinlay Kunchup	(1948-1950)

For political reasons, there was no formal recognition of Shamar Rinpoche. To have done so would have incurred the wrath of the ruling Gelugs, who had seized all the monasteries and property of Shamar Tulku. The XVIth Karmapa said, "Merit is becoming smaller and smaller. There is much political interference. Black is becoming white. The real is becoming unreal." At that time it was not practical to have any Shamar recognised or enthroned. Everything was under wraps. The reincarnations appeared, but were not publicly revealed.

Choskyi Lodru, the XIIIth Kunzig Shamar Rinpoche, foremost lama of the Kagyu order, after the Gyalwa Karmapa, was traditionally enthroned in Sikkim after about two centuries of political banishment.

The installation of the Kunzig Shamar Rinpoche by the XVIth Karmapa in the Rumtek monastery in 1963, attended by religious and political figures in the state, was obviously not liked by Situ Rinpoche's administration. It preferred to forget the history and tradition behind the reincarnation of Shamar Rinpoche. In several *sutras* and *tantras*, the Kunzig Shamar Rinpoches are described as emanations of Amitabha in the same way as the Gyalwa Karmapas are described as emanations of the Avalokiteshwara. The IInd Karmapa, Karma Pakshi, had prophesied their appearances as the Black Hat Lama Karmapa and the Red Hat Lama Karmapa, who would take different bodily manifestation but would share the same midstream. During the turn of the thirteenth century, the unsurpassable IIIrd Gyalwa Karmapa, Ranjung Dorje, presented to the Ist Kunzig Shamar, Trakpa Senge, a ruby-red crown, the exact replica of his own black crown. It was to be a symbol of his identity. The Tibetan title of Shamar means 'the lama of the ruby-red crown'. In the *Good Kalpa Sutra*, the Buddha said, "In the future, a *mahabodhisattva* with a ruby-red crown shall come to the multitude of beings, leading them out of the cyclic ignorance and suffering." Historically, in Tibet, the Gyalwa Karmapas and the Kunzig Shamars are compared to the sun and the moon. Similarly, the Vth Shamar, Kunchok Yenlak foretold: "At times the Black Hat Karmapas and the Red Hat Karmapas will act as spiritual masters of each other and at times they will be students of each other. In one instance, they will be related as father and son and in another instance, they will be related as uncle and nephew. Showing respect to the Shamar is tantamount to showing respect to the Karmapa for they are inseparable manifestations."

The prophecy proved true as the present Shamar Rinpoche is the nephew of the XVIth Karmapa who had recognised and installed him. On many occasions, the XVIth Karmapa said that he and the Shamar were inseparable in body, speech and mind.

The Situ Lineage

Reincarnations:

Ist	Chokyi Gyaltshen	(1377-1448)
IInd	Tashi Namgyal	(1450-1497)
IIIrd	Tashi Paljor	(1498-1541)
IVth	Chokyi Gocha	(1542-1585)
Vth	Chokyi Gyaltsen Palsang	(1586-1657)
VIth	Mipham Chogyal Rabten	(1658-1682)
VIIth	Mawe Nyima	(1683-1698)
VIIIth	Chokyi Jungne	(1700-1774)
IXth	Pema Nyinje Wangpo	(1854-1885)
Xth	Pema Wangchok Gyalpo	(1886-1952)
XIth	Pema Tonyo Nyinje	(1954-present)

Prior to the first Situ Tulku the lineage was formed by three great *yogis*: Drogon Rechen (1088-1158), Naljor Yeshe Wangpo (1220-1281), and Rigowa Ratnabhadra (1281-1343).

Jamgon Kongtrul Reincarnations:

Ist	Lodro Thaye	(1813-1901)
IInd	Khyentse Oser	(1904-1953)
IIIrd	Lodro Chokyi Senge Tenpai Gocha	(1954-1992)

Gyaltshab Reincarnations:

Ist	Goshir Paljor Dondrup	(1427-1489)
IInd	Tashi Namgyal	(1490-1518)
IIIrd	Trakpa Paljor	(1519-1549)
IVth	Trakpa Dodrup	(1550-1617)
Vth	Trakpa Chos Yang	(1618-1658)
VIth	Norbu Zangpo	(1659-1698)
VIIth	Kunchok Oser	(1699-1765)

VIIIth	Chospal Zangpo	(1766-1820)
IXth	Trakpa Yeshe	(1821-1876)
Xth	Tenpai Nyima	(1877-1901)
XIth	Trakpa Gyamtso	(1902-1959)
XIIth	Trakpa Tenpai Yaphel	(1960-present)

Pawo Reincarnations:

Ist	Choswang Lhundrup	(1440-1503)
IInd	Tsuklak Trengwa	(1504-1566)
IIIrd	Tsuklak Gyamtso	(1567-1633)
IVth	Tsuklak Kunzang	(1633-1649)
Vth	Tsuklak Tinlay Gyamtso	(1649-1699)
VIth	Tsuklak Chokyi Dodrup	(1701-NA)
VIIth	Tsuklak Gawa	(NA-1781)
VIIIth	Tsuklak Chokyi Gyalpo	(NA)
IXth	Tsuklak Nyingche	(NA-1911)
Xth	Tsuklak Nawa Wangchuk	(1912-NA)

Other High Lamas of the Kagyu Order:

Trungpa Tulku

The Lineage:

1. Trung Mase Tokden
2. Kunga Zangpo
3. Kunga Osel
4. Kunga Namgyal
5. Tenzin Chogyal
6. Lodro Tenphel
7. Jampal Chogyal
8. Gyurme Tenphel
9. Karma Tenphel
10. Choskyi Nyinje
11. Choskyi Gyamtso

Other Important Lama Lineages:

1. Kalu Rinpoche
2. Sangye Nyenpa Tulku
3. Ponlop Rinpoche
4. Khyentse Rinpoche
5. Drupon Rinpoche
6. Dabzang Rinpoche
7. Khenpo Trangu
8. Sabchu Rinpoche
9. Traleg Rinpoche
10. Dorje Lopon Tenga Rinpoche
11. Trungram Gyaldrul Rinpoche
12. Akong Rinpoche
13. Bokar Rinpoche
14. Chokyi Nyima Rinpoche
15. Khamtrul Rinopoche

The list below gives the status of religious dignitaries of the Kagyu School in the order of their importance. It has been written on the fifteenth day of the twelfth month of the Fire Sheep Year according to the Tsurphu Calendar.

Listed below are the names according to the importance of the status of the reincarnated masters that have been able to leave Tibet for India.

I. Heads of the Kagyu School of Tibetan Buddhism:
   1. Kunzig Shamar Rinpoche
   2. Khyenzig Drugchen Rinpoche*
   3. Tsungme Jamgon Situ Rinpoche
   4. Tsungme Chogtrul Taglung Rinpoche*

II. The Second Ranking Religious Dignitaries of the Kagyu School:
   1. Chogtrul Jamgon Rinpoche
   2. Chogtrul Gyaltsab Rinpoche
   3. Chogtrul Pawo Rinpoche

III. The Third Ranking Religious Dignitaries of the Kagyu School:

1. Chortle Joe Won Ponlop Rinpoche
2. Chortle Palpung Khyentse Rinpoche
3. Chogtrul Drungsar Khyentse Rinpoche
4. Chogtrul Surmang Rinpoche
5. Chogtrul Palpung Ongen Rinpoche
6. Chogtrul Sangye Nyenpa Rinpoche
7. Chogtrul Traleg Rinpoche
8. Chogtrul Surmang Trungpa Rinpoche
9. Chogtrul Decho Yangdzin Rinpoche
10. Chogtrul Dilyag Dabsang Rinpoche
11. Garchen Tripa Dorje Lopon (However, the Garchen Tripa Dorje Lopon can also be included within the group of second ranking religious dignitaries because, in the same way as the Garchen Tripa in the Gelug School is the status of the head of the main seat of that school, Garchen Tripa Dorje Lopon is the head of the main seat of the Kagyu school.)

IV. The Fourth ranking Religious Dignitaries of the Kagyu School:

1. Kentruul Thrangu Rinpoche
2. Bagyo Tulku Rinpoche
3. Drupon Tulku Rinpoche
4. Dilyag Urgen Rinpoche
5. Dilyag Sabchu Rinpoche
6. Tulku Ongen Mingyr Rinpoche
7. Chogling Tulku Rinpoche
8. Gyalse Tulku Rinpoche

V. The Fifth Ranking Religious Dignitaries of the Kagyu School:

1. Salche Tulku
2. Tenga Tulku
3. Palme Tulku
4. Bardo Tulku
5. Drung Tulku
6. Tragar Tulku
7. Yoldrag Tulku

There are many more lower reincarnations.

Signed and sealed by H.H. 16th Karmapa, Rangjung Rigpae Dorje in 1967.

***Translator's Note 1:**

At that time the head of the Dringung Kagyu and the head of the Taglung Kagyu had not been able to come to India. For that reason, they are not included in the list given below.

***Note 2:**

Drukchen Rinpoche and Taklung Rinpoche are the Supreme Heads of the Drukpa Kagyu School and the Taklung Kagyu School. As a matter of courtesy, the status 'spiritual leader of Karma Kagyu' was offered to them.

Divisions within the Kagyu Order

(I) The Drukpa Branch

The Drukpa-Kargyud is composed of three sections, being termed the 'top', the 'bottom' and the 'middle'.

The 'top' was founded by Gyalwa Ling Repa, who passed on the teachings on to Drogan Tsangpa Gyare (founder of the Tsangpa subsect). He in turn passed them on to Go Tsangpa Gonpo Dorje, whose foremost disciple was Siddha Urgyen (the teacher of the IIIrd Karmapa). Siddha Urgyen passed them on to his disciple Gyalwa Yang Gonpa. This section became known as the 'Namkhye Karma' or 'State of Heaven'. It was very large.

The 'bottom' was founded by Siddha Lorepa, who went to Bhutan and there met Tsangpa Gyare, from whom he received all the teachings by the time he was seven. At the age of thirteen he went to Khara and meditated there for three years. He travelled to Nam Tso, where there is an island in the middle of a lake and two caves on the island, both of which he used for prolonged meditation. He had only one load of barley flour and had to eat his animal-skin clothing, yet he was able to spend many years there and ultimately attained perfection. One summer he performed a miracle of creating a path of ice from the island to the shore. As he walked across it, a shepherd saw the ice melting behind him and thus his fame spread far. He had about a thousand disciples and founded two monasteries, Karpo Chos Ling in Tibet and Tarpa Ling in Bhutan. He passed away at the age of 64 in 1250. This section became known as the 'Sayi Tsi Shing', or 'Tree Branches'.

The 'middle' was founded by Wonres Dharma Senge, the nephew of Tsangpa Gyare. Born in 1177, he received all the ordinations and initiations from his uncle. He prophesied the coming of a flood but stopped it by leaving his footprint on a rock in front of the great Ralang monastery. Then he repaired the monastery, constructed many new shrines and built great statues. He passed away at the age of 61 leaving eight successors in charge of the monastery. They were: (1) Zhonu Senge, (2) Nyima Senge, (3) Senge Sherab, (4) Senge Nyinche, (5) Chosje Senge Gyalpo, (6) Jambyang Kunga Senge, (7) Lodru Senge and (8) Sherab Senge.

The elder brother of Sherab Senge, Yeshe Rinchan, spent fifty years as their spiritual leader and was succeeded by:

The Ist Drukchen Rinpoche: Gyalwang Kunga Paljor, who was born in 1368, was the first teacher of the 'Drukchen Chyabgon' sect of the Karma-Kargyudpas. He succeeded as Abbot at Ralang. At the age of fifty-nine, he made a prediction concerning his future incarnation. He was an incarnation of Marpa and helped to spread *dharma* widely. At the age of 76 he passed away.

The IInd Drukchen Rinpoche: Jambyang Choskyi Trakpa was born in Jayal, according to the prediction of his predecessor. He became a disciple of Ngawang Chokyi Gyalpo, the nephew of the Ist Drukchen Rinpoche. Perfecting his meditation he became a *siddha*, leaving many footprints permanently on rocks and was able to levitate in the air in the lotus-posture of a Buddha. In accordance with the instructions of *dakini* Sukhasiddhi, he founded the Tashi Thong Mon Ling monastery. He performed many miracles and passed away at the age of 45.

The IIIrd Drukchen Rinpoche: Padma Karpo was born in 1527. He had many teachers. Very soon, he became a *siddha*.

He founded the Sang Nga Chos Ling monastery and wrote many books.

The IVth Drukchen Rinpoche: Mipham Wangpo.

The Vth Drukchen Rinpoche: Paksam Wangpo.

The VIth Drukchen Rinpoche: Tinlay Shingta.

The VIIth Drukchen Rinpoche: Kunzig Chosnang.

The VIIIth Drukchen Rinpoche: Jigme Migyur Wangyal.

The IXth Drukchen Rinpoche: Mipham Choskyi Wangpo.

The Xth Drukchen Rinpoche: Kedrup Yeshe Gyamtso.

The XIth Drukchen Rinpoche: Jigme Migyur Wangkyi Dorje, the present incarnation, who was predicted and recognised by the XVIth Gyalwa Karmapa, lives at his monastery in the Mem Tea Estate, below Sukhia Pokhri in Darjeeling.

(II) The Kham Branch

The first Khamtrul Rinpoche: Karma Tenphel (1598-1638), was a great teacher. He produced an incarnate line.

The second Khamtrul Rinpoche: Kunga Tenphel (1639-1679) had a fine disciple called Dzigar Sonam Gyamtso, the first Dzigar Choktrul Rinpoche.

The IIIrd Khamtrul Rinpoche: Kunga Tenzin (1680-1729)

The IVth Khamtrul Rinpoche: Choskyi Nyima (1730-1780).

The Vth Khamtrul Rinpoche: Dupjud Nyima (1781-1847).

The VIth Khamtrul Rinpoche: Tenpai Nyima (1848-1907).

The VIIth Khamtrul Rinpoche: Sangye Tenzin (1908-1929).

The VIIIth Khamtrul Rinpoche: Donjud Nuima (born 1930), the present incarnation, lives in Tshijong (Himachal Pradesh) where he has established a Tibetan art and craft centre.

(III) The Bhutan Branch

As per a prediction by Drogon Tsangpa Gyare, his disciple Sangye Won took a disciple called Phajo Drogon. This disciple went to Bhutan. There, he founded the Tan Go monastery and spread *dharma* widely.

(IV) The Drigung Branch

It was founded by Jigten Sumgun, of Khams. He founded the Drigung monastery in 1179 and had many fine disciples. He attained perfection and became a great Siddha.

> "Half the Tibetan people are Drukpas,
> Half the Drukpas are begging ascetics,
> Half the begging ascetics are Saints"

(A popular Tibetan saying).

Appendix D

Fiery Dragons: A Brief History of Tibet

The present-day loyalties, rivalries and acrimony amongst the Himalaya's lamas in exile in India have a direct connection with what happened in Tibet and China during the last millennium and before that. Their mentalities and actions are governed, to a large extent, by episodes from the past.

It dates back to the *Mahabharat* period. During the mythological war of *Mahabharat* between the five Pandavas and the twelve legions of the Kauravas, a prince, named Rupati, deserted the battlefield and fled towards the snowy country of Tibet. Fearful of being pursued by the enemy or by his suzerain for deserting the field, he donned female attire, and with about 1000 followers took shelter in Tibet. He reached the country Pugyal (the ancient name of Tibet, which in later times was called Bod.) The land was inhabited predominantly by a race still in a primitive state. The inhabitants welcomed him and adopted him as their king. His mild and peaceful manners won him their affection and he ruled over them for many years.

Under his and his descendants' rule, the people enjoyed prosperity and developed the arts. From Rupati to the foundation of monarchy in Tibet by Nahthi Tsanpo, in the beginning of the fourth century before the birth of Christ (BC), the history of Tibet is very obscure. During this long interval, after the fall of the house of Rupati, the country was partitioned into several petty states, ruled by insignificant native chieftains and princes.

Among the Tibetan ancient records, the *Debther-Nonpo* and the *Chho Jun* are unique and rare historical records as their authors appear to have been less influenced by love for fanaticism and miracles, which marks all early oriental writings. According to the records, the country was peopled at the same time as India, in the beginning of the present *kalpa*, a fact accepted by most modern native historians. The *Gyal-rab* or royal pedigree, written by the Vth Gyalwa Karmapa Rinpoche, and *Mani Kahbum*, one of the oldest legendary works, ascribed to King Srongtsan Gampo, besides other works of historical fiction, give altogether a different and fabulous account of the origin of the Tibetans.

Bon Period (416 BC to 617 AD)

In 416 BC, 417 years after the *nirvana* of the Buddha, Nahthi Tsanpo, the first of the Tibetan kings who established universal sway over Tibet, was born in India. He was the fifth son of King Prasanjit of Kosala. Endowed with obliquely drawn eyes and light blue irises, the colour of turquoise, he was born into a royal family of undefiled race in order to spread Buddhism in Tibet. The spirit of Cheenressig entered into him to make him one of the dynasty-holders of Prasanjit.

At birth, the infant was found possessed of webbed fingers and two rows of teeth, fully developed, and white as a conch shell. Apprehending great evil from such ominous signs in the infant, the parents packed him up in a copper vessel and dumped it in the river Ganga. The vessel was found by a farmer. He carried it to his wife who nursed the infant. Being a simple-hearted man, the farmer did not try to pass off the child as his own and revealed the truth; and the strange story of the foundling spread like wildfire.

Informed of the antecedents of his life, how he had been thrown into the Ganga by his royal parents and nursed by the good farmer's wife, the young mind was overcast with sorrow. Born a prince, he could not bring himself to adapt to the lowly pursuits of a farmer's life. After great anxiety and melancholy, he quit the farmer's house, bidding his country a mournful farewell, with a firm determination to either reign as a king or not live at all.

He proceeded northward to the Himalayan mountains where he subsisted on wild fruit. Unmindful of the difficulties of a mountainous journey or of death, he travelled further and further north till by the blessing of Cheenressig (Avalokiteshwara) he arrived at the summit of the Lhari, snowy mountains of Tibet. His heart was gladdened by the sight of land on the north which was gradually descending as it were from heaven. Down the slopes, he arrived at Tsanthan, a great plateau with four passages on its four sides. Here he met many natives, who were struck by the graceful looks of the stranger. They asked him respectfully who he was and where he came from. He replied to them by signs (for he did not know their language) that he was a prince, and pointing his finger towards the top of Lhari, he showed the direction he had come from. The Tibetans, who were sure they had seen him coming from the direction of heaven, took him for a god who had descended from the celestial regions.

Prostrating before him, they entreated him to be their king, an offer which he gladly accepted. Then placing him on a chair, they carried him in a solemn procession to the central part of the country. From being borne on the back of men, seated on a chair, he was called by the name of Nahthi Tsanpo. He renovated the great palace of Yumbu Lagan, on the site of which Lhasa was built in later days. He married a Tibetan woman named Nam Mug-mug who, says the legend, was a fairy. He was succeeded by his son, Digum Tsanpo who was killed by his own minister in an internecine war.

The minister, Lonam, married one of the widows of the late king, usurped the throne and obliged the three princes to fly towards Konpo. The usurper reigned for several years. The widow of the late king and mother of the three princes, by invoking the goblin Yarlha Sampo, got a son, who eventually rose to the post of minister and killed the usurper. He now invited the three exiled princes from Konpo, the eldest of whom ascended his ancestral throne. These kings are said to have ascended to the skies, being carried there by their queens who were regarded as celestial beings, in consequence of which their mortal relics were not left on earth. The ancient Tibetans, while giving an Aryan origin to their first sovereigns, did not fail to show greater regard for their country by giving their princes an altogether divine origin. All the queens of the monarchs were believed to be superhuman beings, such as fairies and sirens, who had assumed human form for enjoyment of earthly pleasures. They were believed to have gone to heaven with their bodies, taking their husbands with them. All the princes were said to be particularly favoured by Cheenressig (Avalokiteshwara), though Buddhism was as yet unknown in Tibet.

In fact, those princesses were not chosen from Tibetan subjects but from the families of the independent sovereign princes of the border countries. In Tibet, a princess is called *Lhmo* (goddess). The queens who came next in succession were generally taken from among the subjects, and were therefore of human origin. The names of all these kings were formed by a combination of the names of their parents, the mother's name generally preceding that of the father.

It was in the 23rd generation of the royal succession that the Bon religion rose to the zenith of its power, and when the sun of Buddhism was shining in its meridian lustre all over Jambudipa, snow-girdled Tibet remained buried in the 'impenetrable darkness' of Bon mysticism.

Bon was a primitive type of religion with the dominating streak of *shamanism*, a kind of sorcery working on psychic levels, a form of nature worship combined with sacrifice to vaguely defined gods of earth and sky. Shamanism is classified by anthropologists as an archaic magico-religious phenomenon in which the *shaman* is the great master of ecstasy. Shamanism is defined as a technique of ecstasy. A *shaman* may exhibit a particular magical speciality (such as control over fire, wind or magical fight). The distinguishing characteristics of *shamanism* are its focus on an ecstatic trance state in which the soul of the *shaman* is believed to leave the body and ascend to the sky (heavens) or descend into the netherworld. The *shaman* employs spirit helpers, with whom he or she communicates, while retaining control over his or her own consciousness. (Example of possession occurs, but is an exception rather than the rule.)

A *shaman* is not just an initiate who has received inner and outer training, but is a master of *shamanic* journeying and techniques (ecstasy). They are the link between this world and the next. This is considered a sacred trust and a service to the community.

In 441 AD was born the famous Tibetan King Lhathothori Nantsan, believed to be the incarnation of Kuntu Tsan. He ascended the throne in the 21st year of his age. When he reached the 80th year of his age, in the year 521 AD, there fell from heaven on the top of the great palace of Yumbu Lagan a precious chest, which was found to contain *sutrantra pitaka*, a golden miniature shrine, a sacred treatise on palmistry and mysticism, and a *chintamani* gem and cup.

Being the first prince who was favoured by heaven with the precious gift of the sacred treasures, Lhathothori Nantsan has been deified by the Tibetans. Once, when the king, sitting in council with his ministers, was debating on the value and merit of the divine gift, there was heard a voice from heaven, saying that in the eighth generation the meaning of the contents should be revealed.

The king, therefore, carefully preserved them under the name of *Sanwa Nanpo* in his palace. Everyday he offered oblations to them. In consequence of such a rare instance of good fortune, the king retained his youthful vigour even at the advanced age of fourscore and ten. He died in 561 AD at the ripe age of 120, after a prosperous reign of a full century.

His great-grandson was disqualified from ascending the throne on account of his blindness. As there was neither a male heir, nor any possibility of the queen giving birth to a second son, the blind boy after a short interregnum was placed on the throne. At his coronation, the sacred treasures called *Sanwa Nanpo* were worshipped, by virtue of which the blind king regained his sight. The first object that he saw being a *nan* (wild sheep) running on the Tagri hill near Lhasa, he was given the name of Tagri Nan Tsig (the seer of *ovis ammon* on the Tagri hills).

During the reign of his son, Namri Lontsan, the Tibetans got their first knowledge of arithmetic and medicine from China. It is said the prosperity and cattle-wealth of the country was so great during this period that the king built his palace with lime moistened with the milk of the cow and the yak. Once, riding his fleet-footed steed which he had obtained from the banks of Bragsum Dinma lake (north of Lhasa, not more than 20 mile round), he arrived at the northern desert plain where he slew a fierce *don* (wild yak) with terrible horns. Riding fast, he dropped the carcass of the yak, which he had bound with the straps of his saddle. In order to take it up, the king alighted from his horse. He found himself on an extensive salt bank. This was the inexhaustible mine which still supplies the large portion of Tibet with salt. Before the discovery of this salt mine, there was a very scanty supply of salt in Tibet. Namri Lontsan died in 629 AD, leaving the throne to his son, Srongtsan Gampo, with whom opened a new era in the history of Tibet.

In the sacred books of Kalchakra, *Manjusri mulatantra* and *Ashta-sahasrika*, the Buddha foretold that his religion would be widely diffused in the snowy country of the north, where many saints would also appear.

With the antiquity of *tantra* tracing back to the Indus civilisation and with Mount Kailash as the focal point in *tantra*, there were regular contacts and exchanges between the *siddhas* on both sides of the Himalayas in pre-Buddhist and even pre-Vedic time. Some scholars surmise that the Indian *tantra* was even developed from the pre-Buddhist native religion of Tibet called Bon. On the other hand, the Tibetans believe that their *tantrayana* was imported from India.

The advent of Buddhism in Tibet opened a fresh chapter not only in the history of Tibet but also in the history of Asia and this chapter closed in the middle of the twentieth century with the occupation of Tibet by China.

Srongtsan, the most illustrious in the Buddhist annals of Tibet, was born around 610 AD. When he was in the womb, his mother had a vision that a saintly prince would be born of her. She, therefore, kept aloof from any defilement or unholy thing, in consequence of which she remained happy and cheerful. During this time the elder queen Namnan, jealous of Queen Kunju, feigned pregnancy by wrapping a cubit's length of cotton rag every day around her belly. When Kunju's time for delivery came, Namnan induced a midwife to give the former anaesthetic liquor. Kunju lost her senses and soon gave birth to a son, which the wicked Namnan removed to her chamber and replaced it with a female child of inferior parentage born the same day. As soon as she recovered her senses, Kunju was surprised to see a daughter instead of a son, about whom she had seen so many things in her dreams. Meanwhile, the news of Queen Namnan giving birth to a son reached the king and his ministers, who all came to witness the blessed child.

Queen Kunju, who was sidelined, strongly suspected her jealous counterpart. But in the absence of witnesses, she was unable to charge Namnan and so kept her grief to herself. Some of the ministers, who knew of the plot, dared not speak against Namnan. Kunju, however, once complained to the king about the probable wickedness, but as Namnan had, by taking some drugs, producd milk in her breasts, Kunju could not establish her case. Consumed with the desire for revenge she tried to bring damnation on Tibet by means of her incantations, and wrote treatises construing astrology in a perverse way.

When the prince was three, the king invited the maternal relatives of the prince and the princess to a grand festive celebration. Before all the nobles, chiefs and ministers of the realm, the king seated the prince and the princess on either side. Taking a cup full of wine in his hand, he addressed the former "My son, take this cup of wine and with your tender hands offer it to your maternal uncle." To the utter amazement of all present, the prince at once presented it to Kunju's brother, the Chinese prince, whom he thus addressed "I, Srongtsan, am thy nephew Namnan is not my mother, though she has nursed me for a period of three years. I now meet my maternal uncle, and my heart rejoices to behold him."

These words of the child prince filled all present with wonder. Namnan's wickedness was at last revealed, and she was overawed with shame. Kunju was overwhelmed with joy when the king presented the child to her. She now exerted herself to avert some of the evils she had brought on Tibet by her incantations; but as she did not fully succeed in correcting astrology, it is said that the Tibetans cannot make correct calculations.

Buddhist Period (630-917 AD)

The first recorded event in Sino-Tibetan relations took place around 635 AD. The thirty-third Tibetan king, Srongtsan Gampo, married a Nepali princess, Belsa (Bhrikuti in Nepali), which brought him seven precious dowers, the images of Aksobhya and Maitreya, a sandal-image of Tara, the gem named Ratnadeva and a mendicant's platter made of Vaidurya. She was said to be the incarnation of goddess Saraswati.

Then, hearing about the extraordinary beauty of the Chinese princess, Gyalsa (Wencheng in Chinese), the daughter of the King Thai-Tsung, son of the founder of the Tang dynasty, the king sent his celebrated minister Gar Tongstan to China. After repeated negotiations the proposal was finalised. There are stories galore about this marriage. According to one, as the number of candidates for the princess's hand was very large and the king, unable to decide whom to choose, at last declared that he would bestow the princess on that prince whose minister by dint of sharpness of sense and quickness of understanding would stand first in merit and intelligence. In the first ordeal, the king laid before the assembled ministers a hollow coil buckler of turquoise, with one end terminating in the centre and the other at the edge. He asked them to pass a string through the aperture of the coil from one end to the other. All failed except the shrewd Tibetan minister Gar Tongstan. He tied one end of the thread to the narrow waist of a queen ant and gently blew it forward through the coil. The ant, dragging the thread easily, came out at the other end to the great wonder of all.

The king, reluctant to send his favourite daughter to such a distant and barbarous country as Tibet, devised repeated trials. However, in all these, the cunning minister acquitted himself well. The reluctance of the king was at last overcome by various contrivances, but he made one last bid to outwit Gar Tongtsan. Five hundred beautiful girls of the princess's age were dressed exactly like her and along with her exhibited before the assembled ambassadors. The shrewd Tibetan had studied the countenance of the princess. Moreover having learnt the king's design, he had taken some tips on how to identify the princess from an old nurse in the royal household. Thus armed, the minister Gar Tongtsan at once recognised the real princess and gently pulling the edge of her robe, claimed her for his liege lord. The trials ended here.

When it was fully settled that the princess should go to Tibet, she addressed the king, "Sire, as it has pleased your Imperial Majesty to send me to Bod, a country where there is no religion, I pray that you will allow me to take with me the great image of the Buddha, and several volumes of Buddhist scriptures, besides a few treatises on medicine and astrology." The king accordingly granted her prayer and gave these as part of her dowry. The Chinese princess was revered as the incarnation of goddess Tara. It was an example of an equal if not weaker sovereign offering his daughter to a stronger one, as Tibet was militarily superior to China at the time. However, Gampo's was not a politically motivated marriage. The Tibetan chronicles emphatically state that the king married two foreign princesses in order to get the two most venerable images of the Buddha for Tibet.

The union of incarnation of Cheenressig (Avalokiteshwara) in Srongtsan, and of the two incarnations of the divine mothers (Saraswati and Tara) in the persons of the two princesses produced great joy and happiness in the palace of Yumbu Lagan. The two princesses coming from two great centres of Buddhism, viz., China and Nepal, jointly exerted their influence for the propagation of Buddhism. They prevailed upon the king to introduce Saddharma, i.e. Buddhism in Tibet, which in course of time became the state religion of Tibet. The king thus became very famous in the history of Tibet and was known as Chosrgyal (Dharmaraja).

Tibet, being situated in the centre of the four great continents, like the heaving breast of a Srinmo (Amazonian woman), the king thought of making it the fountain of religion by filling it with monasteries. In 639 AD the king founded Lhasa, the renowned capital of Tibet. The hill called Chagpori was considered the heart of the country. The king erected his new palace upon it. Srongtsan died in 649 AD and was succeeded by his grandson, Mangsong Mantsen, who was still a child. In 654 AD Gar Tongtsan, in the name of the Tibetan *tsanpo* (emperor), composed the first Tibetan legal code, established military administrative divisions, and prepared a census of Tibetan subjects and a measurement of agricultural fields for purposes of taxation. Mantsen died in 667 AD. Sino-Tibet conflicts were frequent in those days.

The Gar clan, which had dominated Tibetan politics for some forty years, was challenged by a strong *tsanpo* (emperor), Khri Dusong Mangje. In 704 AD Dusong died. His successor, Tride Tsugtsen, was a minor. Therefore, his mother, Trimalo, served as regent. Trimalo, a devout Buddhist, took the initiative to arrange peace with the Chinese by means of another marriage alliance. Her son, however, was not inclined towards this policy. He sent his armies to invade China. But the Tibetans were repulsed. Subsequently, an immense Chinese army marched upon Tibet with great uproar. Panic seized the Tibetans. They concealed the gold image of Sakya, brought by the Chinese princess, in the southern niches of the great temple near the gate called Melonchan, and deserted Lhasa. Soon after, the Chinese army overran the city and set ablaze the palace of Yumbu Lagan. They also succeeded in carrying Aksobhya's image for some distance, but because of its unwieldiness they left it behind. King Tsugtsen died at the early age of 27.

Trimalo was now able to revive her desire to improve relations with China and enter into matrimonial alliance with China. She did it on behalf of Tride Tsugtsen's son, and her grandson, Megasthom. The Tang Emperor, who was dominated by the Empress Dowager, a devout Buddhist, granted the request in 707 AD, and the princess, Jincheng, was sent to Tibet.

Megasthom discovered an inscription of his illustrious forefather which contained the prophecy that in the eighth generation Buddhism would greatly flourish. Megasthom's son Jantsha Lha was famous for his extraordinary beauty. The king sent messengers all over Tibet to find a match for the prince but to no avail. At last, he sent an ambassador to China, to propose a marriage between his son and the accomplished princess Kyimshan Kunju, the daughter of the Emperor Waijun. The princess, hearing the account of the extraordinary beauty of the Tibetan prince, prayed to her father to consent to the marriage, to which he at last acceded; and the princess started for Tibet. In the meantime one of the Tibetan chiefs, enraged at his king for not selecting his daughter as the prince's wife, treacherously murdered the prince. The king dispatched messengers to convey the bad news to the princess who was on her way to Tibet.

The princess, though deeply disappointed, did not want to return to China. Her fancy was captured by the snowy country of Tibet, and more especially the celebrated image of Sakya. She continued her journey to Tibet, where she was warmly welcomed by the king. She brought to light the hidden image of Sakya which had received no offerings for the last three generations, having been concealed near the gate Melonchan. Her beauty so charmed the king that he at once proposed to marry her. The princess at first declined, but after long deliberation she yielded, and to the great wonder and joy of the people the betrothed daughter-in-law became the bride of the father. She gave birth to the famous monarch Khri Srong Detsan, believed to be the incarnation of Manjusri, the god of wisdom and learning.

However, the Buddhist presence in Tibet remained superficial for another century. In fact, the progress of Buddhism was by no means smooth for the first 200 years as it had to reckon with the hostility of the Bon, the native religion. It was deeply rooted not only in the mind of the common man but was also strongly entrenched in the court itself. Ministers and even members of the royalty were often ambivalent and some of them continued to be diehard. The Bon priests disputed the authority of the Indian monks and challenged them to polemics and mysteries. Victory in doctrinal debates was easy for the scholar-monks who no doubt emphasized the doctrine of salvation for all. The field of magic was, however, not convenient for the monks from India as only a few of them were adepts in *tantra*.

During the reign of Detsan (756-97), the Buddhist monks failed to match the Bon priests in performing miracles. The Bon elements in the court proclaimed the foreigners' defeat and reconverted the bulk of the population into their native faith. But the king did not yield and invited the Indian monk

Santaraksita to establish the first monastery at Samye. In order to accomplish his purpose, Santaraksita is said to have had to call on another Indian *yogi*, and famous master of *tantra*, Guru Padmasambhava, who was considered as an emanation of Manju-Ghosa. The Guru answered the call and reached Samye or Lhasa, overcoming en route the demons set up by the Bon magicians, and, in a number of bouts, conclusively proved the superiority of Buddhist *tantra*. For example, he could divert a hailstorm conjured up by the native priests while the latter could not contain a similar scourge set by the Guru. In short, the superiority of Buddhist magic was indisputable and *dharma* emerged victorious in the field of mysteries also. Ambivalent believers soon sought refuge in Buddhism.

Another story says that his ministers were divided into two factions, designated the 'Buddhist' and the 'Heretic' ministers. The first faction, or *chhoilon*, advised the young king to encourage Buddhism, while their antagonists exhorted him to extirpate Buddhism from Tibet, which according to them had been productive of pernicious consequences. Despite opposition, the king, because of his great inclination towards Buddhism, sided with the former. The Buddhist party now, with the king's connivance, entered into a conspiracy against the life of Mashan, the minister. They managed the soothsayers and astrologers to declare that some great calamity was imminent over the king which could only be averted by two of the high officers of the kingdom entering grave-like cells and remaining there for a period of three months. The king, therefore, offered large presents to those who would undergo this self-sacrifice. The minister Mashan volunteered to do so, and was followed by the Buddhist minister. They both entered the cell, the depth of which was three times a man's height. At midnight, the Buddhist minister's friends threw a rope into the cell by means of which he climbed up and escaped. The unfortunate Mashan was left alone there, to realise the horrors of the cell. His mortal enemies, the 'Buddhist ministers', blocked the mouth of the cell with a huge rock and buried him alive.

In the meantime, King Detsan applied himself to study and undertake the critical examination of the ancient records in the archives of the state. The Buddhism introduced by him was not its pure form, but was an admixture of Buddhism and Shamanism prevalent in the Himalayan regions. But Buddhism which was introduced in Tibet by Padmasambhava was Mahayana with elements of *tantra* therein.

On Detsan's forehead there was an excrescence believed to be a symbolic representation of the Amitabha, the Buddha of Boundless Light. Though bright and lustrous, he kept it covered with a red satin headband. During his reign were discovered, in certain caverns of rocks and recesses of mountains, many self-created images of Cheenressig (Avalokiteshwara), the divine mother Tara, Hayagriva and other gods, besides many inscriptions including the six mystic syllables *Om-mani-padme-hum*.

The king made obeisance to these images. Toiling personally, he enlisted his subjects to build a lofty nine-storeyed palace atop the hill, where Potala now stands like a phoenix. He was a learned man and warlike too. He extended his conquests to the surrounding countries, and brought the neighbouring princes under his suzerainty. Having attended to matters military, he devoted his attention to the propagation of Buddhism in Tibet. Through royal edicts, he made his subjects to observe the ten virtues: (a) not to commit murder; (b) not to commit theft; (c) not to commit adultery; (d) not to utter lies; (e) not to speak evil or utter abusive language; (f) not to talk nonsense; (g) not to slander; (h) not to be covetous; (i) not to think on injury; and (j) not to be averse to truth; besides the sixteen moral virtues: to have faith in *Konchhog* (god), study religious observance, to honour one's parents, to respect the meritorious and promote the talented, honour the elders as well as those who are of high birth, pay attention to relatives and friends, be patriotic and useful to one's own country, be honest and upright, know the good use of food and wealth, follow the example of the good, be grateful and return the kindness to benefactors, use just weights and measures, be free from jealousy by establishing concord and harmony with all, not to listen to the words of women, be gentle and polite in speech and acquire skill in conversation, and to bear sufferings and distress with patience and meekness.

Santarakshita undertook the responsibility of explaining to his pupils the sacred literature ranging from the Vinaya to the Madhyamaka philosophy. Padmasambhava and his colleagues taught the *tantras* to a few intelligent pupils, which enabled a few pious persons to obtain sainthood. Padmasambhava is still worshipped as the second Buddha and his image finds place by the side of the Buddha in some parts of Tibet, Sikkim and Bhutan in *lhakhangs* (temples) and *gompas* (monasteries).

Buddhism as a universal religion acclimatized itself to the native genius of the country and the Guru's cult of Vajra undoubtedly became the national cult of Tibet. Under this impact even the Bon priests had to admit ideas and images of Buddhism into their creed, though a contra or wrong meaning was read into each adaptation. Thus Buddhism did come to stay in Tibet in one form or the other.

The few Chinese exponents of *dharma*, who used to visit Tibet from the time of Srongtsan Gampo's marriage with a Chinese princess, failed to comprehend the moral and spiritual needs of the 'barbarian' of Tibet. A Chinese sage named Hwashan came to Tibet to preach a strange form of sophistry. He held that the pursuit of evil as well as of good binds men equally to a course of recurring existence, and therefore affords no means of emancipation. In illustration of this theory, he observed — "Your condition remains the same whether you are bound by an iron or a golden chain; you are not liberated. Therefore, if the mind is purged of all thoughts, deliverance from recurring existence is secured." The doctrine which he promulgated was accepted by Tibetans; and for a time the philosophy and doctrine of the former Indian pandits such as Santarakshita were displaced, for the Chinese sage vanquished all in disputation by his powerful logic. The followers of Santarakshita and other Indian philosophers diminished in number. In order to counter Hwashan's philosophy, the king invited Kamalasila, a very learned sage of that age, for a debate with the Chinese philosopher. In the final debate, the assembly of believers voted for the Indian exponent. Both views, it is now found, were correct but the Indian master had spoken the Tibetan mind. Hwashan was defeated in disputation, and his fallacies were exposed by Kamalasila in three series of books on meditative science. Kamalasila thus re-established the Indian school, its ritual and philosophy. The Tibetans ceremoniously expelled the Chinese exponent and banned the propagation of the Chinese brand of *dharma* in Tibet forever.

Both Santarakshita and Kamalasila belonged to the Svatantra-madhyamaka school. Srongtsan, who was a devout follower of Santarakshita, forbade his subjects by royal proclamation from following Hwashan's theories under penalty of death. He ordered everyone to follow the Madhyamaka school. Although certain Indian pandits of the Yogacharya school had visited Tibet, they failed to displace the anciently propagated Svatantra-madhyamaka school, which prevailed in Tibet till the accession of Langdarma to the monarchy of Tibet, when the last vestige of Buddhism disappeared from Tibet.

Padmasambhava came to be adored as Guru Rimpoche, that is, Guru Ratna. Guru Rimpoche was indeed the saviour of Buddhism in Tibet. While his miracles are a matter of belief, his achievements are factual. Besides proving the superiority of Buddhism over Bon, the Guru handled the great problem of a foreign religion with high statesmanship. He felt the imperative need for nationalising the church. Aided by Santaraksita, he ordained the first seven natives into the *sangha*, thereby, founding the Lamaist Order. The Guru and Santarakshita helped the king build a monastery on the river Tsangpo (Brahamputra); it was modelled on Odantapuri and named after Achintyapuri as Samye. Significantly enough some Bon mystic practices which, if not identical with, were not unlike the rituals of *tantra*.

Detsan had several wives, among whom Tshepon Ssah was his favourite, by whom he had three sons. After a prosperous reign of 46 years, at the age of 59, he ascended to heaven. The eldest prince, Muni Tsanpo, succeeded Detsan to the throne. But before a year and nine months passed after his demonstration of devotion to the monastery, the promising king was poisoned by his mother, who wished to place her youngest son on the throne. The second son's accession to the throne being considered inauspicious by the astrologers and soothsayers, the youngest son, Mutig Tsanpo, a boy eight or nine years old, was crowned. He is said to have miraculously received his lesson in sacred literature from the venerable Padmasambhava. He died at a ripe old age, leaving five sons. The eldest two seemed to have reigned, if they reigned at all, for a few years, having fallen victims to the intrigues of the Buddhist ministers.

The youngest Ralpacan, even from his childhood, gave excellent proof of his intelligence and ability. His assiduity and aptitude for learning were very great. At the age of 18, he was raised to the throne by the Buddhist ministers who were very powerful, opposition being nearly extinct through the continued and rigorous persecution of the late kings.

Ralpacan, the fortieth king, was a Buddhist devotee, but a sickly and weak ruler who neglected state affairs. He invaded western China at the beginning of the ninth century. However, Chinese monks and Tibetan lamas mediated to bring peace. Lake Kokonor was declared the Sino-Tibetan border in the east, and the boundary was marked by stone pillars, erected in 821 AD. Similar pillars were erected in front of the imperial Palace in Changan and the Potala Palace in Lhasa. Mutual pledges were inscribed on these pillars both in Chinese and Tibetan stating that neither China nor Tibet should violate the newly-defined borderline. During his reign King Ralpacan organised the Buddhist Sangha and erected many temples and monasteries. He also invited several Indian pandits for translating religious books into Tibetan.

Contemporary chronicles describe King Ralpacan's expanded kingdom in poetic terms: 'Solong-Shen mountain like a curtain of white silk was the (eastern) frontier with the Chinese king of astrology; an iron pillar near the river Ganga was the (southern) frontier with the Indian king of *dharma*; the gate of Pata Shadung was the (western) frontier with the Persian king of wealth; and the ridge of sand resembling the back of Nyamangma was the (northern) frontier with the king of Beta.'

But he met an unnatural death. Two ruffians, hired by the corrupt ministers, assassinated the king by twisting his neck to the back at the instigation of his brother, Langdarma, whose claim to the throne had earlier been set aside by the 'pious' ministers. After the assassination of Ralpacan, his younger brother, Tamo (Darma), succeeded to the throne. Tamo was fond of wine, a lover of field sports, and devoted to women, cruel, tyrannical, and ungracious. No wonder the troubles of the state increased.

The events that brought Ralpacan's brother, Langdarma, to power in 839 AD also resulted in the downfall of the Tibetan dynasty. In contrast to Ralpacan, Langdarma persecuted Buddhism and the clans that supported Buddhism in favour of Bon and its proponents. To slander the Buddha in blasphemous language was his great delight, and in no discourse did he indulge himself so much as in reviling the holy personage. Not content with demolishing the temples and monasteries of the country, he wreaked havoc even on the sacred shrines of Akshobhya and Sakya. He tried to throw those two images into water. However, he was restrained by some of his 'pious' ministers who pointed out to him the difficulty of lifting those heavy statues. He then contented himself by burying them in sand. On the verge of demolishing the temples of Sakya and Akshobhya, in Lhasa and Samye, respectively, he was forewarned that the guardian demons of those places would send plagues and ruin upon him if he destroyed the temples. Afraid of exciting the wrath of those dreaded spirits, he spared their charges, and satisfied himself with sealing their doors with mud walls. To please him, his ministers and flatterers painted those walls with abominable depictions of the drunken and lustful moods of human depravity.

While the King was thus engaged in overthrowing the sacred religion as well as its relics, saint Lhalunpal Dorje, sitting in deep contemplation in Yarpalbari mountain, had a vision. Goddess Palden Lhamo descending from heaven appeared before him and exhorted him in the following terms: "Oh saint, in these days there is none so powerful as thou. Wouldst thou deliver the country from the hands of that sinful tyrant Langdarma?" Next morning, the saint asked his servant about the condition of Tibet. The servant told him of the cruelties practised by Langdarma. The saint then mounted his white charger whose body he besmeared with charcoal. Clad in a black robe with white lining, with no other weapons than an arrow and a bow in his hands, he reached Lhasa.

The sleeves of the saint's robe were unusually wide so as to make room for the bow and arrow. The king was surrounded by his ministers when the saint arrived, dancing and leaping frantically. All ran to witness the curious dance. The king asked him to come near. The saint pretended to prostrate before the king. In the first prostration he set the arrow and the bow right, in the second he fitted the arrow to the bow, and in the third killed the king with it. Hence the origin of the lama war dance and the use of broad-sleeved robes by the Tibetan lamas.

The arrow shot at the king's back pierced right through his body. The lama then exclaimed, "I am the demon Yasher, and this is the way of killing a sinful king." He leaped on his horse and sped away. As the king fell, his ministers and attendants cried, "the king is dead, the king is dead," and the mob ran after the assassin, but the saint, spurring his horse, shot away like a meteor. While crossing a river the coal-black colour of the horse was washed away, revealing its white coat. The saint turned his robe inside out so as to show the white, flew as God Namtheo Karpo and escaped, leaving his pursuers far behind.

The king pulled out the fatal arrow with his hands, and in the agonies of the death, when his proud heart was subdued with anguish, exclaimed — "Why was I not killed three years back that I might not have committed so much sin and mischief, or three years hence, to enable me to root out Buddhism from the country." These were the last words he was fated to utter. His head sunk on his chest and he died.

With Langdarma ended the monarchy of Tibet founded by Nahthi Tsanpo, and his descendants henceforth ceased to exercise universal authority over the whole of Tibet. The sun of royalty had set, and there rose up numerous petty princes to shine with faded lustre in the pale realm of snowy Tibet.

917 to 1270 AD

The wicked Langdarma had two wives, the elder of whom, perceiving that the other was in the family way, shammed pregnancy. She also tried to secretly kill the newly-born, delivered at dusk. Failing to kill it, she tried to steal the baby but again was thwarted due to a lighted lamp in the room. The child was therefore given the name of Namdo Hodsrun (one protected by light). The elder queen then bought a beggar's child and declared she had given birth to it the previous evening. The minister was aghast as to how a newly-born child could have its teeth fully grown. But not daring to contradict the elder queen, they gave the name Thide Yumten (one upheld by his mother) to the fake newly-born.

During the interregnum, the Buddhist ministers directed the affairs of the state. They endeavoured to revive all the religious institutions that were nearly extinct. They reinstated images in their former places and rebuilt demolished monasteries and temples. Notwithstanding their feeble efforts to rebuild the edifice ruthlessly pulled down by Langdarma, Buddhism did not reach its former condition until 70 years after the death of Ralpacan.

As soon as the princes came of age, they quarrelled and bickered for the possession of the throne. At last they divided the kingdom into two parts. Hodsrun took possession of western Tibet, and Yumten of the eastern provinces. The partition generated incessant quarrels and disturbances, with the brothers constantly engaging in wars against each other. Thus the descendants of Nahthi Tsanpo ceased to exercise universal sway over Tibet.

But this period witnessed the revival of Buddhism in Tibet. Tibetan Buddhist tradition identifies three kings as the primary promoters of Buddhism: Srongtsan Gampo (629-649), Khri Srong Detsan (754-797) and Ralpacan (815-838). In addition, the father of Khri Srong Detsan, Megasthom (704-754), and the father of Ralpacan, Sadnaleg (804-815) were known to have favoured and promoted Buddhism.

Chyan Chhub-hod, a ruler, acquired great proficiency both in Buddhism and heretical philosophies. Greatly interested in restoring Buddhism to its pristine glory, he searched for an eminent Indian pandit profoundly versed in all the *shastras* and particularly qualified in the three branches of Buddhism, viz. theory, meditation and practice of rites and observances, besides possessing a thorough acquaintance with all aspects of Buddhist learning. His emissaries sought out and exhorted Dipankara Atisha Srijnana, a Bengali monk of the 11th century (983-1054 AD) to reform Tibetan Buddhism which was becoming decadent. Atisha left India for Tibet in 1042 AD at the age of 59. Journeying through Tsang (western Tibet), he came across a little village in the state of Zangtu. At that time, Tibet had disintegrated into numerous petty states and principalities. There a miracle occurred. Atisha beheld a miraculously white, enormous disc, glowing with mystic symbols of the god Avalokiteshwara and the god Manjusri, on the centre of Ponto Hill. The hill formed a natural canopied backdrop to this blessed village. Dismounting, Atisha prostrated himself before the sacred signs. Today, a few weather-worn, yellowish mud-brick *chortens* (pagodas) stand as living monuments to Atisha's mystic trance. This place is called Chaktsal Gyap, the Pass of Prostration. At the place where the divine revelation took place is a conspicuous spot of white earth — *sakya* is the Tibetan for 'white earth'. He died at the age of 78 in 1055 AD.

Not till the arrival of Atisha did the condition of Buddhism in Tibet improve. Until then it had remained practically in a moribund condition. Atisha was renowned for his learning, renunciation and wide travel. He also brought with him *tantrik* Buddhism and reformed Buddhism in Tibet. As a consequence, there originated a new sect known as the Kadampa sect.

The sages Marpa, Milarepa, Gampopa, and Pandit Sakya Sri of Kashmir, besides many other Indian pandits who furthered the cause of Buddhism, belonged to the following centuries. Through translations of the *sutras* and *shastras*, Pandit Sakya Sri greatly promoted the diffusion of Buddhism. The ritual vow introduced by him was called *panchhen domgyum*. Similarly, the rituals introduced by Lachhen of Amdo were called *lachhen domgyum*. Buddhism managed to revive and flourish because by persecution the enemies of Buddhism had only succeeded in putting down the external observances and ritual of the clergy, while the real *dharma* and moral discipline continued to be secretly practised even under adverse circumstances. The basis of Buddhism being *vinaya* or moral discipline, the system of Domgyum is only necessary as an external observance.

Buddhism progressed more and more, branching out into numerous different orders as the result of its extraordinary growth. These, like the eighteen divisions of the Vaibhashika school of ancient India, were designated after the names of their respective teachers and places of origin. Some of the Tibetan lamas deriving their religious knowledge from Indian pandits and feeling great veneration for the theories themselves, named their respective sects after them. They did not follow the Indian patriarchs in their nomenclature, for all Indian Buddhist schools were designated after the general sense of their philosophies. For instance, the Sakya-pa, Jonan-pa, Shan-pa and Digun-pa sects of Tibet were designated after the names of the localities where they were taught and orginiated; the Karma-pa and Bulug-pa sects, after the names of their respective teachers; the Kadam-pa, Dsogchhen-pa, Chhyag-chhen-pa and Shi-chye-pa sects after their respective rituals or external *kriya*.

All the various Buddhist orders of Tibet are classified under two schools: the Ancient school and the Gelug or the Reformed school. The difference between the schools lies in the *tantras* only while the *sutras* remain the same in both.

Sakya Hierarchy (1270-1340 AD)

That Tibet was a great military power in Central Asia from the seventh to the ninth centuries is indisputable. The impact of Lamaism in every sphere of life in Tibet came to predominate. Lamaism killed the military spirit of Tibetans, and Tibet as a great military nation vanished forever. This change from the conquest of other nations to the conquest of the human mind was extremely sudden. The religious Tibetan will pray earnestly: 'May I be born in the land of Buddhism, Holy Tibet' — an attitude that indicates the spiritual height to which Tibet had been elevated. Mahayana Buddhism had been safely uprooted from its birthplace, India, and transplanted remarkably well in the alien cultural climate of Tibet. There it miraculously flourished.

Scores of pandits from India and Nepal spent their lives in Tibet, helping the Tibetan lamas translate Buddhist scriptures from Sanskrit into Tibetan; Tibetans studied Buddhism in India and returned home to transmit their knowledge. Tibet had certain rare Buddhist scriptures that were not available even in Sanskrit. Little wonder it was that Tibet came to be regarded as an 'abode of Buddhism', and that the Sakya lamas, Karmapas and, subsequently, the Dalai Lamas were thought to be *bodhisattvas*.

Tibet's status as the abode of Buddhisrn was maintained even at a time when it was split and rendered impotent after the reign of Langdarma. But this status was bound to be affected as a result of what then occurred — Chinghiz Khan's conquest and the rise of the Mongolian Empire.

Tibet crumbled and succumbed to the mighty warrior in the beginning of the thirteenth century. In the whole of Tibet, without much resistance, the different chieftains and petty princes became his abject vassals.

The Mongols under Chinghiz Khan attacked the Tangut in China in 1227. He was killed during the campaign, in retaliation for which the Tangut state was almost completely destroyed. Some of the residents of Tangut fled to Tibet. Chinghiz was succeeded by his son, Ogadai. By 1234, the Mongols had conquered all of northern China. In 1236, Godan, the son of Ogadai, led a campaign against two provinces of China. In 1240, Godan again sent an expeditionary force. In 1241, all Mongol activities were suspended due to the death of Ogadai. Godan's forces withdrew from Tibet. Sakya Pandit arrived at the Mongol camp in 1245, but apparently met Godan only in 1247. Sakya Pandit then made his submission to Godan, and agreed to become the representative of the Mongol authority in Tibet.

It was the grandson of Chinghiz, Mongke Khan, who established an administrative centre at Hochow, in the present province of Kansu, and the pacification bureaus at six places, all along the western border of present Szechwan.

Khubilai, who had commanded the forces that overran eastern Tibet on his way in 1253 to conquer Ta-li (in Yunnan), enforced the pacification policy of the Mongke Khan with even greater energy. In 1269, he established a pacification bureau in Wussutsang, which was further in the interior of Tibet and dominated the two principal provinces, Dbus (U) and Gtsang (Tsang). Later, he divided Tibet into districts (Chun and Hsein) as in China and established various offices and a system of local government.

Apparently, Khubilai Khan found the turbulent and warlike Tibetans a difficult people to rule. He resolved to reduce them to a condition of docility through the influence of religion. Buddhism was reaffirmed as the religion best calculated to tame the wild tribesmen of Tibet, and as it had already secured a firm foothold there, the project was by no means an impractical one. The policy was effectively enforced, and the cooperation of the Sakya Pandit of the large monastery at Sakya was secured by extending invitation to him to the Mongolian court.

According to the Chinese records, Sakya Pandit's nephew Phagspa went to see Khubilai in 1253. Upon the return of Phagspa, Khubilai invited Karma Pakshi, the IInd Karmapa. He was known as a famous miracle-worker, and was reported to have astonished Khubilai by performing innumerable miracles. Khubilai is said to have entertained doubts that the Sakyas, represented by Phagspa, were as powerful as the Karmapa. Phagspa also performed an impressive miracle.

Phagspa asked for a sword and said, 'I shall transform my limbs into the five classes of Buddha, and you, Khan and ministers will get your request to be reborn in whichever of the five Buddha's fields you desire. If you do not so believe, visit where my limbless body rests on my bed!' He made the head Vairocana. The four limbs he transformed into the four other classes, and thus emerged the five classes of Buddhas. In 1254, or shortly thereafter, Phagspa conferred upon Khubilai initiations into the rites of Buddhism. Khubilai accepted Phagspa as his guru, or teacher in religious matters.

The Khan asked, "What precepts must be observed?" Phagspa replied, "Having requested initiation, the lama takes the higher seat. The devotee physically prostates (himself to the teacher) and heeds whatever he says; and (the devotee) must not act contrary to the thoughs (of the teacher)." The Khan said,

"I would not be able to observe such precepts." The dispute was mediated by Chabi, Khubilai's favourite wife. She had already been initiated by Phagspa; she had become a Buddhist and a strong supporter of Phagspa. She proposed, "There is a solution to that. The teacher shall occupy the higher seat when giving teachings and when (only) a few people are present. The Khan shall take the higher seat when there are large assemblies of men such as vassal rulers and lords. The affairs concerning Tibetan regions shall be done according to the words (of the teacher). The Khan shall not give orders without consulting the lama. Apart from that, in all other affairs, big or small, the lama need not be consulted."

Khubilai made a 'donation' to Phagspa of the thirteen myriarchies of western and central Tibet. As a second offering, Phagspa was given the three districts of Tibet: U-Tsang (central and western Tibet), Dotoh (Kham) and Domei (Amdo).

When Mongke died in 1259, Khubilai emerged victorious in the succession war between him and his younger brother. In 1260, Khubilai named Phagspa "National Preceptor" and conferred the title of Tisri on him. Then onwards Tibet came to be ruled by the Sakya lamas as a theocratic state. Phagspa was granted hereditary title to the throne and his successors the right to independent accession. He had received all the highest honours that could be conferred on a lama. He had a seat in Tibet called Sakya Jong. Eventually Tibetan blood-thirstyness was converted and submerged into a passion for spiritual satisfaction.

Phagspa died in 1280, at the age of forty-five. It was suspected that he was poisoned. The title 'Tisri' passed to another member of his family. The Sakya lamahood was hereditary. Twenty-eight such lamas in succession ruled over Tibet. They appointed their own subordinates without imperial consent. They established their own government, functioning quite independently in Sakya. During their reign, a number of Indian pandits visited Tibet, and Tibet's cultural relations with India became stronger than those with China. However, the tradition of sending a brother or son of the reigning Sakya lama to China as China's national mentor continued throughout the Sakya era.

Of all the Sakya lamas, Phagspa was undoubtedly the most illustrious and fortunate. But under his successors, things altered for the worse. Due to the imbecility of the regents, the prosperity of the people was greatly impeded, with chiefs and nobles fighting and quarrelling with each other. The Sakya hierarchies were mostly puppets in the hands of the regents. The regents frequently embroiled the country in feuds, and themselves in war with each other. Quarrelling, not to speak of insubordination, was the order of the day. Conspiracy, assassination and murder were rampant. One Mongol preferred one order, while his successor showered special favours to a different one, usually by means of giving land together with thousands of families for the maintenance of the monasteries under their charge. Numerous feudal chiefs were thus created. The Sakya priest-kings were reduced to mere figureheads.

China did not intervene in any way when in 1358 the twenty-eighth Sakya ruler was dethroned by the monk Changchub Gyaltsan, whose line ruled Tibet until 1435. This line ended in another struggle for supremacy. The founder of the new regime, Changchub Gyaltsan, better known by his name of Phagmodu, was a member of the famous Kagyu order, although he visited the Sakya monastery at the age of 14 and stayed there for some time. During a dispute with the chiefs, nobles, and lamas of U and Tsang, the Chinese emperor decided in his favour, and bestowed on him, to be enjoyed as hereditary possessions, the province of U, leaving Tsang to the Sakyas. Five years later, he defeated the Sakyas and other rivals on the battlefield and annexed Tsang and became the undisputed master of the whole of Tibet. As the Chinese emperor made an extensive search for learned lamas, he could not have missed the great reformer Je Tsongkhapa (1357-1419), the Luther of Tibet. The Emperor invited him to the court but the latter excused himself on the pretext of illness. In 1413 the Emperor again sent an envoy asking the great reformer to dispatch a disciple on his behalf, if he himself could not come. At this, Tsongkhapa complied and sent one of his outstanding disciples.

Earlier, in 1403, the Chinese ruler Ming Cheng-tsu invited the Vth Karmapa, Dheshim Shegpa, to his court to perform the

Buddhist faith and rebirth ritual for his predecessor. Cheng-tsu offered to send the Karmapa back to Tibet with titles and military escorts sufficient to establish the predominance of his sect over others in Tibet. The Karmapa refused the offer.

Tsongkhapa reformed Tibetan Buddhism drastically, and established a new order known as Gelug or the 'yellow hats'. (The Dalai and Panchen Lamas belong to this order.) Tsongkhapa was the most famous lama reformer; and his order was the most popular in Central Asia from the fourteenth century onwards.

During the civil strife, the Yellow order at first met with reverses in their struggle for power on account of the help which the powerful Chief of Tsang gave to the Red order. The Yellow order then sought the help of the Mongolian hordes, who helped them wrest back their lost territorial endowments and their beloved monasteries. The Chief of Tsang, failing in his military enterprise, also sought in vain help from Mongolian chiefs.

In the ensuing further bloodshed, the new dynasty founded by Kagyus of Tsang province to replace the Sakya was overthrown by the Mongolian army under Gushri Khan who, at the earnest entreaties of the Yellow order, marched into Tibet to punish their enemies. Victorious over an 40,000-strong Tartar army of Chogthu Khan of Kokonor, who espoused the cause of the Red order, and reinforced by his annihilation of King Beri of Kham, who followed the Bon religion and who, like Langdarma, had destroyed all the Buddhist institutions of Kham belonging to the Red and the Yellow orders, the formidable Gushri Khan had little difficulty overcoming the resistance of Tsang. He put the defeated monarch to death, proclaimed his authority over the whole country and made the Vth Dalai Lama, Ngawang Lobzang Gyatso, the undisputed spiritual ruler of Tibet.

Four kings of the Ringpong dynasty had ruled in succession from 1435 to 1565, followed by three Tsangpa kings between 1566 and 1645. In an otherwise almost static society, the only dynamism came from the Tibetan religious orders. These orders, founded obviously by the best available brains in Tibet, were responsible for every great movement in the country's cultural history.

The new order spread like wildfire in Mongolia. In 1578, Sonam Gyatso, the third 'pope' of the Yellow Hats, received the title 'Dalai Lama' from the Mongol ruler Altan Khan. 'Dalai' is Mongol for 'ocean', and refers to the extent of Sonam Gyatso's knowledge. The Dalai Lama is neither the formal head of Tibetan Buddhism — a kind of Tibetan Buddhist equivalent to the Pope — nor the head of the Gelug order. The Khan became a dedicated follower of the Yellow Hats, and his subjects readily followed his example. With the help of the Mongols, in the 1640s the Vth Dalai Lama established supremacy over the other orders; and so the Dalai Lama ruled Tibet until the 1959.

Even in historical records, we find descriptions that at the time, the religious protocol dictated that the IIIrd Dalai Lama, Sonam Gyatso, would have to pay obeisance firstly to the IXth Gyalwa Karmapa, Wangchuk Dorje, and then to the Vth Kunzig Shamar, Kunchok Yenlak, by doing prostrations before their thrones during the religious ceremonies. However, all that was about to change in the seventeenth century, when in no time the Mongolian warlord invited by the Vth Dalai Lama flattened several Nyingma monasteries, slew the Desi Tsangpa and at least 250 Kagyu monasteries were violently turned into Gelug strongholds. Within a short span of less than three centuries, there had been three major struggles for supremacy in Tibet, all among the Tibetans themselves.

Right after the Gelug leaders became the rulers of Tibet, political intimidation and religious restrictions were directed at the Nyingma, Sakya and Kagyu traditions in particular. Together with high taxes, derogatory laws were passed against those schools while exempting the ruling Gelug. The hostility and paranoia of losing power again led the ministers of the Dalai Lama to pass on harsh laws against his potential enemies. For example, the ministers of the Vth Dalai Lama, Lobzang Gyatso, decided that the Tsurphu monastery of the Karmapas could ordain no more than three monks a year. The recognition of *tulkus* carried out by the orders other than the Gelug have been, and are totally, independent of the Dalai Lama and his ministers. Ample evidence of this are the hundreds of incarnations autonomously recognised and enthroned by their respective spiritual hierarchs in the Nyingma, Kagyu and Sakya orders. In 1682, the Vth Dalai Lama died. Within the corridors of the Potala political intrigues lurked at every corner and the regent, Sangye Gyatso (reputed to have been the son of the Dalai Lama), kept the death of the pontiff a closely-guarded secret for about 15 years.

The VIth Dalai Lama, Lobsang Rigdzin Tshangyang Gyatsho, was a controversial figure. Instead of devoting himself to the study and practice of Buddhism, he spent his youth composing erotic verses. He would more often sneak away from the palace and make merry in the taverns of Lhasa. The name given to him by the Panchen Lama is translated as 'Precious Ocean of Pure Melody' and one wonders if the Panchen Lama had premonition that the young pontiff would one day be a writer of many songs. He was a true lover of wine, women and song, and of the latter he wrote many. His poems and songs were not pedantic but simple and expressive of the turmoil he was passing through. He wrote:

I went to my teacher, with devotion filled
To learn of the Lord Buddha
My teacher taught, but what he said escaped
For my mind was full of compassion,
Full of that Compassionate One who loves me,
She has stolen my mind.

He was the most enigmatic character in the history of Central Asia. Another unusual thing about him was that he was not Tibet-born but was from Tawang in Arunachal Pradesh, a state in India. He was extraordinary in many ways. He was a *tantrik*, an architect, an exponent of Tibetan monastic opera and, most of all, he was a man with human frailities. His antics and behaviour made the Tibetans and Mongols suspicious of his reincarnation. In 1706, the Chinese and Mongols murdered the young Dalai Lama, and installed a 25-year-old lama as the true incarnation. The Tibetans refused to recognise him, and discovered a new incarnation in Litang in eastern Tibet. The Mongols also seconded the Tibetan choice.

Fearing a Mongol-Tibetan alliance, the Chinese Emperor Kang Hsi dispatched an army in 1718, but the Tibetans and Mongols defeated the Chinese troops. Hence the Tibetan nominee was enthroned as the VIth Dalai Lama, disallowing Tsangyang Gyatso's tenure of office. However, Tsangyang Gyatso had then been reinstated as the VIth Dalai Lama, and his successor was known as the VIIth. The Chinese imperial army remained in Tibet until 1723, when the new Emperor Yung Ch'eng ordered their evacuation and handed back territory annexed by China during the crisis over the VIth Dalai Lama. The Chinese left behind two *ambans* (resident representatives of the emperor) with a small military escort in Lhasa.

In 1791, the Gurkhas of Nepal invaded Tibet and captured Shigatse. They were, however, defeated the following year by a combined Chinese-Tibetan army. The victory pillar erected by the Chinese in Lhasa states that the troops were composed of men from Solong, a district in the Tibetan province of Gyarong.

After the defeat of the Gurkhas, the Chinese *ambans* naturally got a stronger grip on the Tibetan administration. *Ambans* were posted at Shigatse, Tingri, Chamdo and Traya, and Tibetan officials, both lay and ecclesiastical, were ordered to submit all vital decisions to them. The Dalai Lamas were highly respected, once they reached maturity; between 1804 and 1876, four of them (the IXth, Xth, XIth and XIIth) died at the ages of nine, twenty-one, eighteen and nineteen, respectively. It is possible that the *ambans* had a hand in these premature deaths, for they could impose their authority on a regent more easily than on the Dalai Lama. The *ambans* were also to assist in the selection of the Dalai and Panchen Lamas, and an imperial order was issued on the procedure of selecting high incarnates. The *ambans* exercised active power from 1720 to about 1840, and thereafter their power was nominal.

When the Limbu tribe of Nepal invaded Tibet, China did not help the Tibetans expel them; nor did she help when a Sikh and Dogra force of about 5,000 under Zorawar Singh invaded western Tibet in 1841. Tibetan troops on their own expelled both the invaders. In 1855, Nepalese forces invaded for the second time, under the pretext that their subjects were being treated shabbily. The Nepalese were victorious, and a treaty was signed by which Nepal gained extraterritorial rights in Tibet. In 1863, the Chinese invaded Gyarong in Eastern Tibet and annexed it to China.

In 1890, the British Government in India wanted to establish trade relations with Tibet, but was uncertain whether to approach China or Tibet. Knowing that the Chinese authority extended in Tibet during the eighteenth century, the British contacted China, and in 1893 signed a convention with her, without Tibet's knowledge. But when Britain applied for concessions, the Tibetan government rejected the convention, and the British came to realise how little influence the Chinese had over Tibet actually. Lord Curzon, Viceroy of India in 1899, was compelled to regard Chinese control over Tibet as a 'constitutional fiction — a political affection which has only been maintained because of its convenience to both parties.'

In 1904, Lord Curzon despatched a military mission under Colonel Francis Younghusband to impose a trade agreement. The Tibetan troops were defeated, and the Dalai Lama's Regent signed a convention with the British in Lhasa. Seals of the Dalai Lama, the *kashag* (ministerial council), national assembly and of the three big monasteries were stamped on the agreement, but the Chinese were not signatories.

The British military expedition and the subsequent convention made the Chinese realise that their power in Tibet had disappeared. So in 1910 China invaded Tibet, and the Dalai Lama fled to India. But Chinese control was short-lived; in China, revolution broke out, and in 1912, the Tibetans drove the remaining Chinese forces out of Tibet. 'With that', writes the Dalai Lama, 'Tibet became completely independent, and from 1912 until the Chinese invasion in 1950 neither the Chinese nor any other state had any power whatsoever in Tibet.'

The International Commission of Jurists' report to the United Nations *The Question of Tibet and the Rule of Law* sums up conclusively: 'Tibet's position on the expulsion of the Chinese in 1912 can fairly be described as one of the de facto independence and there are, as explained, strong legal grounds for thinking that any form of legal subservience to China had vanished. It is, therefore, submitted that the events of 1911-12 made the re-emergence of Tibet as a fully sovereign state independent, in fact as well as in law, of Chinese control.'

For 38 years Tibet enjoyed de facto independence. She took no part in the Sino-Japanese war, refused permission to transport war supplies from India to China through Tibet during the Second World War, and participated in the conference of Asian countries held in Delhi. In 1948, she sent an official trade delegation with Tibetan passports which were recognised by India, China, France, Italy, Britain and the USA.

It was not only the fanatic and ignorant lamas but also the aristocrats, and specially the government officials, who were responsible for the tragedy of Tibet. Indifferent to their duty, they indulged in petty political squabbles and loose ways of living. It is said that, when the Amdo garrison fell to the invading Chinese army in 1950, an urgent message was sent to Lhasa. When the messenger arrived, he found the officials busy playing *mahjong* (a Tibetan indoor game). He was shouted down, told not to interrupt, and made to wait until they had finished their game.

After the XIIIth Dalai Lama's death in 1933, ill-feeling between the monks of the Sera monastery and the Lhasa government prevailed for years. Ultimately, the acrimony erupted in an armed clash. The abbot of the Reting monastery was appointed regent. Under him, his monastic staff made the most of the opportunity to make the Reting monastery rich and powerful, and it was rumoured that the abbot wanted to continue his rule indefinitely. Finally, in 1947, his political antagonists put him under arrest, and he died under mysterious circumstances.

The Tibetans are deeply religious. They perceive the Dalai Lama as the symbol of their religion, their culture and civilisation, if not political sovereignty, albeit it is psychological. Because, although the Tibetans both in and outside Tibet popularly perceive the Dalai Lama as their legitimate ruler, this does not mean the restoration of the ancient regime.

In the post-1950 period Sino-Tibetan conflicts, the Dalai Lama has increasingly figured as a pan-Tibetan figure, symbolising Tibetan cultural value and popular aspirations. He appears as the rallying point for ethnic mobilisation and opposition. As the head of the Tibetan government-in-exile and as a teacher of great spiritual authority in his own right, the present Dalai Lama remains a force for the Tibetan community's devotion and respect.

During the 1980s the portrait of the Dalai Lama became a symbol of Tibetan resistance. There grew a personality cult around the Dalai Lama and his family. The present Dalai Lama is a well-known media personality. He has also been conferred the coveted Nobel Prize for peace. Blessed with the good fortune of having authored and published ghost-written books, the constant Western mass media exposure has made him an instant hero in the present credulous and media-oriented age. A pastmaster at capturing the international media headlines, he has a charismatic influence among the Tibetans.

Panchen Lama

In the feudal power struggle, a characteristic of Tibet, the story of the Panchen Lama deserves mention in the annals of Tibet. In the time of the IIIrd Dalai Lama, the administration of the Tashilhunpo monastery at Shigatse was entrusted to a series of senior lamas who came to be regarded later as the predecessors of the Panchen Lamas. However, the formalisation and institutionalisation of the Panchen Lama owes its origin to the Vth Dalai Lama who declared that his tutor, Choekyi Gyaltsen (1570-1662), would reincarnate as the IInd Panchen Lama, and so the line continues up to this day. Before the Vth Dalai Lama's recognition, Tashilhunpo was headed by senior abbots, and not by reincarnates. They were simply called Panchen, a hybrid of two syllables: 'pan(dita)', a Sanskrit word meaning 'scholar' and 'chen(po)', Tibetan for 'great'. At that time, Tashilhunpo was endowed with three estates as its source of income.

In 1728, the then Panchen Lama was given considerable political power. During the Dzungar invasion (during which the then Tibetan authorities requested the Qing emperor to intervene on their behalf) the VIIth Dalai Lama and his family sided with the Dzungar forces. Partly to punish the Dalai Lama and partly to have a counter-balancing force within the Gelug hierarchy, the Qing emperor arranged that the Panchen should be made a ruler of Tsang (western Tibet). A special administrative office called *Chizong* (spyi-rzon) was established next to Tashilhunpo, administering sixteen districts in western Tibet from Shigatse. This was the beginning of the Chinese policy of divide and rule during the Gelug period of Tibetan history, which continues to this day.

When the XIIIth Dalai Lama began to consolidate his power and set in motion a certain degree of centralisation, the IXth Panchen Lama and Tashilhunpo were one of the first targets of the Tibetan government in Lhasa, as Tashilhunpo had been growing since 1728 as an autonomous local power centre due to Chinese and British encouragement. The XIIIth Dalai Lama's government sought to curtail the Panchen Lama's growing influence. Several of his estates were confiscated and political privileges of his court reduced. This created tension between Lhasa and Shigatse, and the IXth Panchen Lama and his entourage escaped to China in 1921. Both the British and the Chinese officials tried to intervene and mediate in this Dalai-Panchen dispute, but without much success, for at the heart of the dispute was a feudal power struggle. The Panchen Lama wanted a return to the earlier system (1728-1920) in which Tashilhunpo functioned autonomously from Lhasa. Besides, he wanted the right to maintain an armed force of his own. It was only after the XIIIth Dalai Lama's death that the IXth Panchen Lama could attempt to return to Tibet. He died en route in Jyejundo on 1 December, 1937.

In the Gelug historical records, the relations between the Dalai and Panchen Lamas are depicted as the 'sun' and the 'moon'; the 'father' and the 'son'. This idealistic state of affairs might have prevailed had the two parties not got embroiled in a political contest in Tibet, especially during the period 1445-1728. At such times, there was a kind of symbiotic or mutually beneficial relationship between the Dalai and Panchen Lamas. The incumbent, senior in age, tended to recognise the junior, giving sanctity and legitimacy to the 'new' lama. Thus, the IVth Panchen Lama recognised the Vth Dalai Lama. Subsequently, the Vth Dalai Lama recognised the Vth Panchen Lama. Later, the VIth Panchen Lama recognised the VIIIth Dalai Lama who, in turn, recognised the VIIth Panchen Lama. The current Dalai Lama's recognition of the XIth Panchen Lama may be said to be in keeping with this spirit of fraternal tradition, as both belong to the same order.

But politics soured the 'father' and 'son' relationship. High lamas, sometimes knowingly, sometimes under manipulation by their ambitious entourage, got entangled in the mundane world of power struggle. In this they were often encouraged by domineering neighbouring powers to promote their own national interest in Central Asia. Because high lamas wielded enormous influence among their followers, external powers found it expedient to pursue their interest in Tibet or Tibetan affairs through such holy men of influence. High lamas may have been men of great influence but they often acted as instruments of the great powers and tended to toe the line so long as their 'political' patrons did not interfere in their religious sphere.

Some time before the British mission to Lhasa, led by Col. F. Younghusband, it was reported to the Dalai Lama's government that the Panchen Lama's father had been murdered and that not only were the sorcerers engaged against the Lhasa administration but were also trying to usurp the authority of the Panchen Lama. Asked about this, the Panchen Lama replied that he wanted a thorough enquiry into the matter. Accordingly, a party of officials headed by Gsr-byung Shappe left Lhasa for that purpose. It discovered that the Panchen Lama's father had been having an affair with the wife of another prominent Tashilhunpo official, the Gnyer-tshang Chenpo. In a bid to marry her paramour, the woman tried to poison the Panchen Lama's deaf and dumb mother. But the plot miscarried and it was the Panchen's father and some of his servants who ate the poisoned food. They were saved only by the skill of a doctor known as Badu Amchi.

A dog, which ate a part of the poisoned food, was less fortunate. It died. The Gnyer-tshang Chenpo's wife tried to pin the blame on her daughter but was found guilty and was banished. She was also fined heavily and flogged as well. The Panchen Lama's father, probably innocent in the matter, was also fined and imprisoned in the *Phuntsholing dzong* (prison). These proceedings were presumably carried out by the Panchen Lama's ministers; but the Gnyer-tshang Chenpo, who was more influential among the ministers, wanted further vengeance. The in-charge of the *Phuntsholing dzong* was prevailed upon to club Panchen Lama's father to death. In the twists and turns to the entire affair, the senior-most minister was charged with attempt to bring the Dalai Lama's government under his influence by means of written magical charms which he kept beneath his seat and also of attempting to usurp the authority of Panchen Lama. Along with Gnyer-tshang Chenpo he was heavily fined and degraded. All the fines were made over to the Panchen Lama.

Younghusband has recorded this incident in his memoirs. A Tibetologist later commented that Younghusband underestimated the Tibetan ability to conceal shrewdness and strength of mind beneath a façade of calm and self-control and an assumed air of simplicity. In January 2000, Ashok Malik echoed the similar opinion when he wrote in *India Today*, a fortnightly magazine, "Tibetans are more secretive than a secret service".

The Xth Panchen Lama, Choekyi Gyaltsen, made a heroic departure in 1959 from this self-serving path and emerged as the hero of the Tibetan people under Chinese domination.

After the IXth Panchen Lama's death, the Tashilhunpo monastery organised searches for the reincarnation, finally short-listing two candidates, one in Amdo and the other in Kham. The former was preferred and declared as the Xth Panchen Lama with the name Lobsang Trinley Lhundrup Choekyi Gyaltsen. But considerable complications preceded his formal recognition. A section of the previous Panchen Lama's court recognised the Amdo child in 1941. But a reincarnation of the Panchen Lama's stature would not be readily and widely accepted unless his authenticity was publicly confirmed by the Dalai Lama. With the then Dalai Lama still a minor, the Tibetan government insisted on the performance of all the traditional tests before the official confirmation. This delayed the Xth Panchen Lama's formal recognition by Lhasa. In 1951, China insisted that Gyaltsen be recognised as the true reincarnation of the Panchen Lama. The Dalai Lama recognised him. Throughout the 1950s, the young

Xth Panchen Lama was considered 'pro-Chinese'. While the Chinese were trying to use him as a rival to the Dalai Lama and a counter-force to Tibetan nationalism, the young reincarnate was quietly undergoing his rigorous spiritual training that would transform a mere boy into a reincarnate lama, befitting the high status of Panchen Lama.

Immediately after the Dalai Lama's escape to India in 1959, the Chinese appointed the Panchen Lama as the acting Chairman of the 'Preparatory Committee for Tibet Autonomous Region' (the replacement of the Tibetan government at Lhasa), an office previously held by the Dalai Lama. The following year, the Chinese appointed him a vice-chairman of the National People's Congress. In the early 1960s, the Panchen Lama assumed the religious responsibilities of the absentee Dalai Lama in Tibet. For this, in 1964, he was deported to Beijing's Qin Cheng prison. For fourteen long years, he suffered such mental and physical agonies which only his prison inmates knew of. At one time he even attempted suicide. The lama refused to take food, saying he did not want to go on living under such terrible prison conditions.

In February 1978, the Chinese official news agency released a report that the Panchen Lama had attended the fifth National Committee of the Chinese People's Political Consultative Conference in Beijing. In 1980, he was reinstated a vice-chairman of the National People's Congress. With the permission of the Chinese authorities, he visited his homeland in June 1982.

During his house arrest in Beijing, which followed soon after his release from prison, the Panchen Lama had lost his celibate status to a Chinese woman. On his homecoming, he was reluctant to re-ascend the Panchen Lama's throne but his entourage urged him to do so. Even then he refused to wear the monk's robes again; in public he was seen wearing a yellow brocade *chuba* (the layman's dress). There was no trace of the Gelug chauvinism in him. He visited Lhasa six or seven times after 1978, and toured various parts of Tibet, including Kham and Amdo. His last visit was in January 1989 when he arrived at his traditional monastic seat, Tashilhunpo, in Shiagatse. On 28 January, 1989, the Xth Panchen Lama, 51, died at the

Tashilhunpo monastery, where his previous incarnations had lived and died.

His death unleashed a fresh controversy. At the heart of the controversy was the political question: Who had the power and authority to recognise the XIth Panchen Lama — the Dalai Lama or the Chinese government? The Dalai Lama's claim was based on religious convention and age-old practice, whereas the Communists based their claim on the legacy of the Qing imperial power. In practice, both used to be involved in the final recognition of a Panchen Lama, but the Dalai Lama more so than the Manchu emperor. The Manchu emperor's rubber stamp might add more prestige and power but it was the Dalai Lama's recognition (*ngos-'zin*) that sanctified and legitimised the reincarnation in the eyes of the Buddhist world.

Ultimately, politics took precedence over piety. The issue remains of much political significance to Beijing. China's claim to rule Tibet largely rests on the imperial tradition of conferring titles on high lamas and on the imperial custom of sending *ambans* (representatives) to be present at the recognition and enthronement ceremonies of high reincarnate lamas. This traditional patron-priest relationship, as the Tibetans perceive it, has now been interpreted by the Communist authorities as China's right to 'appoint' high lamas to their posts.

Communist China claims that the presentation of a golden urn by the Manchu emperor Ch'ien-lung in 1792 (the lots drawing system) marked the height of Manchu influence in Tibet. That is why China takes the golden urn presentation in 1792 as the historic basis of its claim to 'confirm' the reincarnations of the Dalai and Panchen lamas.

Whereas, in fact, *tagril* is an ancient Tibetan tradition long predating the Manchu empire. This ancient Tibetan method involves encasing the names of candidates in dough balls of equal size and weight. The balls are put into a container and the container is rotated until one of them pops out. The candidate lucky enough to have his name inscribed on the ejected ball is declared the successful candidate.

With the subsequent spread of Buddhism, certain other Buddhist elements were added, such as praying to the Buddha and other deities and rotating the urn clockwise. Emperor Ch'ien-lung merely presented a golden urn which would hopefully replace the ordinary container. Tibetan lamas have sparingly used the emperor's urn since then. They mostly continue to adhere to their traditional practice. There have been six Dalai Lamas since Emperor Ch'ien-lung presented the urn in the eighteenth century, but it was used in confirming only three of them.

Soon after the Panchen Lama's death in 1989, Beijing appointed Chadrel Rinpoche, abbot of Tashilhunpo, chairman of the Search Committee. The official procedure between the abbot and Chinese authorities included the steps: (i) mystical signs to identify the child candidate, (ii) tests with objects to identify the most likely candidate, (iii) oracles and divination to 'reconfirm' the final candidate, (iv) the golden urn (lottery system), drawn by a government official, to single out the candidate from the short list and (v) approval of the final decision by the Central government.

As a pre-emptive as well as unilateral step, the Dalai Lama announced Gedhun Choekyi Nyima as the reincarnation of the XIth Panchen Lama on 14 May, 1995. The abbot was detained by the Chinese authorities after three days of the announcement. In the following months, 48 Tibetans were arrested on suspicion of helping the abbot send messages about the child (Gedhun Choekyi Nyima) to the Dalai Lama in exile in India. At the same time, the Chinese authorities appointed pro-Chinese Communist 'lamas' such as Sengchen Lobsang Gyaltsen as the head of Tashilhunpo and Bomi, and as the head of the Gelug sect in order to facilitate the staging of the Chinese candidate with some semblance of 'traditional procedures'.

Without the Dalai Lama's sanctification and legitimation, China bypassed the duly constituted search committee's recommendations and announced the name of Gyaltsen Norbu on 29 November,1995 as the XIth Panchen Lama. The decision was to 'invalidate' the Dalai Lama's candidate. It seems that China would have 'approved' Gedhun Choekyi Nyima had it not been for the pre-emptive action of the Dalai Lama. Fully aroused to this fresh peril, the Dalai Lama dispensed with traditional procedures and took the whole issue in his hand. Such a departure, he might have felt, was in keeping with his unconventional spiritualism.

The Tashilhunpo monastery-in-exile in Mysore in India asked for the Dalai Lama's permission thrice to start the search, but the latter kept dilly-dallying. Later, the monks from the monastery were brought to Delhi to support the Dalai Lama's decision after China announced its candidate.

The Dalai Lama says he received over 30 names of potential candidates from 18 different places, both in Tibet and India. His divination in 1991 revealed that the reincarnation had been born in Tibet, but one performed in August of the same year indicated that the popularly believed reincarnation was not true. However, his divinations in 1993 and 1994 indicated that the time for the search was not ripe. The Nechung and Gatong oracles in early 1994 also prophesied that the Panchen's reincarnation would soon be found in Tibet. Spurred by the oracles' hints, the Dalai Lama speeded up the process. A divination performed on 3 December, 1994 suggested that the search process should begin, and in January 1995 the divination revealed that Gedhun Choekyi Nyima was an 'extremely' good candidate. This was verified and confirmed by two more divinations performed in January 1995 at Dharamsala. As to the auspicious date of announcement of the reincarnation, the final divination performed on 13 May, 1995 declared 15 May, 1995 as being most auspicious. The state-run Chinese news agency Xinhua says that the nine-year-old Panchen Lama, picked up by the Chinese government, visited Lhasa in June 1999. It claims that lamas from major Tibetan temples and ordinary Buddhist believers welcomed him. As expected, the Dalai Lama's government-in-exile criticised China and said "the litmus test will be to take the Panchen Lama to the sacred Tashilhunpo monastery in Shigatse and see how many locals come to see him. If there is no fear of the gun, nobody will go."

In other words, the Dalai Lama chose the divination method to select the Panchen Lama reincarnation, a method which enabled him to take personal control over the whole process. Whether the Dalai Lama's divination was the right method or not, the whereabouts of the six-year-old Gedhun Choekyi Nyima, who disappeared from public view under 'official protection' are not known to this day.

It is surprising that the Dalai Lama acted in the way he did which ultimately served neither the Buddhist purpose nor the Tibetan cause. The Chinese authorities had nodded their approval to the Tashilhunpo monastery search party to seek the Dalai Lama's cooperation at the purely religious level, as was done in the Karmapa case.

The boy who was identified as the reincarnation of the Panchen Lama should have been smuggled out of Tibet at an early stage. Such smuggling is not impossible; several monasteries in exile have done so since the early 1980s. As a seasoned politician, the Dalai Lama could not have been ignorant of the fact that one of the most important roles of the Panchen Lama was to identify the reincarnation of the Dalai Lama, a point clearly recognised by Beijing.

In February 2000, a few weeks after the lama boy 'fled' from the Chinese captivity, the nine-year-old boy picked up by China as the reincarnation of the Panchen Lama appeared on the Chinese Television and said, "I will be a living Buddha who is patriotic, who cherishes education, who protects the nation and benefits the people." Swatched in red robes, the chuuby-cheeked, XIth Panchen Lama added, " In recent years, no matter whether I have been in Tibet or in the motherland's interior, my life and studies have been very joyful. I have deeply felt the care of the motherland's large family." The boy turned 10 on 13 February 2000.

Glossary

Ali-kali: The vowels and consonants, the structural elements of all *mantras*. In the *tantras* it has been said that 'the whole universe is nothing but *ali-kali*'. The esoteric significance of these sounds is the inner relationship between the left and right subtle nerves (*nadis*) of the *yoga*-body.

Amban: Resident representative of the Chinese emperor in Tibet.

Amitabha: The Buddha of boundless light and discriminating wisdom; one of the five *dhyani* Buddhas.

Avalokitshwara: The great compassionate manifestion of the Buddha.

Bakhor: Corridor.

Bhikhu: Monk.

Bodhisattva: Manifestation of Buddha; one who is freed from the notion of self and works for the liberation of all beings.

Chang: Hooch or brewed liquor.

Cheenressig: The Buddha of mercy and compassion.

Chema: Butter.

Chorten: A structure usually built to house funeral relics or other precious remains; built as a symbol of the subtle *yoga*-body; pagoda or stupa.

Dakini: Heavenly goddess, 'angel'; guardians of the esoteric teachings, personifications of the cosmic feminine energy sometimes creative, sometimes destructive. A *dakini* plays and important part in the *tantric* hierarchy.

Dharma: Religious doctrines; the Buddhist law governing all aspects of existence; the underlying law of reality; the teaching of the Buddha.

Dhuche: Committee.

Dragon: Mythological creatures, part crocodile, part serpent.

Drubdra: Retreat Centre.

Dungche: Secretary.

Gau: An amulet-box; reliquary, usually made of metal.

Gonkhang: Monasteries.

Guru: Teacher

Hayagriva: A horse-headed tantric deity.

Hevajra: An important *tantric* tutelary deity, the mystic aspect of the teacher. *Hevajra* means 'the indestructible', 'the adamantine one', depicted usually blue of colour, dancing, with sixteen arms, embracing his consort *nairatma* (non-self). It is also the name of a *tantra* which gives the explanations and mystic symbolism of this form.

Kalachakra: An important *tantric* tutelary deity, the mystic aspect of the teacher. It means 'cycle of time', and is depicted blue of colour, with twenty-four arms, embracing his consort; also the name of a *tantra*, which gives the relationship between the *yoga*-body and the astrological patterns and cycles.

Kalon: Minister.

Kang-Rimpoche: Mount Kailash in western Tibet. The main place of pilgrimage for both Buddhists and Hindus. This mountain can be understood as an initiatory *mandala*.

Kanjur: Canonical literature; 'translation of the Buddha's word' consisting of *vinaya sutras*, the *prajnaparamita*, the *mahayana* sutras and various meditative and ritual instructions (*tantras*). About one hundred volumes in entirety, attributed to Lord Buddha himself.

Karma: Action and reaction, understood as one; the course of events; destiny good and bad actions of body, speech and mind whose pleasant and unpleasant results are experienced in this and subsequent lives.

Kashag: Parliament.

Khampa: Residents of the Kham region in Tibet
Khenpo: Abbot of a monastery, and in charge of monastic and academic studies.
Kriya: Action
Kundenling: Government.
Labrang: Administration.
Lama: Teacher, a superior man.
Lhakhang: Temple.
Madhyamaka: A philosophical concept, as expounded by the Siddha Nagarjuna; the 'middle way' of Buddhism; alongside Yogacara, one of the two principal schools of Mahayana Buddhist thought.
Madhyamika: A follower of Madhyamaka.
Mahanirvana: Death, enlightenment.
Mahakala: The Great Time deity, a *tantric* protector, especially of the Kagyu order. He is usually depicted as being extremely wrathful, black of colour, and holding a skull-cap and chopper; a guardian of deep secrets; his consort is the *Mahakali*.
Mahamaya: The Great Illusion. The name of a tutelary deity and the teachings concerning the overcoming of illusion.
Mahamudra: The Great Sign; great symbol; the inexpressible; the highest teaching; a mystic concept, especially held by the Kagyus.
Mantra: Mystic sound-syllables, composed of vowels and consonants understood as the component vibrations of the universe; used for controlling the mind and for transforming it.
Mudra: Gesture; 'seal'; consort; a mystic term, with many meanings in different contexts; as 'Mahamudra', the higher teaching.
Naga: A snake or serpent; guardians of the underworld, treasures and certain esoteric secrets.
Nirvana: Enlightenment; the 'blowing out' of the fires of greed, hatred, and delusion; the ultimate goal of Buddhist practice; the unconditioned.
Oracle: Oracle is a necromancer. They — both male and female, monks and laity — reply the questions posed to

them after going into a trance. Some spirits or deities come into their beings and help them see the future or the past. It is a profession, very popular in Tibet. In almost every monastery there, one can find an oracle. They are also in the towns and big cities. The high lamas can make a particular person a good oracle by bringing a particular deity into his/her being. Offering gifts to the oracles is not a necessity but people, out of reverence, present them something, especially the dress worn by them.

The oracles cannot remain in the trance for a longer period but for a short duration like 10 to 15 minutes. After coming out of the trance, they generally say "what did he/she tell you?" rather than "What did I tell you."

Pandit: Scholar-teacher; a learned man of great repute.

Prajnaparamita: 'Perfection of wisdom'; a class of Mahayana Buddhist literature.

Pratimoksha: A treatise concerning monastic rules; the Buddhist monastic rule contained in the Vinaya.

Puja: Prayer.

Reincarnation: *Autar,* tulku.

Rinchen Terdzod: Empowerment.

Rinpoche: Literally 'precious one', the honorific given to high lamas and teachers.

Sangha: The Buddhist monastic order of monks and nuns

Sarma: New.

Shastra: A commentarial or exegetical manual as distinct from the 'word of the Buddha' contained in the sutras.

Shedra: Institute

Siddha: A perfected being; a saint.

Siddhi: Yogic powers, attained through inner development.

Stupa: See *chorten*.

Sutra: Discourses attributed to the Buddha; A scriptural book in verse; One of the three main divisions of the ancient Buddhist canon.

Sutrayana: A commentarial or exegetical manual containing sutras.

Svatantra-Madhyamaka: A branch of Madhyamaka school.

Tagril: Lottery system.

Tantra: Teachings outlining mystic practices as the most direct way to enlightenment. The esoteric teachings are specific for the Kalyug (the present dark age); a class of esoteric rituals and meditational Buddhist texts used in Vajrayana/ Mantrayana Buddhism.

Tantrayana: A commentarial or exegetical manual containing *tantra* teachings.

Tathagata: Gautama, Lord Buddha, Literally 'He who exists only as such'; 'the thus gone/come'; an epithet of the Buddha.

Tenjyur: Canonical literature, consisting of translated works of individual Indian masters (*siddhas*), being the commentaries on the *sutras* and *tantras*. Various later theories and practices are also included in them, which generally comprise about two hundred volumes.

Terton: An individual who reveals the hidden treasure or teachings, usually an incarnate lama.

Thanka: Tibetan religious scroll painting.

Tsampa: Roasted and crushed barley soaked in milk or tea.

Tulku: An incarnate lama.

Vajra Mukut: The black *vajra* hat, presented to the Vth Karmapa by the Chinese emperor Tai Ming Chen; the mere sight of this hat is said to confer deliverance-on-sight to all living beings who behold it.

Vajrayana: 'The diamond/thunderbolt vehicle', commonly referred to as tantric Buddhism.

Vinaya: '(Monastic) discipline'; one of the three main divisions of the ancient Buddhist canon.

Vira: A male keeper of esoteric secrets; hero (English)

Yarney: Rainy season six-week retreat.

Yoga: Cosmic union; the aim of all spiritual endeavour.

Yogi: One who practises *yoga*.

Yogini: A female *yogi*.

Index